CARING FOR
YOUR PARENTS

CARING FOR
YOUR PARENTS

The Complete AARP Guide

Hugh Delehanty & Elinor Ginzler

Foreword by Mary Pipher, Ph.D.

STERLING PUBLISHING CO., INC.

AARP Books publishes a wide range of titles on health, personal finance, lifestyle, and other subjects to enrich the lives of older Americans. For more information, go to www.aarp.org/books

AARP, established in 1958, is a nonprofit organization with more than 35 million members age 50 and older.

Library of Congress Cataloging-in-Publication Data Available

2 4 6 8 10 9 7 5 3 1

Published in paperback in 2006 by Sterling Publishing Co., Inc.
387 Park Avenue South, New York, NY 10016
© AARP 2005

Photo credits appear on page 221 and constitute an extension of this copyright page.

Distributed in Canada by Sterling Publishing
c/o Canadian Manda Group, 165 Dufferin Street
Toronto, Ontario, Canada M6K 3H6

Distributed in the United Kingdom by GMC Distribution Services
Castle Place, 166 High Street, Lewes, East Sussex, England BN7 1XU
Distributed in Australia by Capricorn Link (Australia) Pty. Ltd.
P.O. Box 704, Windsor, NSW 2756, Australia

Sterling ISBN-13: 978-1-4027-1739-0 Hardcover
         ISBN-10: 1-4027-1739-3

         ISBN-13: 978-1-4027-3559-2 Paperback
         ISBN-10: 1-4027-3559-6

For information about custom editions, special sales, or premium and corporate purchases, please contact the Sterling Special Sales Department at 800-805-5489 or specialsales@sterlingpub.com

To our parents

Contents

FOREWORD *by Mary Pipher*   *xi*

INTRODUCTION *by Hugh Delehanty*   *1*

1   Bringing Up the Subject   *11*

The Art of Conversation | Beyond Either/Or | The Pre-Talk Talk | What Could They Be Thinking? | Stage One: Breaking the Ice | Stage Two: Organizing a Family Meeting | Stage Three: The Actual Talk | Caregiving at a Distance | Sibling Rivalry, Take Two | Resources

SIDEBARS: 'MAY YOU LIVE LONG AND PROSPER' · WHO ARE THE CAREGIVERS? · *LIFE STORY:* DECISIONS FOR THE FUTURE · CARING COUPONS · *FIRST PERSON:* THE BEST-LAID PLANS · PRACTICALLY SPEAKING · GERIATRIC CARE MANAGERS

2   Your Parent's Best Advocate   *31*

Old Family Scripts | The Organized Advocate | Managing Health Care | Hospital Bills and Insurance Claims | Dealing with Nursing Homes | Scam Alert | Lawyering Up | Resources

SIDEBARS: LAYING THE GROUNDWORK · *FIRST PERSON:* WHEN THINGS FALL APART · QUESTIONS FOR THE DOCTOR · DECODING A PRESCRIPTION · A PATIENT'S BILL OF RIGHTS · COPING WITH HOSPITAL BILLS · A NURSING HOME RESIDENT'S BILL OF RIGHTS · SHRED, DON'T TOSS

3   Money Matters   *53*

Sizing Up the Situation | And the Bottom Line Is . . . | Things Look Good for Now—What's Next? | The Question of Long-Term Care | Do Your Homework | Reality Knocks | Resources

SIDEBARS: KEY QUESTIONS · SHOULD YOU WORRY? · MAKING ENDS MEET (SORT OF) · BE A FRAUD DETECTOR · CHOOSING A FINANCIAL PLANNER · LONG-TERM CARE INSURANCE COSTS · *FIRST PERSON:* ACROSS THE CULTURAL DIVIDE

4 The Body 71

What Is 'Normal' Aging? | *Choosing a Doctor* | *A Pound of Prevention* |
The Changing Senses | *Common Ailments* | *Didn't Sleep a Wink* | *Resources*

SIDEBARS: THE MAGIC CALL BUTTON · THE 'I' WORD · A TEST IN TIME ·
LIFE STORY: MOUNTAIN MAN · PREVENTING FALLS · *LIFE STORY:* THE UNSINKABLE
WALLY RISTOW · WARNING SIGNS 1 · WARNING SIGNS 2 · GETTING SOME SHUT-EYE

5 The Brain 91

The Truth About Depression | *No Turning Back* | *'Everything Has an
Air of Strangeness'* | *The Road Ahead* | *Resources*

SIDEBARS: *FIRST PERSON:* MY FATHER'S BLOG · SIGNS OF DEPRESSION · IS IT
ALZHEIMER'S? · BRAIN ATTACK! · *PRACTICAL STRATEGIES:* ROUTINE THERAPY ·
DESIGN FOR LIVING WITH DEMENTIA · *PRACTICAL STRATEGIES:* AT THE CROSSROADS

6 The Medicare Maze 109

The ABCDs of Medicare | *Medicare Part A: Hospital Insurance* |
Medicare Part B: Medical Insurance | *Medicare Part C: Medicare Advantage* |
Medicare Part D: Prescription Drug Benefit | *Filling the (Medi)Gap* |
Blinded by the Fine Print | *Resources*

SIDEBARS: ARE YOUR PARENTS COVERED? · NAMES & NUMBERS YOU'LL NEED ·
CHECK LIST OF CHOICES · *PRACTICAL STRATEGIES:* HOW TO DECIPHER A SUMMARY
NOTICE · WHO YOU GONNA CALL?

7 Living Arrangements 125

Staying Put | *Day-Tripping* | *Making Room for Mom or Dad* |
Independent Living 101 | *When a Nursing Home Makes Sense* | *Resources*

SIDEBARS: WHO LIVES WHERE · HOW SAFE IS YOUR PARENT'S HOME? · *FIRST PERSON:*
TRADITION VS. REALITY · *LIFE STORY:* SISTER DONNA

8 Caring for the Caregiver   143

The Hidden Patients | *The Stress Factor* | *Making Yourself a Priority* | *Lightening the Load* | *Give the Pros a Chance* | *Resources*

SIDEBARS: TAKE A BREATH · REWRITE YOUR INNER SCRIPT · SHARE THE CARE · *LIFE STORY*: THE ART OF SELF-PRESERVATION · FINDING CLARITY · CHOOSING ADULT DAY CENTER PROGRAMS

9 Saying Good-bye   157

A New Intimacy | *Making Arrangements Ahead of Time* | *Achieving Closure* | *The Hospice Solution* | *Getting Down to 'What Was Good'* | *Resources*

SIDEBARS: MANAGING PAIN · CHOOSING HOSPICE CARE · *FIRST PERSON*: LETTING GO · AS THE END NEARS · *FIRST PERSON*: 'TIME TO GO TO BALFRON?' · THE LAST DETAILS

10 The Alchemy of Sorrow   173

The Phases of Grief | *Variations on a Theme* | *Yourself and Others* | *The Virtue of Ritual* | *The Stages of Healing* | *A New Shape to Life* | *Resources*

SIDEBARS: WHEN TO SEEK HELP · THE ONE LEFT BEHIND · CHILDREN AND GRIEF · FACING THE HOLIDAYS · *PRACTICAL STRATEGIES*: GRIEVING WELL · *FIRST PERSON*: ROCK-A-BYE BABY

AFTERWORD *by Elinor Ginzler*   187

APPENDIX   193

GLOSSARY   211

ABOUT THE AUTHORS   215

ACKNOWLEDGMENTS   216

INDEX   217

PHOTOGRAPHY CREDITS   221

Foreword

SUNDAY MORNING, AUGUST 24. Last week my husband and I were in Alaska flying over the deep blue crevasses of glaciers, picking wild blueberries and scouting for moose and grizzlies. We watched alpenglow on Denali and waded in the McKinley River. We indulged in one of those lovely trips that middle-aged people with good health and incomes can enjoy.

We returned to an avalanche of e-mails and phone calls and a mountain of errands and chores. We helped our daughter pack and depart for graduate school. Jim had a pre-op examination for his scheduled hernia surgery. We were surprised by some good news: My son and daughter-in-law were expecting again, and they were coming to visit us soon. That is my current definition of wealth—the number of days a year my adult children and grandchildren visit us.

We were also pummeled by bad news. My mother-in-law was hospitalized dehydrated, vomiting, and in pain. Phyllis and my father-in-law are in their 80s, with multiple health problems. They live at home in Blair, the small Nebraska town where they grew up and raised their children. Phyllis is in a wheelchair and Bernie, who is thin and arthritic, cares for her. Sometimes, he accidentally drops Phyllis. The volunteer fire department or the sheriff's office sends someone over to help her back into bed.

My sister Jane also was hospitalized this week with congestive heart failure, kidney failure, and high blood pressure. She may be dying. My sister Toni, who lives near Jane, calls me every day with updates. I cannot call Jane in the ICU, so I send her e-mails, which I try to make loving and cheerful. Toni reads them aloud to Jane, then stacks them neatly on her nightstand.

The day before Jim's surgery, we drove to the Blair hospital to see his mother.

In her younger years, Phyllis was a beautiful woman—a tall, thin brunette, a lawyer's daughter who had elegant clothes even during the Depression. In college, she sometimes scheduled three dates in one night in order to fit in all her suitors. Bernie felt incredibly lucky to win her. He still feels lucky.

In the hospital, Phyllis wore no makeup and had gray bed-hair. Her gown was bloodstained and wrinkled. Bernie hovered nearby, massaging her feet, adjusting her pillows, critiquing her lunch. "That spinach looks like pond scum. The custard pie looks all right."

Bernie—an attorney, a Mason, and a church elder—wore blue shorts cinched up with a wide white belt. His weight had dropped from 185 to 135 pounds and he was all bones and saggy skin. He fussed over Phyllis energetically, but when she was not watching him, his chin drooped wearily onto his chest. Soon my husband must once again broach the topic of assisted living. Whenever he does this, Bernie changes the subject.

I feel beset by a perfect storm of medical problems. With three family members likely in the hospital at once, I am not even sure where I should be. I want to fly south to be with my sister, but I am the only one who can care for Jim after his surgery. Phyllis will be okay without me, unless she worsens, which is indeed possible with her fragile health. Meanwhile, I have three weeks of work piled up and a manuscript due. I want to see my grandchildren and tend my runaway garden. My situation is not tragic. It's not even unusual; it is the lot of many people my age. This is what 56 looks like.

Time doesn't kid around. By the time we are in our 50s, life can be complicated indeed. Old soldiers are falling and even some in our own ranks are dropping away. This last decade I've lost five of my eight aunts and uncles.

My parents died when I was younger. My father had his first debilitating stroke at age 50, and then many more before he died at age 65. The summer of my sophomore year in college I returned home to help him learn to talk again. In October of that year he had another stroke and lost our summer's work. He lived those last 15 years half-blind, crippled, and paralyzed. Except for swear words and the word "cigarette," which stood for anything he wanted, he was difficult to understand. More than once, when he slipped out alone, his speech was so slurred that he was arrested for public drunkenness.

My mother was hospitalized for the last eight months of her life. Toward the end she often hallucinated that she was delivering babies or cooking spaghetti dinners. I spent a great deal of time with her, and at night we often pretended we were camping in the Rockies, beside clear water, smelling the pines and looking at the stars. The artificial respirators gurgling nearby made waterfall sounds.

Many of my friends are just now experiencing parents with significant medical conditions. And we boomers are coming to grips with our own emerging health issues. We schedule physicals with doctors who are younger than we are. We monitor our cholesterol, bone density, blood pressure, and short-term memories. Almost everyone my age is worried about something. We ponder our futures and look into wills and estate planning. We read ads for retirement villages or talk to our friends about communal living.

The Bittersweet Season

Late middle age is a bittersweet season. Mostly we boomers are healthy and having fun. We enjoy friends, family, travel, book clubs, and recreation centers or gyms. We backpack, kayak, bird-watch, and quilt. Many of us finally have the time to take college courses or do the volunteer work we have always wanted to do. However, shadows are beginning to fall across our lives. As Bob Dylan put it, "It's not dark yet, but it's getting there."

We are entering a hard season when our lessons will be about endurance, loss, love, and letting go. Our parents are entering their most challenging developmental stage—old-old age—with its issues around autonomy, change, and the acceptance of the inevitable. Work issues wane, but relationship issues wax more fully than in any season except early childhood.

From now on, it is all about taking care of ourselves and those we love. Often our relationships grow richer and more beautiful. We appreciate our life partners on an organic level. Jim and I will be married 30 years this October. That seems like a very long time. Given current longevity rates, however, our marriage may be only half over. There are many challenges for us that involve making things new, keeping our personal growth coordinated, and perhaps even accepting that indeed each of us is becoming more like our own parents.

Most of us truly want to be good and to do the right things for our aging relatives, but nothing in our culture is organized to make things easy. One friend lives hundreds of miles away from her mother, who has breast cancer. My doctor's father needs physical therapy but is ineligible for benefits.

Many friends' parents cannot afford medications. My friends could offer to pay for these out of pocket, but they have college expenses to cover for their own children. Jobs, finances, children, and problems with time and distance can keep us from giving our parents the kind of attention they truly deserve.

My neighbor Lily, one of five daughters, didn't quite make it to her father's deathbed in an ICU in Boston. Neither did her four sisters. He fell ill quite suddenly; by the time the daughters could make family, job, and travel arrangements, it was over. The oldest sister would have made it, but a snarl at O'Hare grounded her during the final few hours of her father's life. The father, a widower, tried to hold on for his girls but could wait no longer. When Lily told me this story she was angry and guilty.

As I listened, I asked myself, "What kind of country is this where the old die alone with their children far away?" Never in the history of the world have families been denied each other's company as they face these ordinary tragedies.

Refugees often remark on Americans' isolation from families, especially from our older relatives. They are appalled by our facilities for the aged. Many of them work in our nursing homes and they pity the lonely old ones who never see their grandchildren. They come from places where old people are revered and lovingly cared for by children. This care is seen not as a burden, but as an honor and privilege.

Institutions fail us. Our medical system is a humongous mess. Housing, transportation, and isolation are common problems. Parents can be stubborn, unrealistic, secretive—and we can lack the time, patience, or knowledge to handle the increasingly complicated webs of problems spun around our lives.

On the other hand, some of my friends are creating new ways to be with their parents. One helped her parents buy a small house in her neighborhood. She and her husband both work, and she wanted her children and parents to be together after school and at other times. Her father is teaching the children carpentry. Her mother is teaching them photography. Another friend bought a duplex near her home for her son's family and her aging mother. The son mows his grandmother's lawn and checks in on her. His young daughters visit their great-grandmother daily, and Sundays they all go to my friend's house for brunch.

In my book *Another Country,* I wrote about time-zone issues. By this I mean that depending on the era in which we were reared, we have different ideas on how to communicate and handle stress. When we talk with people of other generations, we often experience very real differences in style and tone. Our parents grew up in a world in which the word "consumption" referred to tuberculosis and Depression was not a mental health problem but an era of economic disaster.

At least in the Midwest, our elders are not likely to be psychologically minded. They don't like to analyze family relationships or openly discuss pain and anxiety. We boomers were socialized to let it all hang out, to emote and take our psychic temperature at every turn. Think Queen Elizabeth vs. Princess Diana. When we try to work through the issues of old-old age, we experience multiple time-zone collisions.

It is important to remember that our differences are not pathological, characterological, or personal; they are generational. Each generation is trying to do the right thing, but we have been educated differently about what the right thing is. Our folks try to buck up and look on the bright side. We consider that denial. But when we share our feelings or "process our experience," they call it whining.

A Chance to Get It Right

As we progress through life's stages, sad stories and bad news accumulate. Unless we are intentional, we are likely to frame these years in terms of stress and problems and thus miss the much more interesting and bigger stories. These middle years, when we care for our parents, are ripe with opportunities for transformation. They can be conceived of as "our call to greatness"—our chance to be heroes in our own lives and to learn life's deepest lessons, our opportunity for redemption and real intimacy with our parents.

These years can be about reconciliation, understanding, and acceptance. If this stage in all our lives is handled properly, we may experience epiphanies and sparkling moments when we see and love each other as we truly are. At last, after decades of squabbling, we may be able to get things right.

Being helpful is not marketed as a pleasure in this culture, but it is in fact one of life's greatest joys. Psychological research shows that people derive more pleasure from being useful than from having fun.

To be good, strong, and useful—these are core human needs. Meeting them allows us to respect and love ourselves more deeply, and to feel that we are truly participants in the dance of life across generations.

Just as middle age is a touchstone developmental stage for us adult children—a time when we have the opportunity to change into stronger, truer versions of ourselves—so too is old-old age a touchstone period for our parents. Under harsh conditions people's true characters are realized. Some elders are patient, some are not. Some become more loving and gentle while others grow querulous and self-centered. Some shrink in intellectual interests and conversational skills while others who are "green on top" become the wisest, most interesting people on Earth. Some face death bravely and with dignity. Others fall apart.

Working with aging parents is a voyage of discovery. As we travel, we learn about us, about them, and about our relationship. We learn about care giving and care receiving. And we learn how we want to handle our own old-old age.

America today is a noisy place, filled with clamor and misinformation, with advice and products designed to make money rather than to genuinely help. Our citizens are educated about aging primarily by people with something to sell—condos by golf courses, lakeside cabins, Viagra, or plastic surgery. Left out of the picture are the truly important discussions—about dignity, social connections, a sense of place, and family commitments.

My hat is off to Hugh Delehanty and Elinor Ginzler, the coauthors of this book, and to AARP for their efforts to provide us with a fuller, more honest education. This book frames our experiences with elders in a way that teaches and deepens our souls.

This book is not just a "how-to" book, but a "how-to-think" book. It helps us ask the right questions and structure discussions properly. It enables us to place all the experiences of this developmental stage into a healthy perspective, one that allows us to love our parents, to make wise choices, to act—and, finally, to let go.

All great truths are paradoxes. Time is everything and nothing. We are all together and we are all alone. Helping our parents in their last developmental stages teaches us that we live in a both/and world, not an either/or world. There is an algebra to aging. As more is lost, that which remains is more deeply valued. "I weep at the beauty of a rose," Abe Maslow said in old age. We learn with our wisest elders—plan carefully, but the moment is everything.

This time in our parents' lives is often the hardest and the saddest, but it's also the time of the greatest victories. Many a bad life has been redeemed by a good death. If we embark freely and willingly on this voyage of discovery, we may find joy, empathy, understanding, and intimacy. We expand our definitions of what it means to be human. We grow our own souls in the garden of time.

Graveyard Flowers

A few weeks after our perfect storm of medical emergencies, Jim and I went camping with my son's family. On a late September afternoon, we staked our tent at Hickory Grove Lake in central Iowa. Kate, who is three, discovered her first toad and followed him around for a long while. Aidan, who is 15 months, experienced his first campfire and s'mores. Afterward he snuggled into me, eyes wide open, and didn't move a muscle for over an hour. He was "melting into richness," as our daughter once put it.

Driving home the next morning, my daughter-in-law, Jamie, spotted an old prairie graveyard high on a hill. We followed a dirt road through bronze and gold fields up to what was called the Pioneer Cemetery. She and I walked among the graves of the first settlers to this part of Iowa and constructed our own narratives about the people buried under the hand-carved headstones.

The first burial was in 1836, the last was in 1899. Until the late 1880s, all the markers had been carved by the same man. No doubt he was buried nearby. Many babies and children were buried. Some couples had lost six to ten children and many men had lost wives to childbirth. These deaths seemed especially poignant as I stood with my pregnant daughter-in-law.

The sky was royal blue, the prairie grasses tall and wine colored. From our vantage point we could see miles of fields and little farms. While we talked of time passing, Aidan frolicked on the graves. He climbed the small, tottering ones and used them for slides. He jumped off the larger graves, shrieking with pleasure. He picked some wild asters and chased a butterfly through the grass. The moment was everything.

I said to Jamie, "They come and they go." To myself I added, "And there is comfort and peace in accepting that." Then I picked up my cuddly grandson and we headed for home.

—MARY PIPHER

Introduction

Growing old is mandatory; growing up is optional.
—CHILI DAVIS

IT WAS THE MOMENT I HAD BEEN DREADING for years, the one that had haunted me a thousand times ever since I'd learned that my father had Parkinson's disease. It was the moment of the death talk.

A few weeks earlier he had fallen and hit his head late at night in his room at the assisted living facility and nearly died en route to the hospital. Dad was so malnourished the doctors inserted a feeding tube and within a week he was shuffling around again, charming everyone in sight. But it didn't last. Shortly after he left the hospital and moved to a nursing home, he started ripping out the feeding tube whenever the nurses were looking the other way. The head nurse called and told me that we either had to reinsert the tube surgically or remove it. Without the feeding tube, he would die in a matter of weeks.

After conferring with my two brothers, I called Joan, a social worker I knew who specialized in end-of-life care, to help me talk the situation over with my dad. Even though he had made it clear in his living will that he didn't want to be kept alive artificially, I wasn't certain how he wanted to die.

My father, a puckish, white-haired man in his 80s with the mischievous charm of a leprechaun, was not particularly religious. The son of Irish immigrants, he had been raised as a Roman Catholic in Fair Haven, Connecticut, and attended parochial school, which made him skeptical about religious dogma for the rest of his life. He went to Mass on Sundays when my brothers

Coauthor Hugh Delehanty with his father, John, in 1993.

and I were kids, but he often fell asleep in the pew and I never once saw him go to confession or take Communion. For him, going to Mass was a familial duty, not an act of spiritual discovery.

Dad was not philosophical either. He had seen a lot of death in World War II as an artillery officer in North Africa and Italy, but he never talked about it. Nor did he have much to say about his brother, James, who fell off a bridge at age five and drowned. This tragedy, which had caused his mother to have a nervous breakdown, must have had an enormous impact on my father, who was three then. Yet when I asked him once what it felt like to lose his brother at such a young age, he stared at me blankly and said he'd been too little at the time to remember. Nobody in his family ever talked about the drowning. Death was not a subject for polite conversation.

Joan ran into a wall of silence at first. Dad wasn't about to get into a serious discussion about such a personal matter with a stranger. When she asked him whether he believed in an afterlife, he recited something he had memorized in catechism class. I figured he was toying with her. As the conversation developed, however, he became more relaxed and matter-of-fact.

At heart, Dad was a pragmatist. He knew his time had come; he just wanted to do it his own way.

"Your son tells me that you want us to take out your feeding tube," said Joan.

"Yes, that's right," he said.

"And if they take out that tube, you're probably going to die. Not today, not tomorrow, but soon."

He nodded.

"You may get to a point in the next few weeks or so when you're not going to be able to make decisions for yourself. Important decisions. Life-and-death decisions. You're going to have to rely on your son. Are you ready for that?"

Another nod.

"I need to hear you say it. Do you trust your son to make those decisions for you?"

"Yes, of course."

At that moment I realized a profound shift had occurred between my father and me.

The generational divide between us used to seem unbridgeable. He was a product of the Depression; I was a wide-eyed baby boomer. I had spent a good part of my life creating as much distance as I could from him because he was stubborn, autocratic, and wanted us to fit into his conventional 1950s vision for the family. I needed the freedom to shape my own identity. So after college, I put 3,000 miles between us by moving to northern California. Sure we talked, but not about anything real. He wasn't interested in the demons I was wrestling with ("all that therapy stuff," as he called it); he just wanted to know how "the Job" was going. Most of our phone calls didn't last very long.

Years later, after I moved with my family to New York, Dad's illness got worse, and my brothers and I decided to split the caregiving duties. My older brother, John, took over the finances and legal matters; my younger brother, Dennis, coordinated the supporting cast of friends and neighbors; and I became my father's health advocate.

A therapist I knew suggested that I spend time hanging out with Dad—nothing special, just sitting around the kitchen table gabbing, as he called it. We talked about my mother, who was his childhood sweetheart, and the 830 letters she wrote him during the war, one for every day that he was away. We talked about his father, a trolley man and a union leader in New Haven, and the lessons he taught Dad about his favorite subject: Irish history. In the course of those conversations

> *Life would be infinitely happier if we could only be born at the age of eighty and gradually approach eighteen.* —Mark Twain

we both changed. Dad allowed himself to become more open and vulnerable, and I became less of a smart-ass and began to allow myself to feel the depth of his love for me.

When Joan, the social worker, asked her question and my father answered, I knew there was no going back. Yes, my father was going to die and I was going to have to give the order to pull the plug. All my life I had been the renegade, the one who tested the rules. That was my role. But with three words—"Yes, of course"—my father liberated me from my past. He trusted me with his life— and death.

The World's Greatest Gift

For most of human history, our elders could expect to spend their final years as respected members of multigenerational households. American Indians speak with reverence for older people, who, they say, "are the link with our past, our present, and our future." Fijians advise each other to "listen to the wisdom of the toothless ones." Arabs often consult their elders on major decisions and view their care as a religious duty because, as one saying goes, "Heaven would be found under the feet of one's mother." And the Chinese consider parental fealty a key to social harmony.

Of course, this is the 21st century, and recent trends in the United States and elsewhere have put a strain on this time-honored tradition. In an increasingly mobile world, adult children often live hundreds, even thousands of miles from their parents, while women—who provide more than half of unpaid caregiving—have entered the workforce in large numbers. The challenge of working outside the home while caring for an elderly parent—and often children as well—adds considerable stress to the lives of women and men alike. Almost half of the so-called sandwich generation—the cohort of Americans between 45 and 55—have children under 21 as well as aging parents or aging in-laws. It's a tight squeeze.

But the rewards of caregiving are many and profound. Not only does it give you an opportunity to repay someone who gave you life and nurtured you when you were a child, it can also bring you closer to estranged loved ones and resolve long-standing emotional conflicts. As author Beth Witrogen McLeod writes, caregiving "has the potential to alter us at the core of our being, opening our heart's capacity to live fully even in the midst of loss." In a recent survey researchers asked caregivers to describe their feelings. "Worry," "sadness," and "frustration" came up a lot, but the words they used most frequently were "loving," "appreciated," and "proud."

'Love Is Paying Attention'

If you're reading this book, you're probably embarking on a caregiving journey of your own. What kind of caregiver will you be? Many people when they're starting out tend to think of caregiving as a fix-it project, says clinical psychologist and Buddhist meditation teacher Tara Brach, the author of *Radical Acceptance: Embracing Your Life with the Heart of a Buddha*, but that perspective has serious limitations. "If you think you're just doing a job, fixing a person who is weaker than you, there will always be a wall between the two of you," she says. "But if you approach it with the point of view that the person you're taking care of is going through a natural process, a profound connection begins to grow."

Sometimes that shift happens when the stress gets unbearable, but, more often than not, it emerges slowly, as it did with my father and me, because a kind of intimacy develops that you've never before experienced. As soon as you realize that your parent isn't going to be around forever, says Brach, "the preciousness of their life becomes very immediate. You stop holding back expressions of love because you know there's not much time."

There's also another dynamic at work. All your life you've envisioned your parent as strong and powerful, so as he or she gets weaker and more dependent, barriers begin to fall away. Our culture places such a high value on self-reliance that aging parents—particularly those who survived the Depression—often resist acknowledging weakness. But when they do, it becomes the ground for

> *Compassion for our parents is the true sign of maturity.* —ANAÏS NIN

a much deeper level of trust. "Trust occurs when somebody's vulnerable and lets you in—and you show up," says Brach. "It often isn't until we're sick and dying that we open up and let that happen."

Caregivers who have the easiest time shifting perspective, says Brach, are those who aren't locked into patterns of denial. "If you're in the habit of avoiding uncomfortable situations, you will probably take the position that something's wrong," she says. "But if you've developed a habit of honestly recognizing your own insecurities, then you'll probably find a place in yourself to tolerate it when someone else is experiencing pain and suffering."

The key is self-forgiveness. Caregivers often punish themselves for not being perfect. But what does "perfect" mean in this situation? No matter how angelic you are, you're not going to save your parent's life or completely ease his or her suffering. "Caregiving is painful," says Brach, "because you can't take away the other person's pain. You can't make everything okay. All you can do is love that person. And the deepest expression of love is paying attention."

That means not only paying attention to what's happening with your parent, but also what's happening to you. When feelings of anger or fear or guilt arise, it's important to be forgiving toward yourself; otherwise, unacknowledged emotions will diminish your ability to be fully present. "The more you're just being with the person, and not trying to fix him or her," says Brach, "the more you'll be able to see them as what Thomas Merton calls, 'the divine that comes through all life.'"

Brach's friend, Susan Stone, had an awakening of this kind several years ago when her mother was diagnosed with terminal non-Hodgkin's lymphoma. A poet and an expert in Asian history and culture, Susan was training at the time to be a Zen monk in California. When she returned to St. Louis to take care of her mother, Blanche, she had elaborate plans. "I thought that I was going to help teach her how to face death," says Susan. "But Mom didn't want any part of that. So I dropped my big mission and started focusing on little things, like folding the laundry together. I realized this was the greatest gift I could give her. Just being with someone—and doing it mindfully—is empowering because you're allowing that person to be who they really are."

Three months before her death, Blanche surprised Susan by writing a poem about the trees in the backyard. Susan said a few encouraging words, but that didn't satisfy her mother. A few days later, Susan relates in her book *At the Eleventh Hour: Caring for My Dying Mother,* Blanche announced, "You keep saying you like my poems, but you don't say anything else. I don't want nice words. I want real criticism. Like the kind of things you talk about in poetry classes."

> *We thought we were running away from the grownups, and now we are the grownups.* —MARGARET ATWOOD

So for the next few weeks, until Blanche grew too feeble, mother and daughter talked about adjectives and line breaks and "the fact that good poetry isn't just about pretty things, but about real things." At one point, Blanche declared, "Where've you been all these years? I never knew this before. And I was satisfied with just my newspapers and my books. You're the only one who could have taught me this, and I really need it now."

After Blanche died, Susan designed a workshop on mindful caregiving based on her experience with her mother. "When I started out as a caregiver, I didn't think I could do it," she says. "But I learned that I didn't have to have all the answers. I just did things step by step, and I found that if I made decisions based on what was needed at the moment, I didn't have to worry. That was very liberating."

In Search of a Second Adulthood

In his groundbreaking book *The Soul and Death,* psychologist Carl Jung argues that the task of midlife is to come to terms with death. "Natural life is the nourishing soil of the soul," he writes. "Anyone who fails to go along with life remains suspended, stiff and rigid in mid-air. That is why so many people get wooden in old age; they look back and cling to the past with a secret fear of death in their hearts. They withdraw from the life process, at least psychologically, and consequently remain fixed like nostalgic pillars of salt, with vivid recollections of youth but no living relation to the present. From the middle of life onward, only he remains vitally alive who is ready to die with life."

Contemporary Western culture doesn't reinforce this point of view. We have replaced the traditional mythic rites of passage with a Peter Pan-like obsession with youth. To cling to the past and remain stuck in the illusion of youthfulness, writes Jung, is as absurd as not being able to outgrow child-sized shoes. "An old man who does not know how to listen to the secrets of the brooks as they tumble down from the peaks to the valleys makes no sense; he is a spiritual mummy who is nothing but a rigid relic of the past. He stands apart from life, mechanically repeating himself to the last triviality."

Caregiving is a way to avoid that trap. The Jungian analyst James Hollis divides life into four psychological stages, each with the power to define a person's identity. The first stage is childhood, which is characterized by the dependency of the ego on the parents' world. The second stage is first adulthood, roughly from puberty to age 40 but it can last a lifetime, when the dependency of childhood is projected onto the roles of adulthood. The third stage is second adulthood, when those projections dissolve and one has a chance to become a true individual, beyond the determinism of parents and cultural conditioning. The fourth stage is mortality, which involves learning to live with the mystery of death.

In his work as a therapist, Hollis has noticed that the elderly generally fall into two categories: "There are those for whom the life remaining is still a challenge, still worthy of the good fight, and those for whom life is full of bitterness, regret and fear," he writes in his book *The Middle Passage: From Misery to Meaning in Midlife*. "The former are invariably those who have gone through some earlier struggle, experienced the death of the first adulthood and accepted greater responsibility for their lives. They spend their last years living more consciously. Those who avoided the first death are haunted by the second, afraid their lives have not been meaningful."

This transition doesn't come easily. It usually requires a major loss or disillusionment that jolts you into consciousness and liberates you from old projections. Taking care of a dying parent can be such a catalyst if it's done consciously. As Tara Brach puts it, "When you're close to someone dying, you realize that you're a living-dying being yourself."

Caregiving is a humbling experience. It forces you to move beyond narcissism to a more inclusive identity. "We spend so much of our time thinking 'How am I going to make myself comfortable?' 'How am I going to handle this future situation?'" says Brach. "But there's a tremendous amount of freedom that comes when you widen the circle of what you're paying attention to and include someone else." It's possible, of course, to find this kind of liberation in other ways. But the day-to-day rigors of caregiving give you direct experience of the alchemy of selflessness. It helps you see, says Brach, that "there's more reality in togetherness than any idea of a separate self."

Now What?

As he neared the end his life, the American novelist William Saroyan quipped, "Everybody has got to die, but I always believed an exception would be made in my case. Now what?" Saroyan was being lighthearted, but his question—Now what?—could also sum up the purpose of this book.

The journey through the later years is likely to bring moments of uncertainty and even bafflement, not just for those making the passage but also for the caregivers helping them down that mysterious road. The specifics may vary, but every adult child taking care of an aging parent faces some version of Saroyan's question. What is coming next? How should I get ready for it? How do I cope? Along the way many difficulties will arise. Caregiving can tear you apart. After all, this is your mother or your father. And you are their child.

I think of my friend Rosemary. She spent much of her adult life trying to free herself from her mother, Arlene, a tough-minded, fiercely independent woman who raised five children on her own after her husband died in a plane crash. Then, one night when Rosemary was in her 40s, Arlene packed a suitcase and wandered away from her house in Brooklyn, hallucinating about a helicopter on her roof and men under her bed. She was later diagnosed with early stage Alzheimer's, and Rosemary, who is a gerontologist, volunteered to become Arlene's primary caregiver (see chapter 5, "The Brain").

There is nothing like returning to a place that remains unchanged to find the ways in which you yourself have altered. —NELSON MANDELA

It has been a wrenching experience. Rosemary moved Arlene to an assisted living facility a few blocks from her apartment in Manhattan and tried desperately to communicate with her. At times Arlene would start screaming and lash out at her for no discernible reason. But, with the help of an Alzheimer's support group and a lot of persistence, Rosemary slowly learned new ways to interact with her mother, and their dynamic changed. "I had to drop what I wanted to do and step into her world," Rosemary recalls. "When I finally did that, the opportunity for love and gentleness grew by leaps and bounds."

Not long after things settled down, Rosemary had to cut back her time with her mother to two days a week to care for her husband, who was diagnosed with cancer. By then, though, Rosemary's connection with Arlene was strong enough to withstand the strain. "When you're a caregiver, a lot of what you do goes unrecognized," Rosemary says. "Then there are times when the eternal mother-daughter roles dissolve. She's softened and I've softened. She's become the loving mother I've always wanted, and I've become the loving daughter I always wanted to be."

Tears start to well in her eyes. "I've finally learned what it really means to love someone."

—HUGH DELEHANTY
Editor in Chief, AARP Publications

1 Bringing Up the Subject

*I hate to bring up a subject that may cause you
to break out in hives....* —Calvin Trillin

TIME WAS WHEN PARENTS and children (adolescents or preteens) squirmed through The Conversation about s-e-x—or, in more recent years, about sex and drinking and drugs. With luck, both parties emerged more or less unscathed, relieved to have gotten it over with. Subsequent conversations on these topics might have been stormier, especially if sparked by real or perceived teenage transgressions. Parents were concerned about their children's health and safety, adolescents about establishing their independence.

Now those adolescents have grown up and probably lived through The Conversation with their own teenagers; the parents are well into their retirement years. The awkward Conversation today is about whether, when, and how these adult children should take on some or all of the care of their older parents. Adult children are concerned about their parents' health and safety, older parents about preserving their independence.

The Conversation is only the beginning of a series of potentially charged discussions that arise as parents get older. Given the emotional stakes, the chances of misunderstandings and bruised feelings are high. No wonder adult children commonly want to put it off as long as possible. But as parents begin to have difficulties with the routines of daily life—unopened bills pile up on the kitchen table, or someone has real trouble walking around— The Conversation becomes unavoidable. In the long run, the discussion will go better if it happens before a crisis forces everyone to make decisions on the fly. Without the pressure of an emergency, family members can work together to ensure that everyone who participates in The Conversation feels fully heard and recognized, that fears and anxieties are addressed, and that no one feels demeaned or diminished.

The Art of Conversation

Psychologists and counselors have long recognized that awkward conversations, no matter what their specific circumstances, have dynamics at work in them that can make the interaction much more difficult than it needs to be. This is especially the case in conversations among family members, where the generations may differ on any number of issues. Older parents, because of the way they were raised by their own parents and because of the experiences they have accumulated in the course of their lives, may view a given subject as simply none of their child's business—while adult children may believe they have reasonable cause for concern. Other times, parents may react negatively less to a given topic than to a particular choice of words or tone of voice, or even to the fact that the conversation is taking place at the old kitchen table with the familiar place mats and dishes. These tangible and intangible factors can have a way of transporting all parties back in time, to the years when the adult daughter was a know-it-all teenager, or even to when the older father was himself a young man answering to his father. "Every little discussion rests on a mountain of history," says Mary Pipher. "Many ghosts are in the room."

The denunciation of the young is a necessary part of the hygiene of older people, and greatly assists in the circulation of their blood....

—LOGAN PEARSALL SMITH

Often the roles everyone has always played in the family can seem inescapable. The baby of the family will still be the baby, with all the baggage that may entail, even if he's now in his 40s and in a position to be the main caregiver. When his mother says, "Oh, Nicksy, don't worry about this!" the son bristles at his mother's use of his baby nickname, hearing it as a denial of his hard-won adult identity.

The eldest daughter, perhaps now through circumstance able to offer only infrequent support, may still be expected to bear the greatest responsibility. In this instance, the daughter may feel immensely conflicted: On the one hand, she resents being expected to take charge when "everyone knows" her circumstances; on the other hand, she is ashamed that she can't do what is

---

'May You Live Long and Prosper'

ONCE UPON A TIME—a time only moderately removed from our own era—long life was a gift for the few. The average life span for someone born in medieval Europe was not much more than 20 years. Worldwide, today's average life expectancy is about 64 years for men, 68 years for women.

Medical advances and a host of improvements in living conditions have greatly accelerated the gains over the past century. Someone born in the United States in 2000 can expect to live about 30 years longer than an American born a hundred years earlier, and life expectancy continues to lengthen.

In the United States and elsewhere, most of the gain reflects declining death rates for children and young adults. But old people are getting older as well. A woman who reaches 65 can now expect to live, on average, to 82.9 years. A 65-year-old man can expect to live to 81.

Meanwhile, many more people are now living to extreme old age: Where once only a very few people made it to their one hundredth birthday, the United States now has 40,000 centenarians. Of the 70 million baby boomers currently en route to being the "elder boomer" generation, three million can expect to reach the age of one hundred.

---

expected of her. And on the third hand, being accustomed to taking charge, she may start bossing her siblings around.

Meanwhile, the once-rebellious younger daughter may want to make up for all the heartache her teenage self caused her parents—but neither her parents nor her siblings trust her to do what she promises. The understandable tendency is for family members to assume they know what other family members are about, what their intentions are, how they'll react in a given situation. Without anyone meaning for it to happen, the ghosts in the room are soon rehashing old issues.

Another human tendency is to believe that one's own version of events—one's own "story"—is right. The consequence, of course, is that anyone else's story has to be wrong. In *Difficult Conversations: How to Discuss What Matters Most,* authors Douglas Stone, Bruce Patton, and Sheila Heen of the Harvard Negotiation Project point out that each of us is influenced by a unique set of experiences and by different implicit "rules" about the way people should behave or how things should be.

The conclusions we reach reflect these experiences and rules, often without our having recognized or articulated them, even to ourselves. At the same time, we don't know what the other person's story is. We may think we do—indeed, we frequently think we do; we easily ascribe motives to them that they would be shocked to hear. In fact, though, each of us is privy to information that no one else has about our own circumstances, feelings, and assumptions—information that would go a long way toward helping another person understand our story.

A first step, the authors say, is to become curious—to shift from being certain about the rightness of our own version of things to wondering what lies beneath our own certainty (what, exactly, makes us so certain?) and then what lies beneath the other person's certainty about the rightness of *their* story. Pausing to uncover our own assumptions is an exercise in humility that is not always easy to carry out, but it is essential to resolving what may seem to be intractable differences.

Beyond Either/Or

A second helpful step is to adopt what Stone and his coauthors call the "And Stance." This approach avoids the characteristic "either/or" situation of feeling that only one story can be "right." For example, Lauren's 76-year-old mother, Frances, although intensely private about her life, will ask Lauren for loans to tide her over from time to time. "She'll make vague references to 'business' that she has," Lauren says, "but when I ask what kind of business, she

---

Who Are the Caregivers?

IN THE UNITED STATES TODAY, family members provide about 80 percent of the care of the elderly. The estimated annual value of this unpaid work is as high as $257 billion. One person usually becomes the primary caregiver, with siblings and perhaps other relatives or friends lending some support. In most cases, the role is assumed by women —a spouse, a daughter (the likeliest, by a wide margin), a daughter-in-law, a granddaughter. Women shoulder this responsibility more often than do men, and on average devote 50 per cent more time to it.

Although every situation is unique, a broad survey can yield a profile of a "typical" caregiver. A 2004 study conducted for AARP and the National Alliance for Caregiving found that the typical caregiver is a 46-year-old woman. She is a high-school graduate, married, and works full-time outside the home, earning $35,000 per year. The recipient of her care is a 77-year-old mother, mother-in-law, or grandmother. The caregiver devotes an average of 18 hours per week to the task and the duration of her caregiving is about 4.5 years.

stonewalls me. 'Just business,' is all she'll say." Lauren's story is that she is worried that her mother is the victim of a financial scam. Frances feels her daughter is trying to take over her affairs. With the And Stance, neither Lauren nor Frances would be required to give up their own stories, only to try to understand each other's. Stone and his colleagues acknowledge that the suggestion to embrace both stories might seem at first hearing like "double-talk." What they have found, however, is that the process allows each person to recognize a powerful truth: Regardless of any "facts" and regardless of whether or not one story influences the other, "both stories matter."

Being mindful of one's own story and remembering the And Stance during conversations with parents and siblings takes conscious effort. It will not necessarily work smoothly right off the bat. But the possible rewards—in deepening understanding and connection between older parents and their adult children, and among adult siblings as they work together to care for their parents—are incalculable.

The Pre-Talk Talk

Before initiating The Conversation, you'll need to make two kinds of evaluations: one about the relationship dynamics in your family and the other about how your parents are doing with the routines of daily life.

On the first score, take some quiet time to think about your lifelong relationship with your parents and how it can help shape your choices going forward. Consider not only how things have gone in recent years but also how they were when you were a child; the dynamics of how you and your parents interacted back then may bubble to the surface again now.

Were you "Daddy's girl"? That may be something you can appeal to as you open discussions with your father about what the future holds. Conversely, you and your mother may find it easy to be frank with one another, whereas conversations between you and your father always seem like a trip through a minefield.

Are you the eldest? Your parents—or your siblings—may look to you to carry the weight of a difficult situation. You may feel comfortable doing so, but consider whether it might be better in the long run for others to take a greater share of the load.

You and your siblings will need to pull together in coming years; if a foundation for cooperation doesn't exist already, it's crucial to establish one now.

Indeed, there may be liabilities in your relationship with your parents that will make it more difficult for them to hear what you have to say; in that case, it might be more productive for a brother or sister—or even a close family friend—to initiate the discussion. If it seems likely that tensions will run high, it can also help to have a neutral third party present, such as a counselor or clergy member.

Your relationship assessment may also involve addressing your family's culture. In some communities, it literally goes without saying that older parents will live with their children. In others, older parents may insist on remaining independent as long as possible. Or perhaps children are expected to take specific roles in caring for the previous generation. "From my experience," says Mei, a 47-year-old Chinese American, "most elderly Chinese parents (especially mothers) prefer to live with their sons and daughters-in-law. However, the same Chinese parents would say they wish for a daughter to be close by because they feel a daughter cares for elderly parents more thoroughly. In my case, my brother is the primary caretaker by nature of his being geographically closer, but I am expected to call home every day, and to be available at a moment's notice. My father had always preferred to have me handle their affairs." Regardless of your own family's culture, it's best not to assume beforehand that all of your family members agree on what "should" happen. Sometimes older parents and adult children have different expectations and desires; one or the other may not want to follow the cultural tradition.

> *Raise children for your old age as you would store up grain against famine.*
>
> — CHINESE PROVERB

After evaluating your relationship with your parents and siblings, you'll need to make a realistic, eyes-wide-open appraisal of how your parents are currently doing with the daily aspects of life. The appraisal should include both physical and mental abilities, with particular attention to any recent changes. The whole purpose in assessing the situation is to gauge what help your parents may need in order to remain independent as long as possible. Consider the following aspects of daily life:

Living arrangements. Can they still care for their home and yard? Are they able to negotiate stairs and walkways? When did they last change the smoke-alarm batteries? You might test the alarm to see if it's working and whether they can hear it from the bedroom.

Day-to-day tasks. Can they take care of their personal needs (bathing, dressing, grooming) on their own? Are they still able to shop and cook for themselves? Is mail being left unopened or trash not being taken out?

Driving. Are they able to drive and to maintain the car? You might offer to check their tires or oil occasionally, to reassure yourself and them that the car is running optimally and safely. Do they often get lost or confused? Have they been in any accidents? They may not mention these, but you might ask if you notice new dents and scratches on the car.

Physical and mental health. What are their medical conditions? Are they taking appropriate medications, and what are they? Has there been any noticeable weight loss or change in appetite? Any unexplained bruises that might indicate a fall? Do they seem depressed or agitated? Have they maintained their friends, hobbies, and activities? Older people tend to nap more during the day and sleep less at night, but have there been more significant changes in sleeping patterns?

Financial status. Are they able to keep up with bills? Is there any difference in their attitude toward money—are they spending less or more than usual? You might want to call attention to this later in order to open the door on financial discussions.

Using the checklist on page 195, make as honest an appraisal as you can of your parents' ability to handle the various aspects of daily life. Check the appropriate column and/or add comments. Make copies of this checklist and plan to reevaluate the situation every few months.

What Could They Be Thinking?

You may already have an inkling of how your parents are going to react to discussing the future, or it may be a complete mystery before you actually broach the subject. Either way, it's a good idea, once it becomes clear, to put a label on that attitude. Not only will this help guide you in how to talk to your parents, but it will also be a valuable tool in charting their adjustment to changing circumstances and how their attitude itself may change. Are they *resistant, reluctant,* or *ready?*

Let's say you've raised the subject, and your mother says, "I just don't want to talk about it." She's *resistant,* and your job will be tougher. Respect her feelings, and don't worry about putting off the discussion for another time, in the near future; it may take several tries. If her health or safety is immediately at risk, be firm but emphasize that you'll do everything you can to maintain her independence. Don't hesitate to seek professional guidance and support.

You open the door about driving, and your father says, "I know I'm going to have to give up the car someday, but I'm still perfectly capable." Your dad is *reluctant,* but not completely closed to discussion. You know now to approach difficult topics gently, leading the discussion and being prepared to encourage whatever willingness your father expresses. You and he can strategize together about that "someday."

Your parents come to you and say, "We need to talk to you about our plans for the future." They're *ready*—and you're lucky. Let them guide you, and offer all the help you can. Again, you'll probably learn much from them that will help prepare you for your own future.

But while we're on the subject of attitudes, what about yours? If you're reading this book, presumably you're not resistant, but you may still be reluctant. Hang in there, though. Remember that you're not the only one in this situation and reach out for moral—and practical—support when you need it. The steps you take here in preparation will help to ease your apprehensions.

Stage One: Breaking the Ice

It's usually best to make The Conversation at least a two-stage process, first opening up a break-the-ice dialogue between your parents and you, just to get the lines of communication going. Later you can arrange for a separate nuts-and-bolts conversation—a family meeting—to discuss specifics. At the very least, doing it in two stages gives everybody involved a chance to take a deep breath. In fact, think of this discussion not as a one-time thing—or even a two-time thing—but as a pattern of communication. Talk early, and talk often. In any event, the first talk will be an excellent guide to how to handle the more challenging specifics later.

The actual first words will hinge on your family's dynamics and on what is going on with your parents. Your relationship assessment should have clarified the best person (which may or may not be you) to initiate the first one-on-one talk with your parents. In the best case, you (or a sibling) will be addressing these matters with your parents before anything serious comes up. In the worst case, you'll be dealing with a crisis. But more than likely you'll be somewhere in the middle: You're doing this because you've noticed some problems and you realize you need to act.

Decisions for the Future

CYNTHIA DYKES INVITED her parents to her California home on Easter Sunday, for a celebration of the holiday and for a discussion she says they "couldn't put off any longer." Her parents—William, 79, and Reita, 75—are in relatively good health, but their daughter is facing a challenge. The 56-year-old artist and middle-school media center director is fighting ovarian cancer and is adamant about addressing her parents' long-term needs in the event she isn't able to care for them herself.

Cynthia notes that they'd had some discussions before. "We've talked more about what would happen in an emergency—an accident, how far to carry something like life support," she says. "At various times, I had said that I wanted to be cremated. Mother had said that, too, and that she wanted her ashes scattered over the High Sierras. During this past year, since my illness began, we've discussed it again sporadically. But I knew it was time to talk seriously together."

They had virtually no problems getting the conversation going. "It's always been easy to talk to Cynthia," says Reita, "and to listen to her. We had touched on these things before, although the subject would often get changed. So a potential caregiver needs to step forward, because it's important to think these things through." Reita also has some advice for others: "Write everything down, or even tape-record it. We realized that even though we'd updated our wills, we need new ones."

There was at least one surprise in store. Cynthia's father, a World War II veteran, had always said he wanted to be buried in a military cemetery. But at the Easter meeting he said that, like his wife and daughter, he too wanted to be cremated, with his ashes scattered in the Sierras. Cynthia doesn't know whether her health situation triggered this change. "I'm sure he wanted to be 'with' Mother," she says. "But in the end, it expresses who he is and what he deeply believes about life. What struck me is that all three of us, individually, said the same thing: We don't want a formal funeral, just a simple memorial—a celebration of life."

Although you'll need to consider the best circumstances for bringing up the subject, don't get frozen waiting for the perfect opportunity. An emergency might beat you to it.

First, a few guidelines for stage one: Don't go in with preconceived notions about what your parents might say; approach with an attitude of listening, not telling. Although it is possible your parents have done no planning, it's also likely that they've given quite a bit of thought to their ability to stay independent as they age and their needs change. They just may not have mentioned their discussions to you. Make references to yourself and your thoughts about your own future. Avoid the word "should." Your ultimate goal is not to tell them they need help, but to have them realize it for themselves (if indeed they do need help at this time). It's often more effective to pose questions than make statements. But try not to turn everything into a question, which can quickly become confrontational, especially if your parents have tended to guard their privacy. Open-ended statements often get the discussion going better. Here are a few ways to start the ball rolling, with some examples of how a conversation might begin.

Be open to openings. Rather than waiting for your parents to bring up the subject, be alert and take quick advantage of any comments they make. Your father might mention that his eyes are bothering him, for example. So you could say, "You know, I just got my prescription adjusted last week—maybe yours needs adjusting, too."

Approach indirectly. In essence, you want them to start thinking about something without yet relating it directly to themselves. If you're both in the car, complaining about traffic as you drive somewhere, you might say, "One of my neighbors told me the other day his car's been in the shop for more than a week. He's been taking the subway to work and says he thinks he might switch permanently. Sometimes I think about doing that myself!"

Ask for help. "I'm starting to think about estate planning," you say. "Do you have any advice?" Your parents have always guided you and still can. You may learn something—and you'll get them thinking about their own situation.

Offer help. This is another way of broaching the subject indirectly. For example, you might ask a question that assumes your parents are addressing an issue they may not yet be. "Hey, you want some help researching the new

---

Caring Coupons

"THE LAST THING any of us need is more 'stuff,'" says 45-year-old Chris. "So a couple of Christmases ago, instead of presents we exchanged coupons: for washing the dishes, or returning rental movies, or breakfast in bed. It was great fun, and a lot of laughs on Christmas morning. But there was a practical side, too. Dad wasn't keeping up with the yardwork at his house. So we agreed to a coupon exchange: I gave him a summer's worth of grass cutting, and he gave me tapes of his reminiscing about his own parents and grandparents. Now I have a precious record of family history, and he gets his grass cut without feeling we're taking over his life. When I'm over there mowing, I always wish him Merry Christmas, even in the middle of July."

Medicare rules on the Internet? I hear it's pretty tough to figure out the different options." Or make a gift of some assistance you know they need; it might provide an opening to further discussion (see "Caring Coupons," page 20).

Be direct, and show your concern. Especially if your parent seems resistant or reluctant, you may need to raise an issue your parent would like to avoid. Don't be confrontational. Instead, use "I" messages. Tell how you are feeling, not what they need to do. Remember, you're in this together. "Dad, I'm really worried about you falling on the stairs; you've tripped a couple of times. How can I help keep you safe?"

Be ready to be "found out." You've tried to be subtle or indirect, and they've seen right through you. Laugh at yourself. It could turn out to be the perfect opening: "Yeah, okay. So much for subtlety. I'm so bad at this stuff. But it's been on my mind and I really think we need to start talking about it."

If your parents are resistant or reluctant, your first attempt may well fall flat. But it's far better to tread softly than to precipitate an argument that could shut off further discussion. You may have to come back to the subject several times before you detect a change in your parents' willingness to move on to more direct talk.

Many people have found it helps to write a letter to their parents, even if they live nearby. Sometimes it is easier to express in writing what is difficult to say or what older parents resist hearing. If all efforts hit a brick wall and the direct talk just isn't happening, don't hesitate to seek support in the community. There's plenty out there (see Resources, page 29).

Stage Two: Organizing a Family Meeting

When you're ready, start planning a family meeting. Keep two fundamental things in mind as you prepare for this nuts-and-bolts discussion. First, do what you can to involve everyone in the family, including your spouse, your children, and out-of-town siblings. Also, "family" can mean close friends, too. Older adults may feel isolated from other members of their generation, so if your parents have friends they have kept in touch with over the years, try to get them involved as well (see "The Best Laid Plans...," page 22).

The second thing to keep in mind is that, starting out, the goal is raising issues, not necessarily finding solutions. The most crucial aspect of bringing up the subject is getting all the concerns on the table. You might consider drawing up a list of questions before the meeting so your parents and the rest of the people involved can think about what they want and how they feel (see "Practically Speaking," opposite). You can and should gather some information—about resources in the community, and about such issues as Medicare, advance directives, living arrangements—but only to encourage the thought process, not necessarily to come up with definitive answers.

Be prepared for some awkwardness at first—maybe a great deal of it. When strong emotions run close to the surface, you and your family members may

---

The Best-Laid Plans

Lauren, 57, lives with her husband in Virginia. About 15 years ago, Lauren's mother and father divorced, and her mother, Frances, moved from San Diego to Virginia to be near Lauren. Scott, Lauren's brother and only sibling, is 55. He and his wife, Carol, live in northern California, where he and Lauren grew up.

I WISH TO HEAVEN Scott and I had held a more formal, sit-down conversation with Mom, maybe with her friends as well. It probably would have saved us the time, money, and angst we spent going down what turned out to be the wrong road.

Several years ago, as Mom neared 70, we began asking her from time to time what she wanted to do and where she wanted to be once she retired. My husband and I plan to move to Monterey in a few years, and I let her know that I was concerned about stranding her on the East Coast. Her general health is okay, but her arthritis was bad when she moved here, and over the years it's gotten worse. She has two artificial hips, her knees are gone, and she can't negotiate stairs or curbs without help. Her answers were always vague: "I don't know. Haven't made up my mind."

About a year ago, I told her that Scott and I were thinking of going in together on a house back home that he and Carol could live in. What if we looked for a house that could have a separate apartment for her? Much to my surprise, she seemed quite enthusiastic. So we bought a house a few months later, and Scott and Carol moved into it. But when we began talking to Mom about moving her there in a few months, she abruptly said she wasn't ready yet, and that she didn't want to live "on the property" in any case.

We were floored. In hindsight I realize that the key decisions had been made in the course of a few brief phone calls, which is typically how my mother and I communicate. I was so surprised when she agreed that I didn't stop to ask questions.

I guess while Scott and I were thinking in terms of "right now," Mom was thinking "maybe someday." It's also clear she hadn't registered that we had planned to split the mortgage payments three ways. Now Scott and I each pay half, which is a stretch for both of us. Mom now says she wants to stay where she is "as long as I'm able."

After that? We have no clue.

stumble over how to say things so as not to hurt feelings or rub someone the wrong way—only to find that feelings get hurt anyway. When this happens, it's helpful to remember the idea of embracing not only your own story but the other person's as well. If you say something that upsets your father, ask him to give you some background on why he had that reaction. Similarly, if someone says something that upsets you, take a moment to look inside; explore the sources of your emotion, then explain why you got upset. The more each of you understands the other's thinking and feeling, the more likely you are to find a way through the impasse together. Each time you do this, it should get easier—and each time you'll learn something to help you move forward. The guidelines below will help you plan this family meeting.

Venue. If possible, hold the meeting at your parents' home or some place where they feel comfortable. You want the setting to facilitate conversation, not shut it down. Holding this discussion on another person's turf may feel like a threat to them before you even get off the ground.

Practically Speaking

HERE ARE SOME SAMPLE TOPICS for discussion at your first family meeting.

☐ How is your parents' health? If they have chronic problems, what are the prospects?

☐ Is their home still a viable place for them to live? Do adjustments need to be made, such as grab rails in the bathroom or a wheelchair ramp at the back door? Should they consider new arrangements?

☐ Do they need some assistance with routine daily chores? Is there a youngster in the neighborhood who can do the yardwork?

☐ What about driving? Are there good alternatives?

☐ What is their financial situation?

☐ Where are their important documents: wills, advance directives, bank and stock certificates?

☐ Is their health insurance adequate?

☐ What are their end-of-life wishes?

Schedule. Try to schedule the meeting at a time when most family members can attend in person. Include those who live far away by arranging a conference call or by using that tool so beloved of teenagers, instant messaging. Don't forget to invite any members of your parents' "family" who might be part of a caregiving team, including partners or close friends.

Facilitator. If your parents have resisted talking about caregiving issues, consider asking a third party to help, such as a clergy member or social worker.

Old business. If you think family members are likely to slip back into patterns and rivalries from your childhood and adolescence, you might try to have a conversation with them ahead of time to call a truce. But if that seems unlikely to succeed, the neutral facilitator can help avoid the pitfalls that come with a resurfacing of longstanding family roles, issues, and conflicts. It's crucial to keep the past from getting in the way of focusing on the most important thing: the long-term health and care of your parents.

New business. Decide in advance what will be discussed. Draw up a list of questions or topics. What's on the list will depend on whether you're in a best-case scenario, planning for the future, or responding to a crisis. But one way or the other, keep in mind that not everything can be resolved in one meeting. You may very well focus this first get-together exclusively on raising issues, not finding solutions.

It is very difficult to live among people you love and hold back from offering them advice. —ANNE TYLER

Remember to ask your parents open-ended questions and avoid statements of the "this is what you should do" variety. It's important to reinforce that getting them help is not about taking away their independence. Rather, it's about giving them support services to remain independent.

To-do list. One of the first things on the list should be locating your parents' critical legal, financial, and medical documents. You will need to ask your parents where they keep their key papers and, with their agreement, help to make an inventory, noting which documents need to be updated and photocopied (see "Key Documents," page 197, and "Inventory," pages 198-199).

Although this may seem a daunting chore, you might find a surprising side benefit. As you go through old papers and documents with your parents, you may see a side of them you've never known. Old photographs, military papers, school records, and the like can trigger stories and memories of your parents' youth that allow you to get a glimpse of them as young men and women, as people of accomplishment and profoundly moving experiences.

Once you've located the necessary papers, it's time to discuss responsibilities, recognizing that talents or abilities—such as legal or financial expertise or medical experience—may naturally lend themselves to specific tasks. In Mei's Chinese American family, for example, the cultural tradition places great value on sons.

"My mother would call my brother first for help with most things because of this and because of his proximity to her home," says Mei. "However, my Chinese language skills are better than his, so I've always been called upon to help with doctors, hospitals, lawyers—any situation where translation is essential. I would travel from Maryland to New York every couple of weeks to tend to my parents' medical needs."

Based on your earlier assessment, draw up a list of tasks that need to be accomplished with a schedule that shows which are pressing, which can wait, and which ones need to be taken care of regularly. These jobs might include acting as medical advocate; providing transportation; preparing meals; performing home repairs; checking in by telephone; helping with bills or insurance claims; or providing hands-on care. Parents should be included in all these conversations if they are healthy enough to participate.

Follow-up. Make arrangements to schedule subsequent meetings and to communicate regularly, especially with family members who live far away. Keeping everyone in the loop will reduce tensions and make it easier to deal with emergencies. Of course, not all families will be able to establish regular family meetings, for many different reasons. Sometimes caregiving really is a family affair; other times only certain family members will be involved. Whatever your situation, regular communication among those who are involved is critical— however many people that may be.

Stage Three: The Actual Talk

To keep the dialogue open and avoid confrontation, start by focusing on your parents' wishes. Ask them to talk about what they would want "in an ideal world." Living arrangements can be a sensitive topic, so don't rush this discussion. Let everyone air their views and concerns. Your father might want something slightly different from what your mother wants; if they haven't discussed this already and settled on a mutually agreeable scenario, this would be a good way to get the topic on the table. You may need to revisit this topic several times before the family reaches a decision.

Don't be surprised if your parents' "ideal world" turns out to be centered on their friends rather than on their family. Friends, it turned out, were the underlying reason Lauren's mother, Frances, didn't want to leave the East Coast, even to be near her children." I have very dear friends and a great support group here," Frances says. Adds Lauren, "It now occurs to me that Mom moved away from home 30 years ago. She and her sister are not particularly close, and she has very few if any friends back there."

At some point you'll move on to end-of-life issues, such as advance directives and funeral preferences. Touching lightly on this now will reassure your parents—and remind you—that they're still in control.

Some adult children may find, of course, that their parents are way ahead of them on this score. Many older parents have been caregivers themselves for their own parents or spouses and are well aware of the challenges involved. Claudine, for instance, an 82-year-old woman living with her daughter, cared first for her father, who had Alzheimer's disease, and then for her husband, who suffered from Parkinson's disease. Although she no longer drives or maintains her own household, she contributes financially to her daughter, manages rental property that she owns, and maintains all her own records. "I've written a letter to each of my executors," she says, "telling them where to find all my important documents. I've done powers of attorney, a will, a living will, and additional health instructions. I added my daughter's name to all my CDs and my bank accounts. You need to make arrangements for someone to make payments on your insurance, your mortgage, and your bills in case something happens to you."

In the course of the conversation, your parents may start to express their concerns and their fears. Again, let this discussion run its course; be prepared to bring it up again, if need be. Remind everyone that while the best may be too much to hope for, the worst is probably too much to fear. Knowing the extremes is a good way to keep a balanced view as you move forward.

Caregiving at a Distance

According to AARP, one-quarter of people caring for elderly relatives do so at a distance. As stressful as this can be for all concerned, many organizations and resources exist for just this situation. Even when faced with a sudden crisis from afar—for example, your parent with Alzheimer's is found wandering in her neighborhood and you and your siblings live 2,000 miles away—you shouldn't rush into any decisions about your parent's care. The whole family will need to assess her situation and needs, evaluate your own lives, get organized, and research your options before taking any big steps.

Geriatric care managers. Your family might want to begin by engaging a geriatric care manager to conduct a thorough assessment of your parent's situation. These professionals can also be the single person in your parent's area to supervise her diverse needs.

The National Association of Professional Geriatric Care Managers provides referrals to these specialists. You should interview candidates and ask for their professional credentials, licenses, and references. Find out if the care managers are available 24 hours a day and how and when they will communicate with the family. Some geriatric care managers provide consumer education and advocacy and can offer counseling and support. They may also provide family or individual therapy, finance management, and assistance with conservatorship or guardianship. Geriatric care managers can be expensive, so be sure to get a clear idea what the care will cost before hiring one.

Building a long-distance team. Even an only child—or an only responsible child—can't and shouldn't try to take care of a parent by herself. She should build a caregiving team with close family members, good friends of her parents, caring neighbors, doctors, clergy, and paid caregivers. If she is visiting her mother's neighborhood, she should introduce herself to her mother's friends and neighbors. If her mother okays it, she can leave a key or two to the residence with trusted friends nearby, making note of all names and contact information and giving her own contact information in turn to her parent's friends and neighbors.

For jobs that family and friends cannot handle, a number of community services, both free and otherwise, can help bridge the gap. Many of them can be found through the Administration on Aging's Eldercare Locator Hotline and the local aging office, as well as through local religious organizations and others (see Resources, page 29). Home-delivered meal services (such as Meals on Wheels), for example, can bring free, or low-cost, meals to a homebound person's door. The volunteers who bring these meals can give their elderly clients a little regular companionship as well as nutrition. Grocery stores also have delivery services. Many community senior centers and religious

---

Geriatric Care Managers

GERIATRIC CARE MANAGERS are counselors, social workers, nurses, gerontologists, or other specialists who can coordinate a wide range of elder care, including:

☐ Assessing the older person's needs

☐ Screening and arranging for different types of in-home help

☐ Reviewing the older person's financial, legal, or medical issues

☐ Providing referrals to physicians who specialize in geriatric medicine

☐ Assisting with moves into nursing homes or long-term care facilities

☐ Overseeing a parent's care in general and acting as a liaison to her family

organizations will provide congregate meals, usually lunches, that offer a chance to socialize as well as eat.

You might also look into free telephone assurance programs that will place phone calls at designated times to older or disabled people living alone; if the resident doesn't answer, they will then call an emergency number provided by the family. A local friendly visitor program can also match a parent with a compatible volunteer, who will pay regular visits simply to provide companionship. Setting up and keeping track of these services long-distance takes some time but can bring great peace of mind.

Sibling Rivalry, Take Two

Adult children often find that sibling relationships become particularly stressed when some live close to an ailing parent and others live far away. Those who are closest, particularly daughters, often take on most of the care by default, even if they are not the ones best equipped to do so. Those at a distance may assume that the nearby sibling is handling matters, and limit their help to occasional phone calls; or they may feel shut out by the busy, yet resentful, nearby caregiver. It's vital not to make assumptions about what siblings are and are not able to do. Families must open the lines of communication early, use them often, and communicate honestly during this process.

Those who live far away may want to set up a regular schedule for visiting their parent, allowing for enough time both to relax with her and to meet with her caregivers in the area. They should schedule any necessary appointments with doctors and such well in advance of their visit. It's also important for them to remember that it is not all about appointments and putting services in place. They are there to visit, too. They shouldn't lose sight of the importance of having some fun with their parent.

No matter how you go about caring for your parents, the experience will entail work and worry, frustrations and fears. But the same can be said of every phase of life, and this phase brings its share of deep satisfactions and joyful moments. The following chapters will help you anticipate what is to come, how to get professional advice and aid, how to cope with crisis, and what to expect at the end.

Resources | Bringing Up the Subject

BOOKS

Stone, Douglas, Bruce Patton, and Sheila Heen. *Difficult Conversations: How to Discuss What Matters Most.* New York: Penguin Books, 2000.

ONLINE SEMINARS AND ARTICLES

Family Caregiving Seminars. AARP *www.aarp.org/learn/course/* A free series of three one-hour seminars; covers "Planning for the Care of Aging Parents," "Options and Strategies for the Care of Your Aging Parents," "Caring for Aging Parents: Managing the Details," and "Navigating Your Way to a Quality Assisted Living Facility."

"Long Distance Caregiving." AARP. *www.aarp.org/life/caregiving/ Articles/a2003-10-27-caregiving-longdistance.html*

"Long Distance Caregiving." UCSB Human Resources Department. *hr.ucsb.edu/Worklife/Elder_Care/ elder_care_longdistance.htm*

"Taking Care of Our Parents." *www.aarpmagazine.org/family/ Articles/a2003-01-21-takingcare.html* A series of articles from *AARP: The Magazine,* available online.

OTHER RESOURCES

Eldercare Locator (Administration on Aging) 800-677-1116 / *www.eldercare.gov/ Eldercare/Public/Home.asp* A first stop for information on services for the elderly.

Family Caregiver Alliance (National Center on Caregiving) 800-445-8106 / *www.caregiver.org* Provides online fact sheets and a downloadable handbook for long-distance caregivers. Fact sheets also available in Spanish and Chinese.

Meals on Wheels Association of America 703-548-5558 / *www.mowaa.org* An association of programs that provide home-delivered and congregate meals.

National Academy of Elder Law Attorneys 520-881-4005 / *www.naela.com* Assists those who provide specialized legal services to the elderly and their caregivers. Points caregivers to local elder law attorneys.

National Association of Professional Geriatric Care Managers 520-881-8008 www.caremanager.org Website explains the role of care managers and points caregivers to local resources.

2 Your Parent's Best Advocate

Do what you can, with what you have,
where you are. —THEODORE ROOSEVELT

WHEN LINDA'S FEISTY Italian American mother moved in with Linda and her husband Tom, they welcomed her into their household. They enjoyed Anne-Marie's lively opinions and her stories about the family, the "sweethearts and the bums." But her presence also placed big demands upon Linda. In addition to working full-time and managing her own household, Linda had to take on her mother's affairs: paying bills, handling insurance, and arranging to become her mother's representative to the outside world.

As Linda discovered, being an advocate—a person who intercedes on another's behalf—is part of being a caregiver. How large a part depends on the older parent's situation and on the caregiver's personality. Most older people are perfectly capable of speaking for themselves, thanks very much, and may not want their children's well-meaning assistance. Others might handle most situations well, but ask for help with specific issues, such as dealing with an insurance company. Those who are seriously ill may need someone to speak for them every day.

Most often, an adult child is called upon to act as her parent's advocate when the parent is unwell and dealing with institutions and bureaucracies, such as hospitals, insurers, and nursing homes. As Anne-Marie's health declined, for example, Linda had to research and find an elder-care facility that could care for her full-time, and then monitor the care her mother received there. It's not an easy task even when a parent and her adult child are in the same region. It's especially difficult at long distance. Karin, the only child of a widowed mother, discovered this when her mother, who lived in Germany, decided to enter a private retirement community there. "In the last two years of her life, I visited three times a year," she says, "and had to constantly challenge the organization about things that had been neglected or that should have been dealt with better. I still struggle with thinking about how things could have been made easier and better for her."

Old Family Scripts

During this difficult period, Karin was fortunate in being able to travel as often as she did. As daunting as practical logistics can be, for many people, emotional issues loom as large as practical ones. Adult children often have trouble accepting that the authority figures of their youth now need their help, so they ignore warning signs until there is a crisis. Parents have a similar problem, albeit in reverse: Why should they seek advice from the son they had to ground as a teenager? Families tend to work from old scripts, with their members cast in old roles. Simply recognizing this dynamic is the first step in dealing with it. Honest communication is the next. It's okay to say, "Mom, I know I couldn't balance a checkbook when I was 18, but I've handled household accounts for 30 years now, so you don't need to worry." Parents have the right to say, "Maybe so, but I'm just not comfortable letting my child speak for me."

Adult children may also find it helpful to keep in mind the life experiences that shaped their parents' attitudes. People who lived through the Depression often have an aversion to being "in debt," even emotionally. "My father used to say that old people should be put on a boat and sent out in the ocean so they wouldn't be a burden on their families," says Susan, who simply disregarded that notion to care for her father as he developed Alzheimer's. "We were raised to be self-sufficient and never lean on anyone nor ask for help. So my father had an ethic of never imposing. He never even liked to visit for more than about three days at a time."

Sure I'm for helping the elderly. I'm going to be old myself some day.

—LILLIAN CARTER, IN HER 80s

Older parents, especially those from traditionally male-dominated cultures, might also have trouble yielding authority to a female child, even while they expect her to be the nurturer. Carla, a Latin woman who cared for her mother after the older woman had a serious accident, says that her mother fought against giving up control over anything to a daughter. Nevertheless, Carla and her mother came to an understanding about allowing Carla to start helping with her medical and financial matters. "She may resent that I take care of her and that she needed to relinquish some control, but she knows I am the one who truly understands her. She knows I have her best interests at heart."

The Organized Advocate

Advocacy requires strong organizational skills and firm but polite assertiveness and persistence when dealing with bureaucracies, so before you take it on yourself, consider which family member has the best skills for the task. You can spread the jobs around—the shy sibling can organize hospital bills and the outgoing one can call the billing department—but it's important for your parent and siblings to agree on a single person to act as advocate with a given institution, so that a doctor, for instance, is not besieged by conflicting requests from different family members.

A critical aid to survival is getting organized early on (see box below). As

---

Laying the Groundwork

SHARING THE WORKLOAD

☐ Don't be afraid to ask for assistance. When colleagues, friends, and neighbors ask if they can help, take them at their word and give them a job to do.

☐ Make a list of tasks and find out what each family member is able to handle.

☐ Siblings who live far away can take on paying bills or researching medical or legal information. The ones closer to home can pick up daily chores.

☐ Those with more money than time can help pay for home care or house-cleaning.

SETTING UP COMMUNICATIONS

☐ Talk with your family members about what works best for keeping in touch— regular phone calls, letters, e-mail?

☐ Don't be afraid to set boundaries: no phone calls on Sundays, for instance, or e-mail just twice a week.

☐ For emergencies, a phone tree is useful so that you don't have to make all the phone calls.

CREATING THE SYSTEMS AT HOME

☐ Create separate files for your parent's medical information, bills, correspondence, and legal papers.

☐ If you have a regular schedule for paying bills, consider whether you will need to allow more time to add your parent's bills to the mix.

☐ Even if you have a relaxed attitude toward your own paperwork, you must be scrupulous and meticulous in managing your parent's affairs.

experienced caretakers will confirm, the initial up-front effort will go a long way toward relieving the stresses of caregiving down the road.

Once you've spoken with your parent and assessed her situation, the next order of business is to look at arranging your own life to accommodate your new responsibilities. (If a parent is facing a medical crisis, however, locating crucial documents may take priority. See pages 197-199.) Throughout the process, be mindful of respecting parental privacy and priorities. Unless your parent is not mentally able to handle her own affairs, you need to work *with* her, not instead of her or despite her. Of course bills need to be paid, and it's important to have certain documents prepared, especially in the event of a medical crisis. But an excess of "help" will feel like interference and she won't appreciate it any more than you would.

A little black book. The first things you should stock up on are thick, sturdy spiral notebooks that fit in a purse or briefcase and small day-to-day calendars (or planners that incorporate both). You must become a note-taking dynamo, keeping track of daily appointments, medication schedules, phone numbers, to-do lists, and other bits and pieces of information. The book is also essential for taking notes on conversations with doctors and other caregivers, with dates attached. Always carry the notebook with you, and refer to it often. As you fill one up, mark its beginning and ending dates, put it where you can find it easily, and start another.

> *Worry often gives a small thing a big shadow.* —SWEDISH PROVERB

Options at work. If you need to take leave or change your work schedule, look into options at your workplace: The Family and Medical Leave Act (FMLA) allows workers to take up to 12 weeks of unpaid leave during any 12-month period to care for close family members with serious health problems—without losing their jobs or health benefits. FMLA does not apply to all employers and employees, however, so check first.

Talk to your supervisor, the human resources department, or both, about your situation and the possibilities for flextime, job sharing, or part time work. Be honest about the demands on your time and consider your employer's needs as well. Most employers are sympathetic to these situations. After all, they have parents, too.

Don't be a martyr. Surprisingly few caregivers—only about 12 percent— actually seek support at their place of employment, according to a study by

When Things Fall Apart

Emma, a 60-year-old retired newspaper editor living in Savannah, Georgia, is an only child who took on the care of both her parents.

A YEAR BEFORE things came to a head, I visited my parents in Atlanta, about an eight-hour drive away. Various comments had gotten me worried. My father was then 88, my mother 84. I realized at once that they'd lost a lot of ground. They'd aged enormously. We had as much of a discussion as was possible. They rejected any idea of assisted living, making the common mistake that their insurance would be adequate for home care if they needed it.

They also made the the mistake of giving each other power of attorney. However, when I asked my father whether my mother could find her way about if he should suddenly die, he said, "She couldn't find her way to the front door." So we went to the family lawyer and arranged for me to have a durable power of attorney. If I had not had this, things would have been almost impossible when the situation deteriorated, late in the summer of 2001.

A neighbor of my parents called to say that Mother had had a fall and fractured her leg. When I arrived in Atlanta, my mother was in the hospital, abruptly withdrawn from alcohol and cigarettes, and terribly confused. She didn't recognize me. My father was even sicker than she. He had a rare blood disorder that prevented his blood from clotting. He'd been bleeding for two days from a minor cut and he, too, had to go into the hospital.

I was much luckier than most. My husband was quite ill, but we had no children. I also had the great good fortune to live across the street from an excellent nursing home in Savannah.

So there was an initial period of two to three weeks, with both parents in the hospital in Atlanta, when I drove back and forth between Atlanta and Savannah, getting things organized. Our friends and neighbors in both places were a huge help, as was my family's accountant and friend, who not only knew everything that had to be done but who was wonderful about doing it.

The nursing home had a rule against admitting out-of-city residents, so first I had to persuade them to take my mother. Then, because only one room was available at the time, I had to make my own house safe for my father to live in temporarily. With a 23-step staircase, this meant installing a chairlift.

While I was getting everything set up, there were issues with my parents at the hospital back in Atlanta. It was so complicated, having to do with satisfying Medicare conditions so that payments for their care would continue. But I had found a wonderful geriatric consultant, who had it under control. He was worth his weight in gold.

Two months and a dozen eight-hour drives later, my mother was installed in the nursing home and my father was strong enough to move. I returned to Savannah to be sure my house was ready. The geriatric consultant took my father to the Atlanta airport. I met him in Savannah and drove him home.

Questions for the Doctor

HAVE YOUR PARENT write these down in advance, then note the answers in writing.

☐ What is wrong with me?

☐ How do you know?

☐ What caused it?

☐ Do I need tests? What do they involve?

☐ How do I prepare for them?

☐ When will I know the results?

☐ Does my insurance cover the costs?

☐ What are my treatment choices and what are the pros and cons of each?

☐ What are the side effects?

☐ What do I do if the treatment fails?

☐ What kind of medication do I take? For how long? What is the dosage? Do I take it until it's finished?

☐ What are the side effects and how does it interact with other medicines?

☐ Should I avoid food or activity while taking the medicine?

☐ Can I take a generic version?

AARP a few years ago. They may be reluctant to do so because they're concerned about appearing not sufficiently committed to their work, or because they believe they simply ought to be able to take care of their father or mother without extra accommodation. But if the strain of trying to juggle the demands of work and family becomes too much and the caregiver falls ill, who will take care of their parents then?

Peter, a 45-year-old who took on his mother's finances after his father died, found that support from his employer was crucial when he had to take time off following his father's death. "He was a real human being who understood what I was going through. Everyone hits that place, at some point. It actually surprised me that there were meaningful events in one's life that other people recognized—no matter what else is going on."

Managing Health Care

If you take on the role of your parent's health-care advocate, careful and constant note taking is essential. However, if note taking is not your forte, another approach is to bring a tape recorder to all appointments. Be sure to ask permission of the doctor before you begin taping. Not only will you capture all the information being delivered, but you also send an important message to the doctor—that you and your parent are highly engaged partners in his health care.

At the doctor's office. Find out if your parent needs, or wants, your help communicating with his doctor. If he doesn't broach the subject himself, you might bring it up by describing your experiences, or those of a friend, when trying to take in information at the doctor's office. You can mention how helpful it is to have a third party present to take notes so that you and the doctor can have a relaxed conversation. If your parent agrees, and requests your presence, have a preliminary talk with him before the appointment so you can write down his questions, concerns, and symptoms in your notebook. Include any new symptoms since the last visit, and any major life changes or stresses, such as the death of a family member or new living arrangements. Bring a list of all his medicines.

If it's the first visit to a new doctor, be sure that any medical records are sent

> *We can lick gravity, but sometimes the paperwork is overwhelming.*
>
> —Wernher von Braun

over from the previous doctor, that your parent has his insurance card, and that you arrive in time to fill out new patient forms. (It's also useful to double check that your parent's health insurance policy has his correct Social Security number and date of birth. A bill from the doctor with the *correct* information will be rejected if the insurance company's records are incorrect.)

Let your parent do the talking, if at all possible, and chime in gently with unanswered questions or concerns when he is done. He might have issues he wants to keep private, so offer to wait outside for part of the time.

When the visit begins, it's perfectly appropriate for your parent or you to ask the doctor how much time she has. Then prioritize your questions, beginning with the most important. If your parent can't cover all his concerns in the time available, ask how he can get more time to address his questions.

Help him overcome white-coat paralysis: If he answers the doctor's "How are you?" with a polite and meaningless "Fine, thank you," you may need to step in: "I think Dad's been bothered by shortness of breath this week, isn't that right, Dad?"

Write down all of the doctor's answers in your notebook. If you don't understand a term, ask her to explain it. And when she's finished, repeat what she's told you—diagnosis, treatment, medicines—to confirm that you've understood her correctly. If you or your parent has an unanswered question after you get home, don't hesitate to call the doctor's office later to follow up.

If you want a second opinion, don't be shy; it is a perfectly reasonable request and doctors will not be surprised by it. For the most objective opinion, look for a second doctor who is not connected to the current doctor's practice.

At the pharmacy. If you will be picking up or doling out your parent's medications, get to know your local pharmacist. He or she can give you good advice about how and when your parent should take the medicine, generic alternatives, side effects, and interactions with other drugs. Make sure the pharmacist has the following information about your parent:

- His age
- His weight
- His ethnicity (some drugs affect certain ethnic groups differently: For example, the ulcer drug Prilosec has a different effect on Asian Americans than it has on Caucasians)
- Other medications he is taking (including over-the-counter drugs, vitamins, and herbal supplements)
- Allergies or difficulties in taking other medicines

Ask if the pill can be crushed or split (you can buy a pill-splitter for just this task). Can the medicine be taken gradually—a little at a time? Should it be taken with or without food? What are the potential side effects, and what can you do to alleviate them? Proofread the prescription label before you take the medicine home. Check the name of the drug, the name of the patient, and the dosage. The box at left gives the meaning of some Latin abbreviations; be sure to ask the pharmacist to explain any others.

At home with your parent, find an appropriate place to keep medicine. A medicine cabinet, oddly enough, is often too warm and moist; a cool, dry drawer is better. You also will want to keep medicine in a place that is convenient, especially if it is to be taken throughout the day. Storing the medicine in an upstairs bedroom will mean several trips up and down stairs, which might be difficult.

If young grandchildren visit, all medications must be secured behind child locks and with child safety caps, if your parent can manage them. Pills must not be left in purses or coat pockets where

Decoding a Prescription

BEFORE LEAVING the pharmacy, take a few minutes to compare the doctor's prescription to the label on the bottle to ensure there are no errors in drugs, dosage, or instructions. Doctors often communicate instructions in Latin, so the mini-dictionary here can help.

ABBREVIATION (LATIN)		MEANING
prn	(pro re nata)	as needed
ac	(ante cibum)	before meals
pc	(post cibum)	after meals
bid	(bis in die)	twice a day
tid	(ter in die)	3 times a day
qid	(quater in die)	4 times a day
q3h	(quaque 3 hora)	every 3 hours
q4h	(quaque 4 hora)	every 4 hours
hs	(hora somni)	at bedtime
po	(per os)	by mouth

children can get at them. More than one-third of accidental childhood poisonings from prescription drugs involve a grandparent's medicine.

If your parent is on several drugs at once, consider organizers and reminder systems, such as electronic pill containers or beepers. Throw out expired drugs.

At the hospital. You will need to call on all of your organizational and advocacy skills if your parent enters the hospital. Even if he has a well spouse who is handling his affairs, that spouse will be under tremendous stress and can use your support.

If your parent has a serious condition, but does not need immediate hospitalization, the first thing to consider is whether the local hospital is the best choice. Although doctors usually have privileges at certain hospitals, ask your parent's doctor and local specialists which hospital they would choose if a relative had the same condition. The Joint Commission on Accreditation of Healthcare Organizations has an online database that provides information about a hospital's specialties. Among the questions you can ask the hospital are:

> *First thing about being a patient— you have to learn patience.*
> —OLIVER SACKS

- Does the hospital provide specialized care in this condition?
- What percentage of the hospital's doctors is board certified?
- What is the average nurse-to-patient ratio? Typical ratios are one nurse to every three to six patients on regular wards and one nurse to every two patients in intensive care.
- What is the RN (registered nurse)-to-LPN (licensed practical nurse) ratio? RNs can perform a wider range of professional services. A typical ratio is four RNs to every LPN.
- What follow-up services does the hospital provide? In today's managed-health-care climate, patients are often discharged "quicker and sicker." Does the hospital provide referrals to home-care agencies or other facilities (such as rehabilitation centers) and help to coordinate this follow-up care? Does it provide training for self-care at home?

Before your parent enters the hospital, confirm that his insurance covers the treatment he's about to receive. You might also have a preliminary conversation with the hospital admission or business office.

Then, on the day your parent checks in, bring the vital information: name, address, Social Security number, Medicare, Medicaid, or other insurance cards. Bring any advance directives, such as living wills or health-care proxies.

A Patient's Bill of Rights

THE AMERICAN HOSPITAL ASSOCIATION adopted a patient's bill of rights in 1973 and recently revised it as "The Patient Care Partnership." Among the things your parent is entitled to expect during a hospital stay are:

☐ The right to considerate and respectful care

☐ The right to know the identity of doctors, nurses, and others involved in care, and the right to know whether they are students or other trainees

☐ The right to a clean and safe environment

☐ The right to understand the benefits and risks of any treatment, including it's long-term financial implications, and the right to know whether it is experimental or part of a research study

☐ The right to consent to or refuse a treatment

☐ The right to have an advance directive concerning treatment honored by the hospital to the extent permitted by law

☐ The right to understand what the patient and family will need to do after leaving the hospital

☐ The right to privacy and confidentiality in treatment

☐ The right to review medical records and have them explained

☐ The right to help when leaving the hospital

☐ The right to help with billing claims

The full list of rights is available through the American Hospital Association (see Resources, page 50).

If at all possible, bring the names and numbers of your parent's doctors and a list of medications and allergies. Your notebook will come in handy here!

When checking in, ask about your parent's room and services. Can he be upgraded to a private room? To a bed next to a window? Does the hospital provide books or newspapers, and, if so, is there a charge? What mundane items in your parent's hospital room are "extras" that the hospital charges for—boxes of tissues, for example?

Once he's settled in his room, get to know the people who will be taking care of him—doctors, the line nurse and charge nurse, and especially aides (also known as patient care assistants). Help them get to know your parent as well, his likes and dislikes, and his family. Let them know that you are your parent's advocate and the go-to person for information about his status and care. Make sure your relatives know this, too, so that the staff does not face discussion or demands from all quarters.

Just as in a doctor's office, don't be afraid to ask questions, whether of doctors or nurses. Make sure that your parent's treatment options are clear to him and to you. Ask about alternatives. If a surgeon is assigned to your parent, find out how many times the surgeon has performed that procedure.

As a patient, your parent has certain rights in the hospital, including the right to review his medical records and to have medical terms explained clearly. Bring your notebook and write everything down: the names of doctors and nurses, tests, results, procedures, instructions.

When problems arise, be firm—but be calm. Try to work with the hospital, not against it. Doctors and nurses are people, too, just as overworked and stressed out as you are. Making enemies of the health care staff certainly will do nothing to improve your parent's care, so do your best to be polite and to treat them respectfully.

Most hospitals have a patient representative; find out who that person is and use her to help cut through red tape, find answers, advocate on your behalf, and help resolve disputes. Most hospitals also have case managers (social workers or RNs) who can help arrange outside services, at-home help, and other follow-up care. If you run into an intractable or urgent issue, try to resolve it first with the person directly involved. But if necessary, you can go to the top: the director of nursing or the hospital administrator. Don't be intimidated by nurses or doctors. Stand your ground.

Sometimes caregivers hire a private-duty nurse to supplement the care their parent is receiving in the hospital, especially if the parent is hooked up to a respirator or other technology (though not while in the intensive-care or coronary-care unit). These nurses may be RNs, LPNs, or aides. Depending on their training, they can help with medical tasks, bathing, getting to the bathroom, and other jobs. Private-duty services can be expensive; check to see if your insurance company covers them. The hospital can direct you to private-duty nurse registries.

Hospital Bills and Insurance Claims

If caring for an ailing parent in the hospital hasn't tested your sanity, coping with his hospital bills surely will. They are notoriously complex and error filled. If you are not organized and good with numbers, this is a fine task to hand off to a family member or friend who has those skills.

If you suspect problems, your parent may ask the hospital for a copy of his medical records. Check the records against the bills. Your insurers can also help review the bills: Call them and ask to speak to the person who reviews questionable charges. You may also pay an agent from a group such as

Coping with Hospital Bills

WHICHEVER FAMILY MEMBER takes this on, he or she should keep all the paperwork organized in files and, if possible, set up a spreadsheet to keep track. Check for these common errors on the bills:

☐ Incorrect name, address, or Social Security number

☐ Incorrect dates of service (which usually should not include the day your parent is discharged)

☐ Wrong or duplicate orders for room fees, medications, tests, or supplies

☐ Excessive operating-room time

Medical Billing Advocates of America to research the bill for you.

Don't put off dealing with hospital bills, no matter how overworked you are or how bizarre they seem. Within 90 days, most hospitals will turn over late bills to collection agencies, and dealing with such agencies is a deeply unpleasant experience.

If your parent is receiving calls from a collection agency, call the hospital billing department and ask to speak to the person in charge of the account. And be aware that collection agencies must follow a set of guidelines about when and where to call, as established by the Fair Debt Collection Practices Act.

Review the insurance notices as they come in as well. If you believe that an insurer is unfairly denying a claim, contact its member services department and ask how to appeal a claim. State and federal laws protect your parent's right to proper health insurance practices. If the insurer is uncooperative, you may file a written complaint with your state insurance regulation bureau.

Dealing with Nursing Homes

If your parent is in a nursing home, chances are that he is not well enough to be his own advocate. Your first task in ensuring that he receives quality nursing home care is to research and visit the available facilities yourself (see chapter 7 "Living Arrangements"). Then, give him some time to get used to the transition—and give yourself time to get acquainted with the staff and the routines. Let them get to know you, too, and make them aware that you are your parent's advocate. Keep your advocate's notebook handy to jot down names, incidents, and conversations with staff.

The most elegant nursing homes are not necessarily the best. Too often, a resident's physical needs are met quite adequately, but his emotional needs are ignored by an overworked staff. Susan found this out at the nursing home where her father, already diagnosed with Alzheimer's disease, was recovering from a stroke.

"They would do everything for him rather than encouraging him to some things for himself," Susan says. "And they wouldn't engage him in conversation," Her husband, Michael, used to talk with her father about everything under the sun, as would Susan. "At dinner at the facility when I visited," she says, "he'd say something like, 'Susan, how soon can they detect pregnancy these days?' He's a veterinarian; he's interested in things like this. I'm a nurse, so I can discuss this with him. But it must have sounded like nonsense to the staff; they just ignored what he said."

Susan and Michael moved her father to a facility that specializes in Alzheimer's disease. "We looked at three places before choosing this one. It's not fancy, but the staff is very loving and they understood the pain of making the decision. I visit three times a week, and he also goes to the AD day care three times a week for the social stimulation."

Problems that arise in nursing homes can range from the minor (your father doesn't like the food) to the major (he shows signs of neglect, improper care, or even abuse). As a nursing home resident, he is legally protected by a resident's bill of rights (see box, below).

A Nursing Home Resident's Bill of Rights

AS A NURSING HOME RESIDENT, your parent has the same rights that he enjoyed as a member of the larger community. In addition, the 1987 Nursing Home Reform Law established a list of resident's rights to protect his dignity and self-determination. Among them are:

☐ The right to be fully informed of services, charges, and rules

☐ The right to know the address and telephone number of the state ombudsman and the state survey agency

☐ The right to receive information in a language he understands

☐ The right to present grievances without fear of reprisal

☐ The right to complain to the ombudsman or state survey agency

☐ The right to adequate care

☐ The right to refuse physical and chemical restraints

☐ The right to private communications, treatment, and personal care

☐ The right to be treated with consideration, respect, and dignity

☐ The right to visits by relatives, friends, and physicians, and the right to refuse such visits

☐ The right to make independent choices

The full list of rights is available through the National Citizens' Coalition for Nursing Home Reform (see Resources, page 50).

Among the symptom of problems you'll want to be on the alert for are:

- Bedsores
- Contractures (stiffening muscles)
- Physical restraints
- Malnutrition
- Dehydration
- Chemical restraints (drugs)

Your first step in dealing with most problems is to talk one-on-one with the person involved. Be friendly, not accusatory, and get their perspectives on the issue. Focus on finding a solution together. You might also take advantage of the facility's regular care-planning meetings or its family-council meetings as a forum for addressing your concerns. Find out when the next session is scheduled to take place and, without making a formal complaint, raise any issues that bother you.

Speak when you are angry—and you will make the best speech you will ever regret. —LAURENCE J. PETER

If talking with the caretakers yields no results, the next step is to go to their supervisors—the director of nursing, for instance. Be as specific as possible: not "so-and-so isn't paying attention to my father," but "yesterday so-and-so left my father sitting in his chair for three hours when he needed to be taken to the toilet." (Note: If you are worried that making these complaints will result in retaliation against your parent, make a point of saying so.)

If spoken communication is not working, file a written complaint with the facility. The nursing home is legally required to have a formal grievance process in place. When you file the complaint, ask how soon you can expect to have a resolution; the law entitles you to a reasonable response.

Outside agencies. If the problem continues, you might need to take it to the long-term care ombudsman for your area. These are state, regional, and/or local advocates who work on behalf of residents to investigate and resolve complaints against long-term care facilities. You can find the nearest ombudsman through your state agency on aging, the National Long Term Care Ombudsman Resource Center, and other sources. You can also file a complaint with the state survey agency that licenses nursing homes; these are often run by a state's department of health.

Reporting serious abuse. Serious abuse should be reported immediately to the proper authorities. Your state may also have a toll-free elder abuse hotline.

If the abuse involves serious injury, sexual abuse, or suspicious death, it is a crime and must be reported to the police as well as to the state department of aging.

Scam Alert

There is more than one kind of abuse, and it can occur outside of a nursing home facility: All too many elderly people suffer the financial battering of con artists. Jane's father, for instance, was scammed by a day laborer who showed up at his door. The man talked him into removing a small, "diseased" cherry tree in his front yard, and then presented him with a bill for $4,000.

"We were able to stop payment on the check only because my brother happened to drop by my dad's house and saw the devastation in the front yard," says Jane. "The tree guy sued my dad for the $4,000. My brother, who is a lawyer, ended up in a courtroom fighting for my dad's money. But we had to spend $2,000 to keep from paying out the $4,000 to the tree guy. It was clearly a case of my dad not realizing he should ask someone else for advice, ask the guy up front how much the service would cost, get other estimates. He was easily confused and alarmed—a perfect victim for a scam artist."

As expensive as it was, at least the tree trimmer was local and identifiable. All too often, scammers are just voices on the telephone or contractors with no fixed address who quickly get out of town. (See "Be A Fraud Detector" on page 59 for more information on scams.) How can you help your parents out of these situations?

Treading delicately. Begin by treading delicately. Your parent may be embarrassed by the incident, or he may simply resent your interference. If you believe he is being victimized by scammers, emphasize the criminal nature of the offense, not your parent's gullibility in falling for it. Scammers are adept professionals who practice their lines until they get really good at talking people out of their money. Your parent is the victim of a surprise attack, just as if he had been mugged on the street.

If he'll allow it, ask to help him balance his checkbook and check his credit card receipts. See if he'd like some help from a daily money manager. If his affairs are desperate and he refuses help, but you have power of attorney or are co-owner of his bank accounts, you may need to take control of those accounts. Without such legal powers, however, you cannot intervene in your parent's financial affairs, and even with those powers you cannot go against his expressed wishes.

If you are not already co-owner of his bank account and don't have power of attorney, your parent may prefer to set up a "convenience" or "agency" checking account, which would give you limited authority to assist with bill paying but would not make you a joint owner on his account.

Reporting fraud. You should report unfair or fraudulent business practices to your state attorney general's office and the Federal Trade Commission's Bureau of Consumer Protection. If your parent has been the victim of Internet or telephone fraud, you can report it as well via the National Fraud Information Center. These agencies will file a report with enforcement agencies, which should investigate the offending parties. However, their investigations may not move fast enough to be of practical help to your parent. If the fraud is local, report it to the police.

One of the most striking differences between a cat and a lie is that a cat has only nine lives. —MARK TWAIN

To help your parent avoid these situations in the first place, help him cut off contact with the usual avenues for fraud. Add his phone number to the National Do Not Call Registry and contact the Direct Marketing Association to opt out of mailing lists. If necessary, he can change his phone number (but remember to add it to the Do Not Call list afterward).

Go-slow policy. Also, encourage him not to sign any contracts or allow even seemingly minor work to begin without getting three estimates (remembering that the lowest estimate may not always be best). While he's at it, he should check with the Better Business Bureau to see if any complaints have been lodged against the contractor.

This is not foolproof, however, as an absence of complaints is no guarantee that the contractor is on the up and up. Finally, urge him to have a written contract with the contractor, containing full details and a clear understanding of the price.

Lawyering Up

As Jane and her brother discovered, some problems end up in court. When you need legal advice and don't have a lawyer, there are several routes you can follow; which one you choose depends on the nature and complexity of your problem. If you're in need of just forms or simple guidelines, many web-based or commercial organizations can provide basic advice and printed matter. There are also some web services that can help with mediation and dispute resolution. AARP's Legal Services Network (LSN), for example, provides access to attorneys who have been screened to meet LSN standards of experience and customer service, and who have agreed to offer their services to AARP members at reduced fees.

Call a hotline. Several states also have free legal hotlines for the elderly. In most cases, relatives or caregivers of people over 60 may also call these phone services and speak to an attorney. The hotline might assist you or your parent with simple services such making referrals to a legal service program or private bar member. Free (pro bono) or low-cost legal aid is available in most locations to low-income people. The American Bar Association, the Legal Services Corporation, and AARP can steer you to directories of these programs (see Resources, pages 50-51).

If you don't want pro bono help or don't qualify for it, you can find a good lawyer through several avenues. A fine, time-tested method is to ask a trusted friend or adviser for a recommendation. There is also the American Bar Association, which has a directory of lawyer referral services, and local county bar associations, which usually maintain a listing of elder law attorneys. Also, your local library will have guides such as the Martindale-Hubbell Law Directory.

You might want to look for a lawyer who specializes in elder law. These attorneys have expertise in matters such as age discrimination, elder abuse, fraud recovery, guardianships (see pages 48-49), Medicare appeals, nursing home issues, and the like. The National Academy of Elder Law Attorneys is a good place to begin your search.

If your parent becomes incapable of making basic personal and financial decisions on her own, and if she has not set up legal directives such as a durable

Shred, Don't Toss

AS YOU WEED THROUGH your parent's papers or mail, don't toss the discards into the wastebasket. Identity thieves are just waiting to get their hands on those goodies. Even cutting across old receipts or checks is an ineffective safeguard. The best way to render those papers unreadable. is with a cross-cut paper shredder, available from office supply stores. Among the items you'll want to destroy are:

☐ Anything with a Social Security number

☐ Anything with driver's license information

☐ Bills, especially with account numbers

☐ Credit-card receipts

☐ Pre-approved credit applications

☐ Loan applications

☐ Checks and deposit slips

☐ Bank statements

☐ Investment account reports

power of attorney, you may need to look into the process of becoming her representative.

Social Security representative payee. If your parent is not competent to manage her Social Security income, a family member, a trusted member of the caregiving team, or a social-service or government agency may apply to become a representative payee. (Power of attorney does not allow the agent to manage someone else's benefit payments.) A representative payee is an individual or organization that receives and manages Social Security and Supplemental Security Income on behalf of a beneficiary.

Because this position is easily subject to abuse, the government takes it quite seriously. Prospective representative payees need to apply to the nearest Social Security Administration office, fill out an application, and go through an interview.

As payees, they have a number of obligations and must keep scrupulously accurate records. They must use the benefits in the beneficiary's best interests to meet her current needs, saving or investing any remainder. Individual payees may not take fees for this service, although organizations such as community groups may collect a fee to cover expenses. The Social Security Administration can provide a full list of requirements and contacts for local offices.

Guardianship. Brought over from England during colonial times, guardianship is used only under narrow circumstances and only as a last resort for someone who is truly mentally incompetent, not just eccentric or spendthrift. Guardianship is painful and expensive. You and your parent will want to avoid it at all costs by ensuring that she has her legal directives, such as a durable power of attorney, in order.

"Guardianship is a godsend and a gulag," says Erica Wood, associate staff director of the American Bar Association's Commission on Law and Aging. "It's a lifesaver and a life stopper. It's an institution that we as a society need. But we need to make it better." Horror stories abound of wards who have been financially exploited by their guardians, of competent elders who have had their freedom wrongfully usurped.

Every state has specific procedures to determine the need for a guardian. If you need to petition the court to become your parent's guardian, you'll need to retain a lawyer, preferably one with an elder law background, to help you through the process. If your parent does not have an attorney representing her, the court will appoint one. The court may also appoint a *guardian ad litem*, a kind of temporary guardian who will see your parent through the legal process. Your parent will be notified of the proceedings and will need to undergo medical evaluations to assess her capacity. At that point, a judge will decide whether guardianship is warranted. Sometimes, a court grants limited guardianship—for instance, the right to make financial decisions, but not medical ones.

Guardians are supervised by the court and must act only according to the ward's best interests. Guardians must also do their best to make the kinds of decisions the ward would make if she were competent—in other words, you must put yourself in your parent's shoes and not substitute your own values for hers. If you have control over your parent's finances, you must protect her assets, keep separate accounts, spend the money only for her needs, and get advance approval from the court for major expenditures.

> *Wisdom is knowing what to do next; virtue is doing it.* —DAVID STARR JORDAN

You will be required to file regular reports to the court and account for your parent's money. As one registered nurse who was the legal guardian for her sister put it, "The protection afforded by guardianship comes with a price. A family member guardian must learn how to live with an invasion of privacy that requires us to document information and to seek the approval of powerful strangers within the system."

Guardianship is the most extreme form of advocacy and one that takes its toll on the caregiver. For most people, the worst aspect is the awful experience of seeing their parents stripped not only of their independence but also of all their rights and privileges as an adult. Your parent may fight you every step of the way, making you feel guilty and angry at once. Well-meaning relatives may also weigh in with arguments. Remind them that the court, not you, will decide if your parent needs a guardian, and remind yourself that going through this difficult period is an expression of your love.

If you must take on this role, don't try to handle it all by yourself. Friends, family, and support groups can validate your experience, give you valuable information and advice based on their own experiences, and help you gain some perspective on the situation. Without losing sight of the critical tasks at hand, try to remember that your role as your parent's advocate is important—but it is not your only role in life.

Resources | Your Parent's Best Advocate

MEDICAL ISSUES

Lynn, Joanne, M.D. and Joan Harold. M.D. *Handbook for Mortals: Guidance for People Facing Serious Illness.* Oxford: Oxford University Press, 2001.
Helpful advice on dealing with doctors.

Austin, Elizabeth. "I'm Afraid I Have Bad News…." *AARP The Magazine.* May-June 2003.
How to handle serious illness.

Wild, Russell. "How to Be Drug Smart." *AARP Modern Maturity.* September-October 2002.
Understanding medicines and pharmacies.

"Decoding Your Hospital Bills."
ConsumerReports.org
www.consumerreports.org
A guide to handling hospital bills and finding common errors.

American Hospital Association
312-422-3000
http://www.aha.org/aha/ptcommunica-tion/partnership/index.html
Information on patient's rights.

Medical Billing Advocates of America
540-387-5870 /*www.billadvocates.com*
Consultants who review medical bills and insurance forms.

Joint Commission on Accreditation of Healthcare Organizations
630-792-5000 / *www.jcaho.org*
Evaluates and accredits health-care organizations in the United States.

LONG-TERM CARE

CarePathways.com
www.carepathways.com/nhg-state-survey-agency.cfm
Links to state nursing home survey agencies and rankings.

National Citizen's Coalition for Nursing Home Reform
202-332-2275
www.nccnhr.org
Offers useful publications and contacts. Includes the National Long Term Care Ombudsman Resource Center.

Nursing Home Compare
http://www.medicare.gov/NH Compare/home.asp
Information about performance of every Medicare and Medicaid certified nursing home in the country.

SCAMS

"Sites to See: Scam Prevention"
AARP Bulletin May 2002
www.aarp.org/bulletin/consumer/ Articles/a2003-06-30-scamsites.html

Direct Marketing Association Mail Preference Service
P.O. Box 643
Carmel, NY 15012
To get off mailing lists, send your name, home address, and signature to this address.

Federal Trade Commission Bureau of Consumer Protection
1-877-382-4357
www.ftc.gov/ftc/consumer/home.html

National Consumer's League
202-835-3323
www.nclnet.org
Advocates for consumers with information about fraud and the elderly.

National Do Not Call registry
www.donotcall.gov
Online registration for removing a phone number from telemarketing lists.

National Fraud Information Center
800-876-7060
www.fraud.org/ info/repoform.htm
To report internet or telephone fraud.

FINDING A LAWYER

AARP legal issues
www.aarp.org/money/legalissues
Links to articles and resources about law and the elderly.

"Finding Affordable Legal Help." AARP
www.aarp.org/Articles/a2004-03-19-li_findingaffordablehelp.html
A list of organizations that can provide free or low-cost legal services.

American Bar Association Directory of Pro Bono Programs
www.abanet.org/legalservices/findlegal-help/probonodirectory.html#
A searchable online directory of free legal services, state by state.

Legal Services Corporation
202-295-1500
www.lsc.gov
A private, nonprofit organization that helps low-income people gain access to legal help for civil (not criminal) cases.

National Academy of Elder Law Attorneys, Inc.
520-881-4005
www.naela.com
Assists lawyers for the elderly; includes a searchable directory of attorneys.

Administration on Aging Elder Rights and Resources
202-619-0724
www.aoa.gov/eldfam/Elder_Rights/Legal_Assistance/Legal_Assistance.asp
Resources for elder care, including links to legal assistance and hotlines.

Nolo.com
www.nolo.com/index.cfm
Legal information, forms, and software.

GUARDIANSHIP

Yeoman, Barry. "Stolen Lives." *AARP The Magazine,* January-February 2004.
An overview of the guardianship process.

National Guardianship Association
520-881-6561
www.guardianship.org
Information and resources on guardianship.

3 Money Matters

Money is better than poverty, if only for financial reasons. —Woody Allen

FEW PEOPLE RELISH the thought of taking an objective look at their financial situation. Fewer still enjoy discussing their finances at all, even with their nearest and dearest (or perhaps *especially* with their nearest and dearest). This can be true of husbands and wives, but the circumstances become considerably more complex when the discussion occurs between adult children and their parents. Politics, religion, and sex may be fair conversational game these days, but money remains off-limits.

Parents often balk at sharing the details of their finances—a reluctance that is not only ingrained in the modern American culture of privacy but also characteristic of the generation that came of age during World War II. It's entirely possible that only one parent was "in the know" about the family's money, while the other remained largely in the dark. In some families, Father kept his salary to himself and paid for everything or gave Mother an allowance for housekeeping expenses. In other families, Mom held the purse strings, doling out appropriate amounts of spending money to Dad and the kids. When the time comes, the caregiving adult child may not be the only one getting a first look at the financial books.

All in all, it shouldn't be surprising if the topic of finances turns out to be the most difficult one for caregivers and their parents to address. Some adult children may learn that their parents have been operating in the red for years and have run up a mountain of debt. Or that Mom and Dad were quietly subsidizing the irresponsible younger brother, dipping into their hard-earned nest egg to keep him afloat. The opposite situation—discovering that parents have robust resources and might even be considered wealthy—can be equally disconcerting for adult children who have been unsuccessfully urging their parents to pay for needed services. Whether or not angry words are spoken, the emotions roil, making it that much harder for all parties to discuss the issue calmly and make rational decisions.

Adult children who want to help often feel like clumsy intruders asking even the simplest questions about their parents' finances. And parents are just as likely to feel intruded upon. A careful, caring approach is crucial, but it is also essential to deal openly and objectively with the subject.

It's important, in anticipation, to remember the different worlds the generations inhabit. Parents now in their 70s and older are, and always will be, children of the Depression. Many of them knew hard times that their own children can barely imagine, and this experience will affect the way they think about their current economic situation. They may start hoarding their nickels and dimes—or hiding extra money under the mattress instead of in a savings account. Or they may suddenly start spending well beyond their means, as if there was no tomorrow. Even in the face of impending financial catastrophe they may tell you not to worry, that everything will be all right. After all, their entire generation adopted that "can-do" attitude to get through the bleakest days. These are emotional reactions—understandable and worth acknowledging, but important to work around and move beyond.

If this subject is too fraught for you and your parents to deal with, don't forge ahead at the risk of jeopardizing your relationship with them. Some families find the best solution is to hire a certified financial planner or accountant (see "Choosing a Financial Planner," page 61). Remember, the goal is to arrive at a clear understanding of the resources available now—and a realistic sense of the resources that will be needed in the future.

Sizing Up the Situation

Assuming you've broached the subject and your parents have indicated they want your involvement, the next thing to do is to find out where their finances stand (see "Key Questions," opposite, and "Should You Worry?", page 56). In the case of Peter, 45, his late father had kept the finances in good order, so it was easy for Peter and his older sister to help their mother carry on. Peter lives six hours from his mother; his sister lives much closer—only five minutes away. When their mother, in her late 60s, began to need more care, Peter, his partner, and his sister sat down with her to talk about the future. Peter's sister now takes care of many practical, day-to-day details; she visits her mother almost every day, knows her doctors, and hires local help when needed.

Peter and his partner, for their part, now deal with the larger financial issues that Peter's father used to handle. When it became clear that Peter's mother was too isolated, for example, they oversaw the details involved in buying her a new house in town.

Handling his mother's money seemed strange to Peter at first. "The oddest thing since my father's passing away is our becoming involved with my mother financially. It's not something that you generally know about your parents—where everything is."

Despite this involvement, Peter has not taken over completely, by any means. His mother, although happy to accept help with more complex financial matters, remains quite independent. At age 74, she still lives on her own—and she still pays her own bills, thank you very much!

Money was not a difficult topic for Peter and his family to discuss, nor did his mother's finances need serious straightening out. But that may not always be the case. With your parents' permission, review their bank account and investing information, insurance policies, mortgages, and other loans. Next, take a look at their daily expenses. If they haven't done so already, you'll want to help them draw up a relatively simple budget, listing the money coming in and the money going out. Later you can help them detail what their future needs are likely to be so you can work with them to ensure they'll have sufficient resources available.

Key Questions

AS YOU BEGIN to help your parents with their finances, keep the following questions in mind. Plan to review them every six months or so.

- ☐ Are your parents currently financially solvent? Are their finances stable?
- ☐ If they manage their own money, has anything changed in their health or mental ability that suggests they now need outside help?
- ☐ Have changing conditions in their own lives—or in the market—necessitated a shift in their investment strategy?
- ☐ Does their current financial strategy still mesh with their plans for the future? Are they still able to fund those plans?
- ☐ Are they able to pay for their needs now and will they be able to do so in the future? Remember that health-care costs are rising and it is likely that their income is fixed.

Should You Worry?

IF YOUR PARENTS are reluctant to discuss their financial situation, watch for warning signs that they may not be on top of things or may be more vulnerable to scams (see "Be a Fraud Detector," page 59). Here are some red flags to look out for:

☐ *Accumulating bills.* Have you come across unpaid bills or noticed overdue notices arriving in their mail? Have any utilities been interrupted for nonpayment?

☐ *Credit card debt.* If your parents owe money on credit cards, is their total out-standing balance growing, shrinking, or staying roughly constant? Credit card debt is increasingly a problem among older adults. With retirement incomes stagnant and rent and medical costs rising, notes Robert D. Manning, a Rochester Institute of Technology professor and the

author of *Credit Card Nation*, credit cards are being unwisely used to patch the fraying social safety net of America's older citizens.

☐ *Spending habits.* Have there been any noticeable changes in these? Are your parents scrimping on basics such as food? Are they cutting back on things they once enjoyed, such as going to the movies or having dinners out? Or have they recently splurged on a big-ticket item they don't really need? Either extreme may signal that your parents are no longer in control of their budget.

☐ *Personal care.* Has your mother skipped her regular visit to the hairdresser? Has your father passed up a new eyeglass prescription even though he clearly needs it?

A simple budget. To get the most accurate picture of your parents' finances, you need to know their monthly and annual expenses and income. Even if they've kept only rudimentary records, you should be able to tell what their expenses are from old bills. To project future costs, keep the current economy in mind; factor in inflation for expenses such as utilities and especially medical bills. (According to U.S. Department of Labor statistics, the cost of medical-care services increased 3.88 percent to 4.09 percent per year between 1994 and 2004—more than twice the rate of increases in the cost of all goods and services combined.)

Make sure you include all forms of income, including small pensions from previous employers and any veterans' benefits. Adapt the worksheet on page 202 to your parents' situation; help them update it every six months. The Resources list on page 69 suggests websites that offer help with a more detailed budget.

Calculating net worth. In addition to working out a budget, you and your parents need to have a handle on their net worth—the difference between all their assets and all their liabilities. Calculating net worth is particularly important if your parents need to adjust their income to cover ongoing expenses. It's also the first place to look for additional sources to pay for future expenses such as long-term care.

Using the form on page 203, list all bank accounts and all stock, mutual fund, and bond holdings. Don't forget the contents of a safe-deposit box. To estimate the fair market value of any property owned, search the Web for good sources of information, such as www.housevaluefinder.com or www.real-estate.com. Be as accurate as you can, but remember this rule of thumb: Be conservative with assets and liberal with liabilities. In other words, underestimate the value of assets and overestimate the cost of liabilities.

And the Bottom Line Is...

You've subtracted income from expenses, and the result is either positive or negative. Your parents are living comfortably within their means—or not. If the result is a negative number, your parents may have been dipping into their savings to make ends meet. This may become apparent when you calculate their net worth. Be prepared for this ahead of time, and by all means remain calm. If your parents are in serious debt, there are several things they can do to remedy the situation and restore their financial stability.

Change the budget equation. Help your parents look for areas in their budget where they can economize. One common example: They may still be paying premiums on life insurance policies they no longer need. If they have amassed significant credit card debt (an increasingly familiar situation for older adults on fixed incomes who face rising costs), it would be wise to seek professional assistance through a bona fide credit counselor. (Proceed with caution; some credit-counseling services are scams.) A legit counselor can tailor a debt-reduction plan that makes sense for your parents. This will reduce their net worth to some extent, but it may balance the monthly books. Other possible changes might include switching to a less expensive long-distance telephone plan or eating out less often. Look for these kinds of solutions before turning to more significant changes, such as moving.

Take out a reverse mortgage. Three out of four families headed by someone over 65 own their home outright. If that's the case for your parents, they

Making Ends Meet (Sort of)

- [ ] In 1999, the average annual Social Security income received by households with householders 65 and over was $12,300.

- [ ] Ninety percent of these households received Social Security income. Only one out of three households with a householder 65 and over had earnings as a source of income, compared with four out of five of all households.

- [ ] Another source of income for the older population, retirement income, averaged $17,900.

- [ ] Less than 50 percent of households with a householder 65 or over received retirement income.

Source: U.S. Census Bureau Special Report. "We the People: Aging in the United States." December 2004.

might consider a reverse mortgage, which allows them to convert their equity into cash. They can choose a lump-sum payment, a line of credit, or monthly payouts, which may be the best option to cover ongoing expenses. Repayment is deferred until the borrowers die, move, or sell their home. Borrowers must be 62 or older to qualify. Use a reverse-mortgage counselor to help make the best choice. (For more information about reverse mortgages, see www.aarp.org/revmort/.)

Sell their home. Yes, it's a big step, but perhaps it's time. Your parents may, in fact, be ready to move into a smaller place, such as an apartment. Or perhaps they're ready to come live with you; in many cultures, especially Asian and Hispanic, this is the normal course of events. In any event, selling the house is an effective way to reduce expenses, and up to $500,000 of the profit your parents make on their home sale can be excluded from capital-gains tax. See Chapter 7, "Living Arrangements," for more information about the options available if your parents choose to sell—and how to handle some of the issues that will undoubtedly arise if they move in with you.

Government assistance. Programs to help low-income seniors exist at many different levels of government. These include Supplemental Security Income—a benefit of the Social Security system—food stamps, and other state and local programs. Your parents may even qualify for assistance on their utility bills. Take a look at AARP's Benefits Outreach Program at www.aarp.org/money/lowincomehelp/ or the National Council on the Aging's "Benefits CheckUp" at www.benefitscheckup.org/.

Things Look Good for Now—What's Next?

Whether you've had to help your parents stabilize their financial situation or have discovered positive numbers at the bottom of the balance sheet, don't stop now. This is the perfect opportunity to talk to them about other steps they can take to ensure they stay in the black.

Simplify. When you were helping your parents pull their budget together, you probably had to add the totals from several different bank accounts, credit cards, or stock portfolios to come up with those one-line figures. The next step is to consider consolidating those accounts, which will greatly simplify their bookkeeping. Help your parents arrange for dividend and interest

Be a Fraud Detector

OLDER AMERICANS COME from a generation that tends to be more trusting. Many are lonely, rendering them especially vulnerable to someone who offers a sympathetic ear. According to AARP research, even active and involved elders routinely fall victim to fraud, be it telemarketing, door-to-door sales, e-mail, or Internet sites. You can help protect your parents from scams by following some of these simple strategies:

☐ *Give examples.* Draw from the "Scam Alert" column of the *AARP Bulletin* or check out AARP's online site: www.aarp.org/money/consumerprotection/scams/. The Federal Trade Commission is also a good source (http://www.ftc.gov/ftc/consumer/media_consumeralerts.html).

☐ *Share your own experiences.* If you're getting financial solicitations over the phone or in the mail, it's likely your parents are too. Let them know that you reject these out of hand.

☐ *Remember the adage "If it's too good to be true ..."* Those surefire deals are almost invariably scams. Remind your parents to avoid anything that sounds too good to be true—especially if they're being pressured to decide "before it's too late!"

☐ *Install caller ID and an answering machine.* Urge your parents to monitor their calls using caller ID and an answering machine. Even if a scammer leaves a message, your parents will have time to seek advice about the offer.

☐ *Opt out.* Suggest that they sign up for the National Do Not Call Registry. They can register online at www.donotcall.gov if they have a working e-mail address, or by calling 888-382-1222 from the number they wish to register. They can also register to opt out of unsolicited credit card offers by calling 888-567-8688.

☐ *Review mail.* Have your parents collect all the offers they get in the mail over a two-week period, recording what they respond to. Review the pile with them, pointing out pieces that look "fishy." Look for patterns in their responses.

☐ *Watch out for the new "best friend."* If your parents suddenly have a helpful new friend, ask questions and arrange for a meeting. A scammer will know that your parent has a real "best friend"—you.

payments from stocks, mutual funds, and other sources to be reinvested automatically or deposited directly into a single checking account. If your parents haven't done so already, help them institute direct deposit of all their wages, pensions, Social Security, and other sources of income.

You can also get some of their regular bills deducted from their bank account automatically, including mortgage payments, insurance premiums, and other bills that are constant amounts from month to month. Certain types of bills, however—credit cards and utilities come to mind—should not be paid automatically. To ensure that all charges are legitimate, credit card statements should always be scrutinized before they are paid. Utility bills, which tend to fluctuate from one month to the next, make similarly poor candidates for automatic bill paying; a higher-than-normal bill will overdraw the checking account, triggering overdraft charges that only compound the problem.

I'm living so far beyond my income that we may almost be said to be living apart. —E E CUMMINGS

If your parents are accustomed to seeing a pension or Social Security check arrive in the mail each month or have always paid their bills by mail, they may resist automation. Not only that, but automatic bill paying limits flexibility in disbursing funds each month. Overall, however, automatic deposits and automatic bill paying combine to reduce the paperwork involved in money management.

Hire a pro. If your parents need help but are uncomfortable with your being involved in their finances, hiring a professional can be a good solution. This may be less costly than you might think. A daily money manager—someone who sees to routine chores such as paying bills on time—will set you back $25 to $60 an hour. Check out the American Association of Daily Money Managers (www.aadmm.com/) for more information or visit www.aarp.org. AARP's Money Management Program uses trained volunteers to help people who can no longer handle their own finances.

If your parents have a variety of investments and other financial holdings, a certified financial planner or an attorney who specializes in wills and estate planning may be the best way to go. A financial planner can help your parents make important decisions about their investments, such as whether they need to diversify more, or how they can start to use their savings for vital expenses ahead such as long-term care. Certified financial planners are more

Choosing a Financial Planner

BE SURE THE PERSON your parents hire is a certified financial planner (CFP). You or your parents can check the status of a financial planner at the website of the Certified Financial Planner Board of Standards, which certifies financial planners (www.cfp.net). The board's toll-free number is 888-237-6275. See Resources on page 69 for other associations of financial advisers.

If your parents have found a certified public accountant (CPA) they want to work with, you or they should check with their state's Board of Public Accountancy to see if the person has an active license to practice in the state. The website of the American Institute of Certified Public Accountants (http://www.aicpa.org) provides links to each state's Board of Public Accountancy.

Your parents should interview at least three planners, meeting each one in person to judge how well they'll work together and to get answers to the following questions:

☐ *What are your credentials?* A licensed CPA is required to pass a number of exams, attend continuing education courses, and have a minimum amount of time in the profession. Your parents should be sure to ask for the planner's license number.

☐ *What is your specialty?* A CFP should have a working knowledge of many areas of financial planning, including taxes, insurance, estate planning, retirement planning, investing, and family budgeting. Your parents should find out if the planner attends classes to keep up-to-date on tax changes and investment strategies.

☐ *What services can I expect?* Financial planners usually prepare written financial plans after analyzing a client's personal and financial history, current situation, and future goals. Your parents should ask to see samples the planner has developed. They should also receive advice tailored to their situation, not a computer printout that could fit anyone.

☐ *What do you charge?* Ask for a written summary of what your parents would be paying in fees and commissions. Think twice about using any planner who is unwilling to provide this report.

☐ *Can you give me references?* Talk to several clients who have worked with the financial planner for at least three years. Ask what, if anything, they would change about their relationship with the adviser.

☐ *Will you act as my fiduciary?* By law, a person designated a "fiduciary"—someone who holds assets in trust for a beneficiary—owes the client the utmost care and loyalty. Ask the planner to write a letter on company letterhead explaining whether he or she will be acting as a fiduciary to your parents—and under what circumstances, if any, he or she will *not* be acting as a fiduciary.

☐ *How will we settle disputes?* If the agreement with a planner stipulates that your parents will go to arbitration in the case of a dispute, this generally means that they will give up their right to settle a dispute in court. The planner should be willing and able to discuss the pros and cons of signing such an agreement.

Long-Term Care Insurance Costs

LONG-TERM CARE INSURANCE PREMIUMS vary with the terms of the policy and the age of the purchaser. Inflation protection will raise the cost of your monthly premium, yet at the same time it can protect you from the rising cost of health care. And, as is the case with many other types of insurance, the younger you are when you sign up for a policy, the less expensive long-term care insurance will be.

The chart below gives some average annual costs based on $150 of daily benefits, four years of coverage, and a 90-day waiting period (also called a deductible period).

AVERAGE ANNUAL PREMIUMS, 2004

$150 Daily Benefit, Four Years' Coverage
90-Day Waiting Period

Age	Annual Basic Premium	Annual Premium Including 5% Inflation Protection
50	$ 564	$1,134
65	$1,337	$2,346
79	$5,330	$7,572

Source: Guide to Long-Term Care Insurance, America's Health Insurance Plans, 2004

expensive—as much as $100 to $200 an hour—but their sound advice may pay for itself. Choosing a good financial planner requires some effort, however (page 61). Be leery of marketing come-ons from so-called professionals; these are a common scam (see "Be a Fraud Detector," page 59).

Cover incapacity. Whether or not you're directly helping your parents with their finances, it's critical to have a candid conversation with them about having a plan—and certain documents—in place should they ever lose the ability to make decisions. For their finances, the single most important document is a durable power of attorney (DPA). If they don't already have one, they should talk to an attorney about drawing one up. In it, your parents designate an agent to make financial decisions for them.

The DPA can go into effect immediately, authorizing both the designated person and your parents, or they can create a "springing" DPA, which takes effect at some specified later date or when a specific event occurs, such as the incapacity of one or both parents. A springing power of attorney must be drafted very carefully to avoid confusion in determining exactly when the "springing" event has occurred. In fact, some banks and other financial institutions may resist accepting a springing DPA because of its potential ambiguity; your parents should check with their bank to see what is required. (See chapter 2, "Your Parent's Best Advocate," for information on durable power of attorney for health care and living wills.)

Your parents should also consider designating someone as an authorized signer on banking and brokerage accounts. This does not make the signer a joint account holder; it does, however, let that person write checks or sell securities for your parents in an emergency. It's also a good idea to know where the keys to any safe-deposit boxes are located, and to ask your parents if they would like to have your name on a signature card at their bank for emergency access.

Stay current. As you and your parents review their legal documents, have them make sure their designation of beneficiaries is up-to-date on all their paperwork, including wills, insurance policies, and the like. They should make it a habit to check these documents regularly—and update them as needed.

The Question of Long-Term Care

Today anyone who reaches age 65 stands a two in three chance of needing assistance with care for some stretch of time during the rest of their lives. By 2020, some 12 million Americans over the age of 65 will need long-term care. This can mean in-home care, assisted living, a temporary stay in a nursing home, or full residence in a retirement or nursing home. As you and your parents look to the future, the issue of their long-term care is probably the most important discussion you'll have that involves their financial situation. It's a big topic, and there are many decisions for them to make—from what kind of care they anticipate they will need to how best to pay for it.

The first step is understanding some basic facts. Most people would prefer to age in place, in their own homes. If they need in-home care, hourly rates today typically run $20 an hour for a home health aide. If they need to enter a nursing home—and Americans over the age of 65 have a 40 percent chance of doing so—current monthly costs average $5,000 a month (double that in some urban areas). Of people in nursing homes, 10 percent stay five years or more. Medicare does not cover such long-term stays. Assisted living costs average $2,400 a month; these, too, are not covered by Medicare or Medigap (see chapter 6). In addition, drugs, supplies, and special services are extra costs generally not included in monthly fees at nursing home and assisted living facilities.

Given this sobering picture, the essential question is: how can you help your parents plan to handle the costs? Many people today are contemplating buying long-term care insurance (LTCI), but this may not make sense—or be financially feasible—depending on your parents' age, health, and financial circumstances. As the box on page 62 shows, premium costs for long-term care policies escalate rapidly with age. Nor, in any case, do these policies cover all the costs involved in long-term care.

So who should consider purchasing long-term care insurance? Your parents may want to consider a plan if:

- they have more than $30,000 in assets, excluding their home. If this is the case, those assests are sufficient to warrant the protection of an LTCI policy;
- their household income is high enough to handle the premiums. LTCI premiums should not cost more the 7 percent of total household income;
- they are still healthy. Applicants who are not in good health may be denied long-term care insurance.

Do Your Homework

Long-term care insurance may or may not be an option for your parents. However, it might be time for you to start thinking about LTCI for yourself. This is especially so if there is uncertainty about your future care. If you are married, for example, would your spouse care for you if you required it? If so, for how long? If your spouse needed care, who would provide it? If you are single, who would care for you if you needed it? If you aren't sure who would take care of you, your spouse, or your parents, you might want to consider long-term care insurance. And, of course, the longer you wait, the more expensive long-term care insurance will be.

So if you're younger and in good health, make a note to revisit the subject at age 60; if at that point you determine you need the coverage, consider buying when you turn 65. (Not only is the average age of people entering nursing homes now 83, but the policy you buy today may not cover new care systems that emerge in the decades between now and the time you finally need the policy's coverage.)

In either case, whether for your parents or yourself, a good place to start doing the necessary homework on the subject is the insurance commissioner in your state. Another good source of information is the State Health

Across the Cultural Divide

Leo, 37, is the only child of elderly Chinese immigrants who came to the United States in 1969 when he was two years old. His father, now 87, and mother, 76, have lived in the same apartment in San Francisco's Chinatown for 27 years. Leo lives on the East Coast.

MY PARENTS ARE MODEST, stoic people, not financially well off. My father worked as a janitor and a restaurant worker and got up every day at 2 a.m. to go to work. My mother worked as a seamstress in many sweatshops in Chinatown and in other factories in the Mission District and in SoMa [South of Market]. In recent years, my dad has had major surgery and my mother has had a heart bypass. My father also has mild dementia. They still need regular checkups, but their health has stabilized. In fact, Mom has a very active social life—she goes out with her friends and is enrolled in a cardiac exercise program at a nearby hospital.

My father needs more care. We're fortunate that he qualifies for a senior healthcare service that allows him to continue to live at home. The service includes an adult day-care program. Three times a week, he is picked up and taken to the center, which provides breakfast and lunch, hosts activities like mah-jongg, and schedules his medical appointments and therapy. Someone from the center also comes to the apartment every morning to help him with his medication. Because he is eligible for Medicare, Medicaid, and Supplemental Security Income benefits, the costs of his care are covered. I speak with the social worker there

quite a bit to monitor what's going on with my father.

There are a lot of cultural and generational barriers. My parents don't speak English, and they don't initiate conversations on important issues. Over the years I've had to figure out their needs, see if they agree with my assessment, and, when needed, advocate for them. We're not a typical Chinese family, certainly for Cantonese speakers, in that our nuclear and extended family is small. We often rely on a network of friends. For people of my parent's generation, though, we're quite typical in other ways. My parents rarely talk about difficult matters related to their declining health or express gratitude for the things I do for them. In traditional Chinese culture, these things are unspoken. Everybody has their role and is expected to play it.

My parents live frugally on their Social Security income. Their apartment—a junior one-bedroom—is very small, but it is rent-controlled; they pay less than $200 a month. They would be more comfortable in a larger space, but they would need help to afford it. I visit every couple of months and pay for things they cannot afford or are not willing to spend their money on.

Recently, however, they managed to eke out money and work their family associations to buy two plots at a cemetery. In our culture this was a very important task, yet they never discussed it with me. I had mixed feelings about it—glad they could show such initiative, but disappointed that I wasn't part of a family decision.

Insurance Assistance Program (SHIP), which offers free counseling on all sorts of insurance-related topics. Find the nearest program by calling the Eldercare Locator at 800-677-1116. You or your parents should purchase insurance only through an established, reputable insurance provider. Never buy insurance from a door-to-door salesperson, and never pay cash. You should also comparison shop—a process that includes checking with rating services that evaluate the safety of financial institutions (see Resources, page 69). Call at least three agencies; some charge a fee. Be sure to ask for an explanation of what the agency's ratings mean, how many different rating categories it has, and what the agency considers to be a good rating.

Although your parents may choose a benefit period of anywhere from two to six years—or even the rest of their lives—experts advise LTCI coverage for four years. Care is covered in different settings, depending on the policy. Keep in mind that the average length of stay in a nursing home is two and a half years. Also remember that care may be needed at home or in an assisted living residence. Read the fine print about a policy's limitations and exclusions: Most policies will not cover long-term care that results from alcohol or drug addiction or attempted suicide; nor will they cover care in facilities outside the United States or its possessions.

In examining policies and providers, look for a number of features:

Elimination period. There should be just one elimination, or waiting, period for the life of the policy. This period ranges from 0 to 100 days, during which your parents must pay all long-term care expenses out of their own pocket. The longer the waiting period, the lower the monthly premium—a good thing very early on in the life of the policy, but not so welcome when your parents must finance their care themselves during that longer time period when they first activate the benefit. Once they begin receiving benefits, the policy should let them stop paying premiums.

Preexisting conditions. The policy should automatically cover preexisting conditions—as long as these were fully disclosed when your parents applied. If your parents have difficulty remembering specifics about their health during the application process, they should refer the insurance company to the doctor who treated them. It's best to be forthcoming; when your parents later file a claim, the insurance company will scrutinize their medical history. Should the company determine your parents were misleading about their health, it could deny their claim.

Inflation protection. Look for a policy that offers 5 percent compound inflation protection. Although general inflation rates in the 21st century have been relatively low, that has not been the case with the cost of health care, nor is it likely to be in the next decade or two. Inflation protection adds to the premium, but it's probably worth it. Be sure to find out if circumstances other than inflation could cause the premiums to rise over time. If your parents are still earning wages now, remember that their income will go down when they stop working, making future increases harder to deal with. If the time comes when they can no longer afford the premiums for the coverage they originally bought, the policy should allow them to downgrade coverage—without having to discontinue the original policy or forfeit premiums already paid.

> *I have enough money to last me the rest of my life, unless I buy something.* —Jackie Mason

Nonforfeiture. Some policies also offer nonforfeiture benefits, which apply if your parents can no longer afford the premiums at all. This will let your parents collect a daily benefit for long-term care up to the amount they paid in. But there's a hefty price: A nonforfeiture benefit can add as much as 100 percent to the policy's cost. Also note that even if they were paying extra for inflation protection, the nonforfeiture benefit will not cover inflation.

Eligibility. The policy should clearly explain when your parents will be eligible for coverage and how their eligibility will be determined. Generally, insurers will not pay for care unless your parents are unable to perform a specified number of "activities of daily living"—bathing, dressing, eating, getting from a bed to a chair, walking, remaining continent, and using a toilet. Look for a policy requiring inability to perform no more than two of these activities. Beware any policy stipulating the policyholder must need "one-on-one continual assistance" in order to qualify for benefits. This restrictive precondition is difficult to meet. Likewise avoid a policy that demands that your parents be screened by the insurer's physician before the company will pay for care—a rule aimed largely at minimizing claims—and shun any policy stipulating they must spend time in a hospital before receiving benefits.

Dementia. Make sure the policy includes coverage for dementia. Companies whose policies do not cover dementia may refuse a claim if an Alzheimer's patient is *physically* capable of performing most of the activities of daily living—even if cognitive impairment prevents her from doing so.

Flexibility. Finally, the best policy will allow your parents to choose from various forms of care when they need it. If they want to remain at home, be sure the policy covers a home health aide and other professional care in the home. They might also choose coverage for a mixture of care options that includes assisted living and adult day care. Some policies today cover needed home modifications, such as the installation of a ramp. Others have become "consumer directed," meaning they offer a cash payment to the insured to use as they wish—including paying family members to care for them.

Reality Knocks

For many, long-term care insurance can mean the difference between peace of mind and financial anguish. You'll need to determine whether a policy best suits your situation. Susan's father, Robert, now 90, was diagnosed with Alzheimer's at the age of 86. He is otherwise physically in good health, and has lived in an Alzheimer's residence care facility since August 2003. Robert's care is being paid for out of his trust account, which includes some small pieces of rural property. "I think he would have wanted to 'pay his own way,'" says Susan, "so as executor of the trust, I try to manage his assets in a way consistent with that." Susan has sold off a couple of pieces of property to pay for Robert's care. She reckons they have enough from these sales to cover costs for another 25 months or so, at which point they may need to sell something else. "If we didn't have the trust, we would need to get all of his children together and decide who could help pay for what is needed. That would be an extreme hardship for some of the children. So far we have not had to deal with that."

Susan, 62, and her husband, Michael, 55, purchased LTCI for themselves five years ago. "My mother and my maternal grandmother both had severe osteoporosis," she says. "I've seen my stepfather enter a nursing home with Alzheimer's, and Michael's mother, who moved into a retirement facility, continues to need a good deal of medical care well into her 90s. I guess when you live with the constant reminders of aging and physical decline, the long-term care option makes especially good sense."

Besides, she jokes, "I once said to my son—who was really good with Robert, knew how to be with him and talk with him—'You're really good with Grandpa.' He looked at me and said, 'I'm practicing!'"

Resources | Money Matters

BOOKS AND PERIODICALS

Burns, Sharon, and Raymond Forgue
*How to Care for Your Parents' Money
While Caring for Your Parents: The
Complete Guide to Managing Your Older
Parents' Finances and Planning for Their
Future.* New York: McGraw-Hill, 2003.

Palermo, Michael T. *AARP Crash Course
in Estate Planning: The Essential Guide to
Wills, Trusts, and Your Personal Legacy.*
New York: AARP Books/Sterling, 2005.

"Scam Alert." *AARP Bulletin.*
Monthly column.
www.aarp.org/bulletin/

OTHER RESOURCES

**AARP Foundation Money
Management Program**
www.aarpmmp.org

**American Association of Daily
Money Managers**
301-593-5462
www.aadmm.com

BenefitsCheckUp
www.benefitscheckup.org

Federal Trade Commission
*www.ftc.gov/bcp/conline/pubs/
services/livtrust.htm.*

Financial Planning Association
800-282-7526
www.fpanet.org/

**Long-Term Care Insurance
Knowledge Center**
hiicap.state.ny.us/ltc/kc

**National Association of
Insurance Commissioners**
www.naic.org

**National Association of Personal
Financial Advisers**
888-333-6659
www.napfa.org

National Family Caregivers Association
800-896-3650
www.nfcacares.org

Nolo Press
*www.nolo.com/lawcenter/
ency/index.cfm*

RATING SERVICES

A. M. Best
908-439-2200, ext. 4742
http://www.ambest.com

Fitch, Inc.
212-908-0800
www.fitchibca.com

Moody's
212-553-0377
www.moodys.com

Standard & Poor's
212-208-1527
www.standardandpoors.com

Weiss Research
800-289-9222
www.weissratings.com

4 The Body

The secret of staying young is to live honestly, eat slowly, and lie about your age. —Lucille Ball

FRED ASTAIRE WAS SKATEBOARDING when he was 80. At the age of 96, Georgia O'Keeffe was making pottery in the New Mexico desert. Too often, older people, their adult children, and even their doctors assume that aging equals illness. But growing numbers of vigorous people in their 70s, 80s, and 90s give the lie to this assumption. Disease and disability are not inevitable parts of growing older, and they should be fought with the same energy that would be brought to bear on such problems when they occur in younger people.

Much of the blame for our dismissive and often negative attitude toward aging may be laid on modern culture. Because Westerners value control and economic productivity, we fear the decline of power and the loss of independence that may come with old age. Rather than associating age with a lifetime of accumulated wisdom, we associate it with death, and we are uneasy around the people who represent that fearful end.

Western (and especially American) mass media, driven by advertisers appealing to the 18-to-35 demographic, portray a world of youthful, fit, and beautiful consumers. When even the vampires on TV look young and sexy, it's no wonder we can be persuaded that age means ugliness and loss.

Different cultures bring different expectations to old age. In traditional African societies, for example, elders are seen as powerful leaders—sources of strength for younger generations. But Chinese Americans, though respected by their children, may be more likely to give up their independence at a relatively young age.

"First- or second-generation Chinese American elderly come to depend on their children a great deal," says Mei. "Moreover, elderly Chinese often consider themselves elderly and feeble much earlier than their Western counterparts, so the pressure on Chinese American children starts earlier. This may be changing in some large, metropolitan areas where there are good social organizations that cater to Chinese American elderly. But it is a slow, painful process to try to convince elderly parents that at age 60 or 62 or 65 one is still vibrant and can live a full and independent life, that one can travel to see children and grandchildren, that one is not simply 'waiting to shrivel up and die.'"

> *Health consists of having the same diseases as one's neighbors.*
>
> —QUENTIN CRISP

Although it's true that some bodily functions decline with age, and that older people are more likely to suffer from certain common maladies, many of these disorders are preventable, treatable, or curable. The first thing adult children can do to help their parents stay healthy, no matter how old they are, is to encourage a positive, proactive attitude toward aging.

What Is 'Normal' Aging?

As life expectancy has increased dramatically over the last hundred years and the numbers of elderly rise, the percentage living in nursing homes has in fact decreased, dropping from 22 percent in 1985 to 19 percent in 1997 for those 85 and older, and from 6 to 5 percent among those aged 75 to 84. Thanks to improvements in vaccines, medicines, and medical technology, the percentage of people over 65 with debilitating diseases has also dropped from 22 percent to 20 percent, as has the proportion over 85 with disabilities (going from 62 percent to 55 percent) .

Nevertheless, as people age, their bodies change and simply do not work as well in various ways. They are increasingly likely to suffer from such chronic conditions as arthritis, heart disease, and diabetes. At least 80 percent of those over 65 have a minimum of one chronic condition; 50 percent have at least two. Three million are so disabled they cannot handle basic activities of daily living, such as bathing or eating. These disabilities will become part of a caregiver's life, too. Fortunately, resources abound to help caregivers and their parents understand and cope with these conditions.

It's important, first of all, to understand which parts of aging come with the territory and which are diseases. "Normal" aging is a bit of a misnomer—what's normal for one person is not always normal for another—but most bodies age in predictable ways. For example, the cells of the body can divide only a limited number of times. This means that, as people grow older, their tissues begin to shrink and lose some functioning as well. Overall body shape changes with age. Older bodies thicken around the middle and shrink in height; men over 50 and women over 70 begin to lose weight, in part because of a loss of muscle tissue. Systems that are affected by age include:

Muscles. Beginning as early as the 20s in men and the 40s in women, muscles lose mass. As muscle fibers shrink, they lose tone and become more rigid. Over time and without intervention, walking may become unsteady.

Skeleton. The bones decline in mass and density with age, particularly in women after menopause. Vertebrae lose minerals as well as some of the fluid between the disks and, as a result, the spine shortens. Joints become stiffer; hip, knee, and finger joints may begin to degenerate.

Skin. Skin becomes thinner, fragile, and wrinkled, with less underlying fat.

Eyes. Around age 40, many people develop presbyopia—the inability to focus well on nearby objects—and need reading glasses.

Ears. As wear and tear take their toll on the delicate structures of the ear, the eardrum thickens. By their 50s, many men and women will lose some sharpness in their hearing and will have more difficulty distinguishing high-pitched sounds and the differences between spoken consonants.

Organs. The bad news here is that organs reach their peak functioning

---

The Magic Call Button

IF YOU OR YOUR PARENT is concerned that she might fall or become ill while alone, consider investing in a medical alert system. Also known as personal response systems (PRS), these can bring peace of mind to you both. A PRS typically consists of a battery-operated pendant worn around the neck. Pressing the button sends a signal to a transmitter near your parent's telephone that calls a response center. Responders then call emergency help if they determine there is a crisis. You can buy or rent the pendant, paying a monthly fee for the service. Medical alert companies are listed in the Yellow Pages and on the Web; also ask your parent's doctor for recommendations. Compare several companies, asking about their training and response time. Finally, test the system with your parent at home to make sure she is comfortable using it.

when people hit their 30s, after which the organs begin to decline. The good news is that they have plenty of extra reserves; half of a liver can be removed without harm, for instance. However, the heart cannot pump quite as well, the lungs become less elastic and deliver less oxygen, and changes in the kidneys and liver mean that the body responds differently to drugs, illness, and toxins than it did in its youth.

Choosing a Doctor

Older people need physicians who have experience with geriatric patients and won't dismiss their illnesses as "just old age," as Nell, who is in her 90s, learned. When she talked to a doctor about her hoarse, fading voice, he refused to take any action. "He said I should expect that at my age," she says, "as if I should just be grateful to be alive at all!" Rather, doctors with geriatric patients need to understand that medications affect older bodies very differently from younger ones, and they should be familiar with the hazards of daily life for the elderly, such as falls, dehydration, and malnutrition. Older people and their advocates should get recommendations for a primary care physician from someone they trust: preferably a board-certified doctor in family or internal medicine, and ideally one with a certification in geriatrics. Then they should set up a brief interview session, asking the doctor how many older

---

The 'I' Word

ONE OF THE MOST HUMILIATING PROBLEMS of old age, incontinence affects up to 35 percent of people over 60, especially women. More than half of those confined to their homes or to nursing homes are incontinent, making it a costly and burdensome issue as well as an embarrassing one. If you see that your parent is incontinent, you can't avoid talking to her about it. Do so in gentle but practical terms and in private.

Many techniques and medicines can treat incontinence. Your mother should talk to her doctor about Kegel exercises to strengthen the urethra, bladder training to increase the time between bathroom trips, and other diet and exercise practices. If she has difficulty moving around, arrange for a portable commode or bedpan by the bed or chair. Your mother should also talk to her doctor about medications that can help in some cases of incontinence—and make sure that the ones she's currently taking aren't making the problem worse. If none of these remedies help, she can wear a specially designed diaper, pad, or catheter.

Don't let her suffer silently. Her doctor and self-help groups can help her understand that she's not alone with this problem.

---

patients she treats, how she feels about treating their diseases, and whether she visits patients in the nursing home or hospital to manage their care.

According to the Centers for Disease Control, two out of three times an older patient visits her doctor, she leaves with one or more drug prescriptions. Eight percent of the time these medications are inappropriate and, for some reason, this problem is worse for women. As people age, their body chemistry changes, and medicines or dosages that worked just fine when they were 30 are toxic when they are 70. Older stomachs, kidneys, and livers don't process drugs as well; the lungs and circulatory system are less efficient. Drugs that need to be monitored in older people include:

- Common pain relievers such as aspirin and ibuprofen
- Antihistamines
- Antianxiety drugs
- Antidepressants
- Blood thinners
- Cardiac medicines
- Bronchodilators
- Antibiotics
- Urinary tract relaxants

Even if your parent sees several doctors and therapists, she should ask her primary care doctor to serve as the conduit for all information regarding her care, ensuring that her treatments and medications are coordinated. Pharmacists are also a great source of information and should be considered partners, along with the physician, in health care. The reason for this vigilance is that some helpful drugs can be fatal in combination: aspirin and blood thinners, for example. Because older people may not tell their doctor all their medications (and the doctor may not ask), adult children may want to keep a comprehensive list in their own notebook (see page 34) of all parental medications and dates prescribed. At a first visit with a new doctor, caregivers should bring the list and all their parent's pill bottles along. They may even want to serve as backup medical managers themselves, looking up their parent's medicines in a medical reference or on the Web. More than one potentially dangerous drug problem has been caught by the caregiver.

If your parent has serious impairments and her primary-care doctor does not seem fully able to treat her, she or her advocate should ask for a referral to a geriatrician. These specialists are trained in care of the elderly and may order a comprehensive assessment. They may ask the patient to work with a health-care team that includes a nurse, social worker, nutritionist, physical therapist, occupational therapist, consultant pharmacist, and gero-psychiatrist (a psychiatrist trained to deal with the mental health of older adults). This team will evaluate all the circumstances of the patient's life, including her social support network and ability to perform daily tasks (see Resources, page 89).

A Pound of Prevention

No one can slow the passage of time, of course, yet it is possible to minimize its effects on the body. Cancer, heart disease, and stroke—leading diseases of older adults—are all linked to lifestyle. According to the Centers for Disease Control, people who follow the practices listed here have half the disability rates of those who do not. A healthy lifestyle can mean a long life without disability. For those with chronic conditions, a healthy lifestyle can slow or prevent further decline. Young and old alike should strive to:

Develop healthy eating habits. Older people, like everyone else, should eat

---

A Test in Time

The following tests are recommended for people over 50. Your parent's doctor can tell you how often they're needed:

□ *Blood pressure.* To check for hypertension

□ *Cholesterol.* To decrease the risk of heart attack, stroke, and vascular disease

□ *Bone density.* To screen for osteopenia or osteoporosis; for women 65 and over

□ *Vision.* For glaucoma, cataracts, and other problems

□ *Hearing.* For age-related hearing loss

□ *Colon.* To test for colorectal cancer; get a sigmoidoscopy every 5 years, a colonoscopy every 10 years.; check stool for blood every year.

□ *Skin.* To check for skin cancers

□ *Thyroid.* To screen for hypothyroidism, hyperthyroidism, and thyroid nodules

□ *Blood glucose.* To screen for diabetes

□ *Prostate.* To test for prostate cancer—blood tests for PSA (prostate specific antigen) and digital exams

□ *Mammogram.* To test for breast cancer

□ *Pap test.* To screen for cervical cancer. Women who have never had one before age 65 should have two, one year apart.

□ *Tuberculosis.* Those in nursing homes are a high-risk group for this disease.

□ *Depression.* This screening typically involves a set of questions from a doctor.

plenty of vegetables, whole-grain cereals and breads, fruits, fish, and lean meats. They should make sure they get enough calcium, but cut down on foods containing large amounts of salt, saturated fats, and trans-fatty acids. Those who are overweight should consult a doctor or nutritionist about how to lose weight safely; ailments from diabetes to heart disease are linked to obesity.

> *To get back my youth I would do anything in the world, except take exercise, get up early, or be respectable.*
>
> —OSCAR WILDE

Exercise. The old adage "use it or lose it" applies to bodies of whatever age. A study done in the 1960s involving members of a national football team showed that just one week of bed rest, even for young men in prime physical condition, caused loss of muscle mass. Not one of them could stand up unaided when they were first allowed out of bed.

Muscles—anyone's muscles—shrink and weaken if they are not used. Similarly, if the ligaments that hold our joints together are not regularly stretched to their fullest, they shorten until we can no longer bend to tie our shoes or turn our necks to look over our shoulders.

Research by AARP shows that although most people in their 70s and older are well aware of the benefits of exercise, they tend to view the activity as either difficult or strenuous. Perhaps this explains why more than 60 percent of the elderly are inactive.

Yet even a moderate amount of physical activity—30 minutes a day, five days a week—can ward off a host of illnesses, from high blood pressure to heart disease, stroke, diabetes, and depression. Older parents who don't feel up to a 30-minute exercise stint can divide it into 10-minute segments, three times a day. Walking briskly is good exercise for anyone. So is stretching, dancing, and tai chi—which, in older adults, has been shown to improve balance and prevent falls.

Weight training works wonders for older men and women as well as for the young and buff. Supervised weight-training programs have been found to increase muscle strength in older people more than 100 percent in 12 weeks. Medical experts recommend exercise even for people with arthritis or back pain, and for those who are recovering from serious surgeries; bed rest can actually worsen many conditions.

Adult children can encourage their parents by helping them understand that even easy, low-stress exercise such as walking can be beneficial.

Quit smoking. It's never too late. According to a study by researchers at Duke University, 65-year-olds who quit smoking increase their life expectancy by one to four years. Those who quit later in life improve cardiovascular functioning and reduce lung infections to say nothing of the risk of lung, mouth and throat cancers, osteoporosis, and eye disease. In older people with Alzheimer's disease or other mental disabilities, smoking is dangerous in another way: Left forgotten, burning cigarettes can start fires.

Practice safe sex. Surprised? Older people with more than one sex partner are part of the post-AIDS world. If parents are out there dating—and mating—they need to use condoms.

Curb alcohol consumption. In general, older people should have no more than one drink a day. Older bodies do not handle alcohol as well as younger ones do, and in the elderly drinking is more likely to cause dizziness and confusion, damage the brain and liver, and precipitate falls or car accidents. Alcohol can also mask the signs of a heart attack and is dangerous for those with certain medical conditions, such as hypertension, liver or kidney disease, pancreatitis, and congestive heart failure. Topping it all off, many

LIFE STORY

Mountain Man

KEIZO MIURA CELEBRATED his 100th birthday skiing at Snowbird, Utah, in February 2004, an event that included four generations of the Miura family. His son Yuichiro—known as The Man Who Skied Down Everest, a feat he performed in 1970—became the oldest person to reach the summit of Everest in May 2003 at age 70. Yuichiro's son Gota competed in the 1994 and 1998 Winter Olympics in freestyle moguls.

Recognized as the oldest active skier in the world, Keizo Miura began skiing when he was 21. Although he keeps no records, he reckons he has averaged 110 days a year on the slopes in the 79 years since then—which adds up to phenomenal

8,690 days, or nearly 24 years of solid skiing.

Miura's daily regimen includes rising at 5 a.m., performing some breathing and stretching exercises, and then taking a 40-minute walk. His eyesight and hearing are failing, but he is otherwise in good health. At 4 feet 11 inches, he maintains his 85 pounds on a diet of rice, fish and chicken (prepared in a pressure cooker to soften the bones, which he eats for the calcium), seaweed and soya. He goes to bed about 9:30 p.m.

At the end of his centennial downhill run, Miura was asked the secret to his long life. Speaking through a translator he said it wasn't the activity of skiing itself: "The reason for my long life is my *passion* for skiing."

medications—among them tranquilizers, aspirin and other painkillers, and antihistamines—interact badly with alcohol. With this in mind, patients and their doctors should together carefully review all their medicines.

Five to twenty percent of the elderly drink more alcohol than is advisable. The percentage of heavy drinkers in the population declines with age, but the current generation of older adults—which came of age during the cigarette and cocktail-hour habits of the 1940s and '50s—drinks more than its parents did. Adult children who know or suspect that a parent drinks excessively may want to talk to her doctor one-on-one. Alcoholism in the United States is seriously underdiagnosed, in part because alcoholics often don't acknowledge the problem to themselves, much less to others, and also because doctors may dismiss its symptoms as signs of old age. Relatives can also find support and education about alcoholism through groups such as Al-Anon.

Get immunized. More than 40,000 people over 65 die each year from influenza and invasive pneumococcal disease. Vaccines will prevent or ameliorate these dangerous illnesses, yet about one-third of the elderly do not get vaccinated when they should. Vaccines your parent should receive include:

- *Influenza.* Once a year, every autumn, before the flu season starts.
- *Pneumococcal pneumonia.* At least once if your parent is 65 or over; she may need to be revaccinated a few years later.
- *Tetanus.* If your parent has never received this vaccine, she should get two injections of the tetanus and diphtheria combination. If she has been vaccinated before, she should at least be vaccinated again at 65—and possibly every 10 years thereafter.
- *Hepatitis B.* One series of three shots is recommended for certain people, including dialysis patients, IV drug users, and those who live in homes for the mentally and physically disabled.

Take steps to prevent injuries. More than one-third of adults over 65 take a tumble each year; 20 to 30 percent suffer injuries as a result. Living spaces can be modified to minimize the likelihood of falls. Everyone should have a working smoke detector and carbon monoxide detector installed in the house—and the alarm on each device should be loud enough to be heard easily. "Granny gown" burns among older women occur when they wear dangling sleeves while working over the stove. Older parents should be encouraged not to wear such clothing while cooking, and not to store frequently used items above the stove. Temperatures on water heaters should stay below

120°F. And, of course, all drivers and passengers should wear seat belts. They really do save lives.

The Changing Senses

All five of the senses—vision, touch, smell, hearing, and taste—need a minimum level of stimulation, called a threshold, before they register a sensation. This threshold rises with age. As the senses no longer respond to delicate stimulation, the resulting dimming of sensation can leave an older person feeling isolated and depressed.

Vision. By middle age, almost everyone experiences age-related changes to vision. Otherwise healthy older people should visit the eye doctor at least once a year; if they have vascular diseases such as diabetes or hypertension, they should go more often.

Normal changes include dry eyes (which can be eased with eye drops), worsening peripheral vision, and decreased visual sharpness, or acuity. Almost everyone over 55 needs glasses at least part of the time, usually for presbyopia (difficulty focusing on objects nearby). Glare and transitions from light to dark or dark to light become more difficult. (Serious problems with night driving may also signal cataracts—eye doctors should screen for these.) The ability to distinguish greens and blues diminishes, so your father's mismatched outfits may be a function of poor vision, not poor taste.

Older people are also at higher risk for cataracts, glaucoma, and macular degeneration, all of which can lead to blindness if untreated. Of these, cataracts, a clouding of the lens of the eye, are the most common affliction— and the easiest to treat: Fifty percent of people 65 to 74 years old and seventy percent of those over 75 have them. Symptoms include:

- Poor night vision
- Cloudy, fuzzy, or foggy vision
- Halos around lights
- Loss of color intensity
- Trouble with glare

A standard eye exam should detect cataracts. Mild cataracts might need no treatment beyond eyeglasses. More serious cataracts usually require outpatient surgery to remove the lens and replace it with an artificial one. These procedures are typically successful; often they confer better vision than the patient has experienced in quite some time.

Preventing Falls

FALLS ARE THE MOST COMMON cause of both fatal and nonfatal injuries among older people. Hip fractures from falls are particularly likely to lead to deaths and institutionalization. You can help your parent prevent falls through awareness of the health conditions that lead to such mishaps and by modifying his living environment. In particular your parent should:

☐ Have his vision tested often

☐ Talk to his doctor about which of his drugs might affect balance and coordination

☐ Limit the amount of alcohol he drinks

☐ Stand up slowly

☐ Avoid getting too hot or too cold

☐ Exercise regularly to maintain strength and balance

In his house, you or he should:

☐ Remove throw rugs and clutter in halls

☐ Use nonslip mats in the bathtub and shower

☐ Install grab bars next to the toilet and in the shower or tub

☐ Put in handrails on both sides of the stairs

☐ Brighten the lighting throughout the home and add night-lights to bathrooms and hallways

Glaucoma is a less common but more serious disease, in which fluid within the eye builds up, putting pressure on the optic nerve. Without treatment, nerve cells can die, resulting in partial or total blindness. There are four kinds of glaucoma. The most common form in older people is chronic glaucoma, which progresses slowly over the years. Its symptoms include:

- Slow loss of peripheral vision
- Blurred or foggy vision
- Seeing a rainbow halo around lights
- Mild headaches

In its early stages, chronic glaucoma has few symptoms. Older adults should have regular eye exams with an ophthalmoscope in order to detect it. Treatment involves either medication or surgery to relieve the fluid pressure.

Macular degeneration is the leading cause of blindness in people over 55. It occurs when the macula—a central portion of the retina at the back of the eye—deteriorates, causing a loss of vision in the center of the visual field.

This disorder comes in two varieties: dry, marked by thinning of the retina, and wet, in which newly formed blood vessels leak fluid into the eye. The main symptom for both kinds of macular degeneration is blurred, wavy, or dimming central vision, usually with clear peripheral vision. The wet form and more severe cases of the dry form can lead to serious vision loss, rendering the patient unable to read or drive.

Unfortunately, there are no good treatments for dry macular degeneration. A combination drug-and-laser therapy can slow the progress of the wet form by destroying the abnormal blood vessels.

Impaired vision can seriously affect an older person's quality of life, so caregivers should help their older parent pursue solutions to the maximum extent possible. Reading tools for the visually impaired range from magnifiers to Kurzweil machines—computerized devices that convert text to speech. Other tools—talking watches, large-display or talking calculators, even specially designed cooking accessories—will help an older parent continue to live safely and productively.

Hearing. Older adults who complain that people mumble when they talk, turn up the television volume to numbing levels, or don't hear the doorbell

---

LIFE STORY

The Unsinkable Wally Ristow

STEVE'S MOTHER DIED about 15 years ago, after a prolonged struggle with pulmonary disease. His father is still going strong at 96, living in his own cottage at an assisted living facility. Although he has enough peripheral vision to get around, macular degeneration has rendered Wally legally blind, and he is hampered by severe arthritis. Yet he remains motivated enough to drive his scooter to the fitness center three days a week for a 30-minute session on an exercise machine. He gets his own breakfast and lunch; for dinner he rides the scooter to the facility's dining room, where the wait staff dotes on him. The rest of the time, he keeps up with news magazines with the aid of a Kurzweil reading machine, listens to books on tape from the library, naps, and listens to the radio or the Sunday talk shows on TV.

Over the years, Wally has been generally healthy. As his vision failed, Steve rigged up a computer that would talk back as Wally typed. About four years ago, Wally finished his autobiography as a gift for his children and grandchildren. Two years ago he had to have lumbar surgery—not once, but twice in less than a month. It took him a year to recover his strength, and he was somewhat depressed for a while. He needs pain medication to manage the arthritis, but he's now back to his old self: irreverent, opinionated, and—macular degeneration notwithstanding—possessed of an unerring eye for "an attractive woman."

ring are probably suffering from age-related hearing loss. In about 30 percent of people over 65, hearing declines significantly, but in most cases, this loss is not serious. Older people may no longer be able to distinguish between consonants such as *s, f,* and *p,* and they may fail to discern high-pitched sounds. Those who were exposed to loud noises in their youth—Woodstock alumni, take note!—are particularly vulnerable to this.

When hearing loss stems from structural deterioration of the eardrum and delicate bones of the inner ear, hearing aids can help dramatically. Deafness due to nerve damage, on the other hand, may not respond as well to standard hearing aids. In either case, people who experience even the faintest symptom of hearing loss should visit an audiologist. Family members can communicate better with their parent if they stand close when they talk to her, reduce background noise, and speak distinctly without shouting.

Common Ailments

Older people can suffer from any number of illnesses, just like younger people. Nevertheless, a few chronic disorders predominate in the elderly. Heart disease, stroke, cancer, diabetes, and chronic lung diseases are leading killers; arthritis, hypertension, and osteoporosis are also major causes of disability in those over 65. But no matter how old the patient is, almost all of these ailments can be treated with some success—or even cured altogether.

Heart disease, stroke, and hypertension. About one-fourth of the U.S. population suffers from some form of heart disease. Although the traditional portrait of a heart-attack victim is a portly, middle-aged man, women are just as likely to suffer from coronary heart disease, often with fewer and milder symptoms than men, making it even more difficult to diagnose.

High blood pressure (hypertension) and high blood cholesterol are two of the leading risk factors for cardiovascular diseases. Hypertension, which begins at readings over 140/90, occurs in more than 60 percent of people over 65, yet a 2003 National Council on Aging survey showed that almost half of Americans did not know their own blood pressure numbers. See to it that your parent gets regular blood pressure checks.

Total blood cholesterol readings above 200 are considered too high. Today, those numbers are typically broken down into subsets, including HDL ("good cholesterol"), which should be above 40, and LDL ("bad cholesterol"), which should be below 130. Diet, exercise, and statin drugs can lower cholesterol effectively; with each 10 percent decrease in total cholesterol numbers, the risk of heart disease drops as much as 30 percent. Adult children and their parents should have their cholesterol checked regularly. The American Heart Association and the Centers for Disease Control also recommend tests for a substance called C-reactive proteins (CRP); its presence in the bloodstream usually indicates inflammation somewhere in the body. High CRP levels are associated with heart attacks, even in people with low cholesterol.

As for me, except for an occasional heart attack, I feel as young as I ever did. —ROBERT BENCHLEY

Heart attacks can also befall those who are free of any known risk factors. Most start slowly, with only mild pain or nausea. Be alert to the symptoms listed in the box at right and get help immediately if they occur:

A stroke (sometimes called a "brain attack") occurs when blood flow to part of the brain is suddenly blocked or when a blood vessel bursts in the brain. People at increased risk for stroke include smokers and those with high blood pressure, high cholesterol, atherosclerosis (hardening of the arteries), or diabetes.

Transient ischemic attacks (TIAs) are "mini-strokes" that have similar symptoms lasting only a few minutes. If a parent shows these signs, even if they seem to fade quickly, he must get to the emergency room as soon as possible. Every second counts in stroke treatment. Early intervention can save lives—and speed recovery.

Diabetes. Diabetes occurs when the body doesn't manufacture enough insulin, or fails to process its insulin well, causing sugar to build up in the blood. Type 1 diabetes is usually present from childhood and requires insulin shots to survive; type 2, accounting for more than 90 percent of all cases, usually occurs in adulthood. Type 2 cases may or may not require insulin shots.

With a general population that is increasingly obese and sedentary, diabetes is on the rise in the United States, and it hits older people the hardest: one in five people over 65 has the disease. Women suffer a disproportionately high toll, as do African American, Hispanic, American Indian, and Alaskan Native populations.

Obesity and physical inactivity are major risk factors for type 2 diabetes in adults. Not coincidentally, most elderly women with diabetes are 20 percent or more over their desired weight.

In addition, about 40 percent of the middle-aged population has prediabetes, meaning they run a higher risk of developing the disease. Tests for blood-sugar levels are an easy and effective means of detecting prediabetes. Otherwise, however, the disease can be hard to spot in its early stages, when it may evince few symptoms, or when its symptoms may not seem serious. These include:

- Frequent urination
- Excessive thirst
- Extreme hunger
- Unusual weight loss
- Increased fatigue
- Irritability

People with some of these symptoms should see a doctor. Sugar in the blood may sound harmless, yet it leads to a host of serious complications, including heart disease, stroke, blindness, kidney failure, lower-extremity amputations, and deaths from flu and pneumonia. The average cost of health care for a diabetic in 2002 was $13,243, compared with $2,560 for a person free of the disease.

Warning Signs 1

HEART ATTACK. Symptoms include:

- ☐ Chest discomfort: pressure, squeezing, or pain
- ☐ Pain in the arms, back, neck, jaw, or stomach
- ☐ Shortness of breath
- ☐ Nausea, cold sweats, or light-headedness

If you suspect a heart attack, call 911 immediately.

STROKE. Symptoms include:

- ☐ Abrupt, severe headache
- ☐ Sudden change in speech, such as inability to get words out, nonsense speech, or slurred speech
- ☐ Weakness or paralysis of one side of the face or body, or one arm or leg
- ☐ Loss of sensation on one side of the face or the body
- ☐ Inability to swallow
- ☐ Sudden mental confusion

Though a cure for diabetes has yet to be discovered, its deadly complications can be prevented or postponed with early detection and careful self-management. Those with diabetes—and their caregivers—must educate themselves about care and be scrupulous about diet, exercise, and doctor's visits. They should have regular eye exams, blood pressure checks, foot exams, dental checkups, and flu and pneumonia vaccinations.

Arthritis. Nearly 50 percent of the elderly suffer from arthritis, the leading cause of disability in adults. For reasons unknown, it affects more women than men. Although more than a hundred forms of the disorder exist, two common kinds predominate: osteoarthritis and rheumatoid arthritis.

Osteoarthritis is the wear-and-tear version. It occurs when cartilage within the joints breaks down, allowing bones to rub against each other. Most often affected are the hips, knees, spine, small joints of the fingers, and base of the thumb and big toe. These areas can become stiff, swollen, and painful, especially first thing in the morning. There is no cure for osteoarthritis, but exercise, physical therapy, and medications can ease its symptoms. People with arthritis should see a rheumatologist—a specialist in arthritis—and work with their doctors to develop a treatment plan. It's also a good idea to stay active; overweight people run a higher risk of arthritis, and losing weight can lower that likelihood.

Rheumatoid arthritis (RA) affects about 1 percent of the population. It is one of a large group of mysterious autoimmune diseases—that is, disorders in which the immune system attacks healthy tissues. In this case, it inflames the lining of the joints. Like osteoarthritis, rheumatoid arthritis is marked by painful, swollen joints; unlike its sister disease, however, it typically begins in one's 30s or 40s, and may be attended by overall feelings of sickness and depression. A rheumatologist can run tests to determine which kind of arthritis the patient has and will prescribe treatments. Although RA has no cure, medicines are available to relieve the pain and inflammation.

Osteoporosis. All too often, the caregiving experience begins when a parent's bones give way. Osteoporosis—the most common type of bone disease—occurs when the body fails to grow enough new bone tissue or reabsorbs too much old bone. About 20 percent of American women over 50 have osteoporosis; another 30 percent have osteopenia, an early stage of the disease, in which bone density reaches low but not critical levels. (Men are less likely to develop osteoporosis, but about 20 percent will have it by age 70.) Fifty percent of elderly women will eventually suffer a hip, wrist, or spinal fracture. About half of those who break their hips will not be able to walk independently again, making such injuries one of the leading reasons for admitting people to nursing homes.

Thin, white women with a family history of the disease are at higher risk for osteoporosis. Other risk factors include early menopause, a history of cigarette smoking, and heavy alcohol consumption.

Early osteoporosis has no symptoms. The best test for it is a bone mineral density (BMD) exam, a painless and harmless X-ray procedure that lasts about 20 minutes. Treatment for osteoporosis includes drugs as well as a change in diet and exercise. Hormone replacement therapy, though effective in preventing fractures, is now believed to increase the risk of heart attacks and strokes; patients should review the pros and cons of this therapy before beginning it. Perhaps the most useful thing a caregiver can do for her mother is to help her prevent falls (see "Preventing Falls," page 81).

Cancer. The probability of developing almost any kind of cancer increases with age; after 60, men have a one in three chance and women have a one in four chance of developing some variety of invasive cancer. According to the American Cancer Society, the most common cancers are prostate in men; breast in women; and lung and colorectal cancers in both sexes. As with other preventive measures, older people should schedule regular screenings to test for these common cancers. Cancer

> ## Warning Signs 2
>
> **CANCER.** Each form of the disease has its own symptoms, but be on the alert for the following:
>
> ☐ Unexplained weight loss (ten pounds or more)
>
> ☐ Fatigue
>
> ☐ Skin changes, such as jaundice
>
> ☐ Changes in bowel habits or bladder function
>
> ☐ Sores that don't heal
>
> ☐ Unusual bleeding or discharge
>
> ☐ A thickening or lump in the breast or other body part
>
> ☐ Difficulty swallowing
>
> ☐ Recent change in a wart or mole
>
> ☐ Nagging cough or hoarseness

remains a complex and frightening disease—or set of diseases. Yet almost one-third of cases stem from diet and lifestyle. This means that everyone, no matter how old, can limit their risk by adopting healthy habits. A diagnosis of cancer is no longer a death knell, but hearing it from a doctor is a disturbing and disorienting experience. Trusted friends or family members should consider visiting the doctor along with cancer patients to serve as their advocates, helping them to absorb information and negotiate tests and treatments.

Didn't Sleep a Wink

For more than a third of people over 65, getting to sleep and staying asleep are nightly challenges. It isn't that people's need for sleep decreases with age but that after about the age of 40 we spend less time in the deeper stages of sleep and thus tend to wake up more easily during the night, often not even realizing it's happening. The situation is exacerbated by stress, inactivity, poor diet, and the hormonal changes that come with age. Restful sleep patterns are

Getting Some Shut-Eye

THE SECRET TO A GOOD night's sleep will be different for everyone. Have your parent try some of the following approaches to see what works for her.

☐ Go to bed and get up at the same time each day to help regulate her body clock.

☐ Go to bed later, rather than earlier.

☐ Limit naps to a single one-hour nap, preferably in the early afternoon.

☐ Go to bed only when ready to sleep; don't read or watch TV in bed.

☐ Eat lightly at dinner and have the meal several hours before bedtime.

☐ Exercise in the afternoon, not right before bedtime.

☐ Listen to a relaxation tape or practice deep slow breaths and relaxing each muscle and joint.

also disrupted by drugs, such as diuretics to control high blood pressure, certain antidepressants, painkillers, or drugs to treat Parkinson's disease. Then there are sleep disorders such as sleep apnea and restless leg syndrome, or periodic leg movements, which jerk a person awake as he is falling asleep.

Sleep apnea, which occurs when the airways are blocked and breathing stops for ten seconds or more, is most common in overweight men. The sleeper wakes when he gasps for breath, but often so briefly that he is not aware of it. However, his bedmate will probably testify to loud snoring at night and he himself will feel inexplicably fatigued during the day. Only testing in a sleep laboratory or clinic will give a certain diagnosis, followed by various possible treatments, ranging from weight loss to medication to surgery.

If your parent complains of insomnia, his doctor should take a look at his medications as well as his overall health habits to determine what remedies make sense. Certainly sleeping pills, going to bed earlier, or downing an alcoholic nightcap—all common folk "remedies" for insomnia—will only worsen the problem. Indeed, sleeping pills should be used only as a last resort because they can cause confusion and anxiety in elderly people.

The question for adult children caring for their parents is not how many hours of sleep do their parents get but whether their mother or father wakes up tired or feeling refreshed and rested. Whatever other health issues a body might be dealing with—and this goes for caregivers as well—they will be more manageable after a good night's sleep.

Resources The Body

BOOKS

Beers, Mark H. *The Merck Manual of Health and Aging.* Whitehouse Station, NJ: Merck Publishing Group, 2004.

Margolis, Simeon. *The Johns Hopkins Medical Guide to Health after 50.* New York: Rebus, 2002.

Directory of Physicians in the United States. Chicago: American Medical Association, 2005.

ONLINE RESOURCES:
GENERAL

"The Pocket Guide to Staying Healthy at 50+" The Agency for Healthcare Research and Quality
ww.ahrq.gov/ppip/50plus/

The American Geriatrics Society
www.americangeriatrics.org/index.shtml

The American Geriatrics Society Foundation for Health in Aging
www.healthinaging.org/

Centers for Disease Control and Prevention
www.cdc.gov/

drkoop.com
www.drkoop.com
Up-to-date health news and a doctor-approved medical encyclopedia.

Healthfinder
www.healthfinder.gov
Information from the National Health Information Center.

MedlinePlus
medlineplus.gov/
Health information from the U.S. National Library of Medicine.

ONLINE RESOURCES:
DISEASES AND CONDITIONS

AARP Health Guide
www.aarp.org/health/healthguide/

American Cancer Society
www.cancer.org

American Diabetes Association
www.diabetes.org

American Heart Association
www.americanheart.org

American Stroke Association
www.strokeassociation.org

Arthritis Foundation. *www.arthritis.org*

Macular Degeneration Foundation
www.eyesight.org/

National Eye Institute. *www.nei.nih.gov/*

National Institute of Arthritis and Musculoskeletal and Skin Diseases.
www.niams.nih.gov

National Institute for Injury Prevention and Control
www.cdc.gov/ncipc/factsheets/falls.htm
Tips on preventing falls.

National Institute of Neurological Disorders and Stroke
www.ninds.nih.gov/health_and_medical/disorders/stroke.htm

National Institutes of Health
ClinicalTrials.gov
Information about federally and privately supported clinical research.

National Osteoporosis Foundation
www.nof.org/

The Simon Foundation
www.simonfoundation.org/html/
Information on incontinence.

5 The Brain

The human brain starts working the moment you are born and never stops until you stand up to speak in public. —GEORGE JESSEL

THE HUMAN BRAIN is one of nature's masterpieces. It monitors and controls everything happening elsewhere in the body, weaves together a ceaseless flood of sensory perceptions, regulates emotions, stores the knowledge and skills accumulated over a lifetime, and finds meaning in everything from a traffic sign to a mathematical equation to a mother's smile. All of this is possible thanks to the brain's dense mesh of nerve cells, or neurons, which communicate by exchanging electrochemical signals.

All through life neurons die off, at different rates in different parts of the brain (as many as 50,000 a day in the cerebral cortex, according to some estimates). Although some new neurons are created, most are not replaced. Over the course of a normal life span, brain weight drops by about 10 percent because of cell death and shrinkage of the neurons themselves. In addition, connections between neurons atrophy, slowing the communication among them. Some decline of mental powers over time is therefore inevitable.

In normal aging, the kind of intelligence that psychologists call "crystalized" holds up well. This term refers to knowledge and practical skills lodged in memory and used repeatedly. Along with facts and experiences, language falls into the category: As the years pass, the ability to speak smoothly and fluently may decline somewhat. Vocabulary, however, remains unchanged, as do comprehension and command of the rules of language. Measured IQ also stays about the same. Even so, people typically start to lose some cognitive abilities around age 30; the loss can be apparent by age 60. As people grow older, their ability to concentrate is reduced. They are more easily distracted. They may have difficulty focusing.

At the same time, there is a falloff in what psychologists term "fluid intelligence," or the ability to deal with new information—absorbing it, holding it in memory for a few seconds, and manipulating it. Solving problems or figuring out the right response to new facts tends to slow with age. Lists and geometric designs become harder to memorize. Finding the right word to describe something may require more effort. This loss of efficiency, however, does not mean a corresponding drop in accuracy; older people may process information less rapidly, but they process it as well as ever. The one constant is that this process happens to everyone with age.

Estimated amount of glucose used by an adult human brain each day, expressed in M&Ms: 250

—HARPER'S INDEX, OCTOBER 1989

For some people, the diminution is so gradual it's scarcely noticeable for decades. Steve's father, Wally (page 82), is a case in point. "Not only can my dad remember the names of old colleagues, he can tell you all about everybody he knows at his assisted living facility—including where their kids went to college!" A few days before his 96th birthday, Wally was honored at a dinner for an organization he helped found 25 years ago, shortly after his retirement. He knew he would be asked to say a few words, so he prepared a graceful speech—all in his head, since he's legally blind and couldn't write anything down—and delivered it when the time came with self-deprecating humor. In the months since then, his children have noticed his increased difficulty with finding words, and it takes him a beat or two to recognize a joke. But then an impish grin comes over his face and he shoots back a riposte of his own. At 96 and a half, he attends philosophy class every Tuesday afternoon, using his reading machine to keep up with assignments.

Not everyone stays so sharp or keeps such a zest for life, of course. The brain, for all its remarkable powers, is a delicate organ, and old age is especially likely to reveal its vulnerability. For example, many older people suffer from depression, which is often viewed as a natural reaction to the problems and losses of old age. Similarly, millions of older Americans suffer from dementia—the technical term for what was once called senility—which is characterized by severe memory loss, difficulties with speaking and counting, persistent confusion, and personality changes. Dementia occurs often enough among the very old that it is sometimes viewed as a normal part of aging.

Such attitudes are profoundly mistaken. Depression and dementia are diseases. They lie outside the normal spectrum of growing older.

The Truth About Depression

The bleak moods that may descend on people in their elder years are not necessarily baseless. They may sorely miss the financial and emotional rewards of work. With advancing age, serious illnesses are more common, and older people have more disabilities—anything from painful arthritis to severe hearing loss. They may have lost a spouse. The accumulation of these cares can make life seem hardly worth living at times.

But if your parent feels this way for a prolonged period of time, she may be suffering from clinical depression. All too often, this serious medical condition goes unreported by those who suffer from it—and unrecognized by doctors focused on physical complaints. The older brain is particularly susceptible because of age-related changes in the interactions of brain chemicals—neuro-

---

FIRST PERSON

My Father's Blog

Sharon, 54 and one of nine children, sent the following e-mail to friends and family.

AS MANY OF YOU may know, my 87-year-old father has spent the past year writing e-mails on political subjects for an ever-expanding group of recipients. His deafness and my mother's death had isolated him—until he learned to use the Internet as his way of communicating with the world.

A lifelong Democrat, my father has led an interesting life for a man from a small town in Wisconsin. He was a member of the state senate of South Dakota and ran for Congress in Wisconsin. Hubert Humphrey ate dinner with us many times, and we met Kennedys and many other politicians. When we were children, he landed on the John Birch Society's hit-list for bringing black children from the Job Corps in Milwaukee's inner city to our home for summer vacations and holidays. He wanted us to learn that all people are the same. In reprisal, fake bombs were planted in our mailbox. Someone dumped a load of horse manure on our front lawn.

One of his readers has recently set him up with a blog. If you want to earn some points in heaven, visit the blog and add a comment. Feel free to disagree with him; he loves nothing better than a debate. You will be making an old man very happy.

transmitters—that influence mood, and perhaps also because of changes affecting the brain's blood supply. Clinical depression among older adults is especially dangerous. In 2001 alone, 5,393 Americans over age 65 committed suicide. (In the next highest age group, young people between the ages of 15 and 24, there were 3,971 suicides.) Some indicators of depression are listed below. If your parent demonstrates any five of them, or if symptoms are so severe that they interfere with daily routines, she should see her doctor or a qualified mental health professional for an assessment and possible treatment.

Lauren's Aunt Rose, 72, has spent the last two years in her room, sleeping or simply curled up in a fetal position. Long afflicted with osteoarthritis, Rose had surgery five years ago to replace both knees. Because the surgery was not a success, Rose is largely confined to a wheelchair, still in considerable pain. Then two of her five grown sons died, one after a long battle with kidney disease, the other after a stroke. Understandably, these losses hit Rose hard. Her husband and remaining sons encourage her to eat, to come out and join family dinners and holiday celebrations, but usually to no avail.

On Lauren's most recent visit, her uncle managed to get Rose to sit up in bed. But she responded only in monosyllables to efforts at conversation, and Lauren was shocked at her aunt's skeletal condition, her unkempt hair. "I urged my cousins to get their mother to a doctor, to get her treated for depression,"

Signs of Depression

THE SYMPTOMS OF clinical depression vary from one person to the next. Seek professional help for anyone who experiences five or more of these symptoms for more than two weeks, or if symptoms interfere with daily routines.

☐ A persistent sad, anxious, or "empty" mood

☐ Sleeping too little or too much

☐ Difficulty concentrating, remembering, or making decisions

☐ Reduced appetite and weight loss, or increased appetite and weight gain

☐ Fatigue or loss of energy

☐ Loss of interest or pleasure in activities once enjoyed

☐ Restlessness or irritability

☐ Persistent physical symptoms that do not respond to treatment; these include headaches, chronic pain, or constipation or other digestive disorders

☐ Feeling guilty, hopeless, or worthless

☐ Thoughts of death or suicide

says Lauren. "But as far as I know, they haven't done so. They act as if there's nothing to be done."

That simply is not true. A caregiver for an elder parent should refuse to accept depression as inevitable or untreatable. Studies indicate that more than 80 percent of those grappling with depression will feel better with treatment. Antidepressant medications, by increasing the level of certain neurotransmitters, can produce dramatic improvements. Psychotherapy may also help—especially in cases of mild or moderate depression.

A recent study suggests a beneficial side effect of treating the depression of people such as Rose: It lessens their chronic pain. In the randomized trial, which involved 1,001 depression sufferers aged 60 or older who also had arthritis, one group of patients received enhanced depression care; this included antidepressant medicines and six to eight psychotherapy sessions. These patients were closely monitored by a depression-care manager, who worked with both the patient and the patient's primary care physician. The care manager met weekly with a supervising psychiatrist and an expert primary care physician to evaluate each patient's clinical progress and adjust their treatment plans accordingly.

Patients in the control group received routine depression treatment. They were prescribed antidepressant medication but were referred to specialty mental health services only if their primary care doctor or the patient thought it necessary; there was no concerted effort to monitor their progress. In neither group was there assessment or treatment of arthritis.

At the end of the year-long study, patients in the experimental group showed not only fewer depressive symptoms than those who had received routine care but also reported lower intensity of arthritis pain. Those in the experimental group also reported better general health and a better quality of life.

This study and many others indicate that depression interacts with chronic pain in a vicious cycle of despair. Careful, monitored treatment with antidepressants can break the cycle, easing pain and renewing an older parent's outlook on life. Depressed elders who are battling serious illnesses such as cancer also tend to fare better in those struggles when their depression is treated.

No Turning Back

Unlike depression, the mental decline of dementia is not reversible. Dementia can take hold over a period of many years or arrive with the sudden ferocity of a thunderbolt—a metaphor the Greek physician Hippocrates used to describe stroke 2,500 years ago. About 60 percent of the time, dementia stems from Alzheimer's disease, a still-baffling degenerative ailment that begins by killing brain cells involved in memory and proceeds to engulf other vital brain structures, ultimately leading to death. In the United States, Alzheimer's disease alone afflicts an estimated 4.5 million people. Another 20 percent of dementia cases are the result of various sorts of strokes that disrupt the blood supply to the brain. Most of the remaining 20 percent may be explained by a mixture of Alzheimer's and multiple strokes. A small fraction may be traceable to tumors, Parkinson's disease, Huntington's disease, Creuztfeldt-Jakob disease, alcohol abuse, vitamin deficiency, profound depression, and a variety of other threats to the brain's sensitive tissues.

If your parent seems more forgetful and confused than was once the case and also shows unusual surges of anger or agitation, begins to dress oddly, or neglects her hygiene, have her evaluated by a doctor—perhaps a neurologist or some other specialist. A series of tests may reveal an underlying vascular disease or other ailment, including Alzheimer's.

> *There is nothing wrong with making mistakes. Just don't respond with encores.* —ANONYMOUS

Alzheimer's disease. The kinds of damage that lead to Alzheimer's probably begin 10 to 20 years before the disease becomes detectable. After diagnosis, the disease takes an average of about eight years to run its course, although the duration may be anywhere from three to twenty years; younger patients usually live longer. On November 5, 1994, former President Ronald Reagan wrote a letter to the American people announcing that he had been diagnosed with the disease. He died a decade later, on June 5, 2004, at the age of 93. The late president's public acknowledgment of his disease and his wife Nancy's calls to accelerate research into its causes and cures have boosted funding for Alzheimer's research and helped remove its stigma.

Physicians can now correctly diagnose Alzheimer's about 90 percent of the time, although absolute certainty isn't possible until brain tissue is examined under a microscope after death. What the tissue would show in the case of a positive diagnosis for Alzheimer's are two sorts of abnormal microstructures, known as plaques and tangles. Both are clearly implicated in the death of brain cells, but their relationship remains uncertain. The disease may in fact involve a whole cascade of reactions—including, perhaps, inflammation as the brain tries to defend itself, only to inflict more damage in the process.

Is It Alzheimer's?

SIGNS OF MENTAL SLIPPAGE in an older parent may mean nothing serious, but at some point you should seek expert opinion. Some of the possible causes of changes in a parent's ability to remember or to navigate while driving are reversible. They include depression, problems with medication, or an overactive thyroid. If the cause is Alzheimer's disease, the march into full-blown dementia will be unstoppable, but early knowledge of the situation allows both patient and family members to make plans about care, living arrangements, and other key issues.

Diagnosis—by specialists such as a geriatrician, a neurologist, or a psychiatrist—is done on an outpatient basis and typically takes more than a day. Steps include:

☐ Interviews focusing on the person's medical history and current functioning. Family members and the patient are interviewed both separately and together.

☐ An assessment of mental status—the patient's awareness of time and place, powers of memory and comprehension, and ability at tests such as spelling a word backward, copying a design, or doing simple calculations.

☐ A complete physical examination, including a hunt for evidence of cardiovascular, thyroid, kidney, and other diseases that might produce symptoms of dementia.

☐ A neurological examination that could reveal tumors, stroke damage, and other brain disorders. Laboratory tests may include MRI or CT scans, a PET scan to show neural activity in different parts of the brain, and an EEG to monitor brain waves.

☐ A psychiatric evaluation to rule out depression or other mental illnesses. The evaluation may include additional tests of memory, reasoning, vision-motor coordination, and other skills.

☐ Although total certainty about Alzheimer's isn't possible until brain tissue is examined under a microscope after death, the diagnostic procedure outlined above yields accurate results about 90 percent of the time.

Adapted from "Steps to Getting a Diagnosis: Finding Out If It's Alzheimer's Disease," the Alzheimer's Association, 1996.

Whatever kills neurons in Alzheimer's disease, it affects a part of the brain called the hippocampus, which is essential to the formation of both short- and long-term memories. Without a properly functioning hippocampus, memories are simply not encoded. This explains why one of the first symptoms of Alzheimer's is the forgetting of experiences, conversations, and incidents that took place just a short time before. This forgetting is total: Because the occurrences never register in the patient's memory, it's as if they never happened. As the disease progresses, the patient will be unable to recognize anyone. Muscles will be stiff, breathing labored, and swallowing all but impossible.

Although medical researchers are accumulating invaluable clues to the possible causes of Alzheimer's, much about the disease remains uncertain. Some researchers think that a person with a genetic predisposition to the disease may be tipped over the edge by additional "hits" on the brain—a stroke, high blood pressure, high cholesterol levels, or reduced blood flow from cardiovascular problems, for example. (The high rate of cardiovascular disease among African Americans may be linked to their higher incidence of Alzheimer's.)

Some recent studies indicate that diabetes may be a risk factor for Alzheimer's disease. Perhaps damage from molecules called free radicals—a product of ordinary metabolism—plays a role.

However it takes hold, the disease cannot be halted. Some medications, however, may help improve memory and other cognitive skills for a while; they can also relieve certain behavioral symptoms. Physicians often describe three stages in the course of the disease; these are outlined on pages 206-207.

Dementia with Lewy Bodies. A number of processes beyond those of Alzheimer's disease can cause the gradual death of neurons. The second most common neurodegenerative disease—and the third most common cause of dementia—is known as Dementia with Lewy Bodies; it victimizes about one-fourth the number of people who suffer from Alzheimer's. The name refers to small, spherical bodies, first described by a Dr. Friedrich Lewy in 1912, that appear along with plaques and tangles. Symptoms resemble those of Alzheimer's, with a somewhat greater likelihood of visual hallucinations and problems with balance and movement.

Parkinson's disease. Another neurodegenerative condition is Parkinson's disease, which afflicts at least half a million people in the United States. On average, it takes hold around age 60 (the incidence rises with advancing age). Parkinson's results from the death of cells in the part of the brain that produces the neurotransmitter dopamine, which is critical to the brain's control of movement. Symptoms include tremors, rigidity, slow movement, and poor balance and coordination—all worsening over time.

About half of all Parkinson's cases eventually progress to dementia, taking their toll chiefly in the form of memory loss and language problems. Other, much rarer diseases that lead to dementia-like symptoms are Creuztfeldt-Jakob disease, Huntington's disease (singer Woody Guthrie was a sufferer), and Pick's disease.

Stroke and vascular dementia. Some dementia is the result of strokes—that is, disruptions of the blood supply to the brain. This type of dementia is categorized as vascular.

Strokes take two main forms, hemorrhagic and ischemic. In a hemorrhagic stroke, an artery serving the brain ruptures. In an ischemic stroke, a blood-vessel blockage deprives brain cells of the oxygen and nutrients they need. Severe constricting of an artery by fatty deposits may be the cause of an ischemic stroke, or the flow may be disrupted by a clot that formed locally or traveled from elsewhere in the body.

About 88 percent of all strokes are ischemic. Depending on the degree of reduction in blood flow and how long it continues, the damage to the brain may be catastrophic: Only heart disease and cancer are bigger killers in the United States, where strokes are the leading cause of long-term disability. At the opposite extreme, the symptoms may pass quickly or even go unnoticed. Blockages that seem to do no lasting harm are called transient ischemic attacks (TIAs) or, less tongue-twistingly, mini-strokes. But even TIAs must be taken seriously: These warning signs indicate risk of a more serious stroke.

> *I don't want to achieve immortality through my work. I want to achieve immortality through not dying.*
>
> —WOODY ALLEN

A variety of symptoms can signal that something bad is happening in the brain (see "Warning Signs 1," page 85) Such symptoms must never be ignored. Stroke is a medical emergency, warranting an immediate 911 call. Treatment within three hours of onset will minimize the damage.

Brain cells destroyed by a stroke are eventually replaced by a fluid-filled cavity known as an infarct. A series of strokes can lead to a condition known as multi-infarct dementia. It is second only to Alzheimer's as a cause of dementia, sometimes has very similar symptoms, and is often combined with it.

The good news: Medications and lifestyle changes can reduce the chance of additional strokes. Among the risk factors are high blood pressure, high cholesterol, heart disease, and diabetes. All can be treated.

'Everything Has an Air of Strangeness'

Whatever its origin and course, dementia is one of the greatest challenges faced by those caring for aging parents. After Susan's father, Robert, was diagnosed with Alzheimer's in 2000, the family realized it had been seeing the symptoms for years without identifying them as signs of the disease. "For example," says Susan, "in 1999 or so, he would try to call my sister or me, and get furious when he got a wrong number. He'd say the phone company kept giving him the wrong number. Or he'd call me three times in an hour and not remember he had just called."

Sometimes it is more important to discover what one cannot do, than what one can do. —LIN YUTANG

Robert, who had been living with Susan's stepsister, went to live with Susan's stepbrother in Houston. "There, he was climbing out of the window, getting lost in the heat of the day or late at night. So they put locks on all the doors. That just made my father furious—and stressed out the family. By the fall of 2001, my brother's wife had had it." In November of that year, Robert moved to California to live with Susan and her husband, Michael.

In many ways, learning the reason for a parent's strange behavior can help. "Once we knew the diagnosis," Susan says, "it was easier to support him. Instead of making light of his memory lapses, we could validate what was going on for him. He would often come to me and say, 'Susan, I think there's something wrong with my brain. Everything has an air of strangeness around it.' I was stunned at how clearly that describes the state of mind."

Loath to distress their parent, many families struggle with the decision of whether or not to inform the parent of his or her own diagnosis. At one point, Susan thought it might help her father to know. "I got a film to show him, then tried to prep him for it by asking if he had ever heard of Alzheimer's.

"He said, 'Yes, that's one of the dementias, isn't it?'

"I said, 'Yes, it affects your memory.'

"He said, 'Well, at least I don't have *that* problem.'

"So I decided not to show him the film, and we don't use the term 'Alzheimer's' around him." However, when a parent realizes they are declining, it is a good idea to explain that they have a disease—and that you will be working with their doctor to arrange the best care possible for them.

Two years later, in June 2003, Robert had a stroke. After he spent a brief period in a nursing home, Susan brought him home. "But he needed a lot more help than he had prior to the stroke—things like dressing himself, which he used to be able to do," she says. "His social screen was gone. He'd take off all his clothes and be naked in the backyard. He tried punching me a couple of times, pushing over furniture. It was really hard for me to watch him decline.

"I used to give him Cheerios for breakfast and he would always make the same joke: 'Well, *this* should improve my disposition!' Now he just sat there staring at the bowl. It was so sad—and I was so distraught. Even if we could have managed time-wise—which we couldn't, really—I was becoming a basket case."

Susan and Michael eventually found an Alzheimer's residential facility for Robert. She now visits him there three times a week.

PRACTICAL STRATEGIES

Routine Therapy

CARING FOR SOMEONE in mental decline can make even routine daily tasks a serious challenge. Coping requires first a willingness to accept that the relationship between parent and child has changed, and that the parent can no longer care for himself without assistance. Second, it requires some advanced planning and clever strategies. Here are a handful:

☐ *Bathing:* Try to do it at the same time every day; substitute a sponge bath some days; be mindful of water temperature; never leave the person alone; use shower benches, grab bars, nonskid mats, and other tools for safety. For those with an extreme reaction to the shower or bathtub, try a bath in a bag: Fill a plastic bag with warm washcloths—some soapy—

and deliver the bath in the bag wherever the person feels most comfortable, such as in their bed or in the den.

☐ *Dressing:* Limit wardrobe choices; choose clothes without buttons; use Velcro on shoes. To encourage your parent to dress himself, arrange the clothes in the order in which they go on.

☐ *Eating:* Limit noise and other distractions at meals; simplify food choices; have healthy snacks on hand; use straws and handled cups; don't put too much food on one plate; use multiple plates, each with a small portion.

☐ *Exercise:* Consider activities you can enjoy doing together; limit your expectations; take walks, sing, and dance; join a special exercise class or activity group.

Design for Living with Dementia

Here are some innovative strategies from environmental gerontologist Rosemary Bakker.

ALZHEIMER'S DISEASE and related dementias significantly change how people interpret what they see, hear, feel, taste, and smell. For people with dementia, the amount, type, and variety of stimuli really matter. Both under- and overstimulation cause confusion, illusions, frustration, and agitation. Even though people with dementia retain many talents and capabilities, these will lie dormant unless they are purposely brought out through appropriate sensory stimulation.

SEEING

Way-finding cues. Visual cues may help people with dementia navigate. For example, to help someone recognize her room, it may be effective to place her name in large, bold type on the door, along with a large photograph of herself from her younger days.

Problems with depth perception, contrast. When walking on carpets with patterns or contrasting borders, people with dementia may try to jump or step over what seems to be a different level in the floor. They may also walk into a wall if there is no contrast between it and the floor, or have difficulty eating from a white plate on a white tablecloth. Strong color contrasts in those situations can help them stay oriented.

Lighting. High levels of glare-free light during the day can be an effective therapy for increasing nighttime sleeping. But reflected glare on glossy surfaces interferes with visual perception among older adults and may cause illusions for people with dementia as well as low vision. Matte finishes on flooring and table tops and appropriate shades on all light fixtures will help reduce glare. Also eliminate dark, shadowy spaces in the room.

HEARING

Reduce distressing sounds. Noise is a known stressor, especially to people with dementia.

Introduce pleasant sounds. Melodies use neural pathways not generally affected by dementia. Familiar music helps people retrieve lost memories and feelings, and can reduce agitation at bath time. However, loud music or discordant sounds, can trigger catastrophic reactions among people with dementia.

TOUCH

Many people enjoy the warm touch of a loved one or caregiver, but others do not and require that permission be granted even for a hug good-bye. Knowing who, when, where, and how to touch is critical. Petting the silky fur of cats and dogs can have a therapeutic effect. Terrycloth robes keep elders from getting chilled after a bath and reduce the need for rubbing a towel against delicate skin.

TASTE AND SMELL

Individuals with dementia often experience a decrease in both taste and smell, with deleterious effects on their nutrition. Appealing choices of food items as well as of texture, portion, and arrangement can encourage appetite. Pleasant smells such as fragrant plants, brewing coffee or baking bread are important for both the caregiver and the person with dementia..

Adapted from "Sensory Loss, Dementia, and Environments," by Rosemary Bakker, *Generations*, Spring 2003, published by the American Society on Aging.

In the early stages of a progressive dementia, adjustments by both caregiver and recipient tend to be fairly minor. Bob's father, for example, has recently been diagnosed with Alzheimer's but still loves to go out to lunch. "It takes more time to get places with Dad," says Bob, "and the mere act of using utensils can sometimes be challenging for him. But I try to offer gentle, matter-of-fact advice where needed, and he seems to take it with a good nature."

Yuki's mother, 91, is also in the early stages of Alzheimer's. "She is still able to bathe and dress herself, although she doesn't wash her hair very often, so I have to do that for her," says Yuki, 66. "And she still remembers most of the immediate family. But her mind is deteriorating. She told the neurologist that this year was 1945."

An aging parent with dementia is desperately trying to make sense out of an increasingly confusing world. As environmental gerontologist Rosemary Bakker conjures the effect, "Not only is your visual acuity less sharp in dim lighting, but you also see frightening images in shadows. It's harder to hear conversations when you're in noisy environments, and loud sounds are agitating. Not only do you forget recent events as if they had never happened, but—frighteningly—you do not know what to expect will happen next. Days and nights blend together because you no longer can impose structure on your day."

All our interior world is reality— and that perhaps more so than our apparent world. — MARC CHAGALL

Caregivers can help by staying calm, being patient, avoiding argument—and not taking odd behavior personally. Communicating clearly can reduce a parent's feelings of confusion. Explain things in step-by-step terms, and keep both tasks and routines simple (see "Routine Therapy," page 101). As Bakker's research shows, calm surroundings are critical(opposite). Noise, glare, and background distractions such as television tend to exacerbate disorientation.

The Road Ahead

For both Bob and Yuki, many hard moments lie ahead as their parents' disease continues. Marked changes in behavior are likely with progressive dementia. As in the case of Susan's father, Robert, aggression, agitation, and anger are not uncommon. Someone with dementia may also pace ceaselessly, repeatedly check door locks and appliances, or tear constantly at tissues. (Susan's husband, Michael, who did the weekly laundry, learned to search the pockets of Robert's clothes for wads of torn tissues.) They may suffer delusions and hallucinations, sudden dreads, extreme jealousy. They may exhibit inappropriate sexual behavior, or issue streams of curses and threats. The symptoms often get worse in the evening—a phenomenon known as "sundowning."

At some point, a person with advancing dementia must no longer be allowed to drive a car. That loss of independence may be fiercely resisted. When your parent refuses to accept that he poses a danger to himself and others, however, you have to take action (opposite). Steps might include disabling the car, parking it in another location where your parent is unlikely to discover it, controlling access to the keys or substituting an entirely different set, asking the doctor to write a "do not drive" prescription, or arranging for alternative transportation. An end-run around the problem may avoid upset, frustration, and an angry confrontation.

> *They tell you that you'll lose your mind when you grow older. What they don't tell you is that you won't miss it very much.* —MALCOLM COWLEY

As your parent's dementia deepens, you can take steps to make the home easier to manage for everyone involved. While your parent is still able to read, it can be helpful to place labels around the house. Signs such as "Garbage here" or "Refrigerator" can help with navigating.

Joanne, whose husband developed Alzheimer's 30 years ago at age 44, was at a loss when he began to have trouble with incontinence. "Physicians now know that nobody with Alzheimer's needs to be incontinent," she says. "You have to make things visible on their terms." Joanne discovered that painting the wall behind the toilet bright red and leaving the bathroom door open helped him find the toilet when he needed it. "His problem had been one of perception," she says. "He didn't see the toilet anymore, and that's why he'd become incontinent. But the red paint drew his attention."

Other steps can keep your loved ones—and your home—safe. Lowering the temperature on the water heater to 110 degrees F. or less will help prevent scalding. It may be necessary to keep matches out of reach and to remove the knobs on the stove. Toxic materials, firearms, and knives should be locked away.

For caregivers of elders with dementia of whatever type, support groups can be an invaluable place to share experiences, find emotional relief, and glean practical skills. Such groups are widely available through hospitals, religious groups, local chapters of the Alzheimer's Association, and other organizations.

At the Crossroads

"MY DAD SHOULDN'T BE DRIVING, but he maintains his license," says Jane. Her father, 78, is in the early stages of Alzheimer's disease and once drove around for 36 hours after suffering a seizure or a stroke. "How do you deal with this?" she asks. "How do you anticipate these crises?"

Many adult children ask the same questions when their parents insist on driving despite the increasing danger. Yet older drivers are not necessarily bad drivers. Most are cautious—and aware of their deficits. If your parent is still driving when he should not be, however, you might be facing an emotional battle. Driving is a powerful symbol of independence.

First, evaluate his skills. If he's willing, ask him to assess himself. AARP and the AAA Foundation have guides that will walk him through questions about his health, driving history, and bothersome traffic situations (see Resources, page 107). You can also ride along with him as a passenger and note whether he is driving at appropriate speeds, responding correctly to other cars and pedestrians, noticing street signs, drifting across lanes, or becoming frustrated or confused.

If his driving is not seriously impaired, your parent might benefit from a refresher course, such as AARP's Driver Safety Program. But if he seems to be in serious trouble, ask his doctor to perform an assessment that measures his strength, reaction time, vision, use of drugs, and mental functioning. If necessary, the doctor can recommend that he stop driving—though rarely do doctors have the legal authority to do more than that.

If these evaluations don't persuade your father to stow the car keys himself, you may have to stage an "intervention." You, your family, health care workers, and concerned friends can confront him firmly but compassionately. The last resort is to literally take away the car keys—or the car itself. If it comes to a pitched battle, your father might simply find another car to drive.

During a transition period, encourage your father not to drive in difficult situations—at night, for instance, or in downtown traffic. Help find other ways to get him where he wants to go. And point out that owning and maintaining a car costs about $6,000 a year—that adds up to a lot of cab rides!

The inescapable reality, as Sandra knows all too well, is that this will be a hard and distressing road. Along with her husband and some professional helpers who come to their home in a suburb of New Orleans, Sandra takes care of her widowed 90-year-old father-in-law Joe, who has Alzheimer's.

A former Marine, Joe fought in World War II and Korea. After working for the telephone company for three decades, Joe suffered a serious stroke in 1998 and is now helpless—dependent on others for his every need. He can still manage scraps of conversation, but mostly he speaks gibberish or moans for hours at a time. From one moment to the next, he remembers very little, and each day seems to take him a little further away.

Joe has since experienced a number of mini-strokes. "He loses some ground each time," says Sandra. "His skin tone gets kind of gray for a few days, he doesn't respond to much, his appetite decreases, and he is very quiet and sleeps a lot. Then he'll come somewhat back to himself—but never fully back. Our goal is to keep him comfortable, well fed, and as socially connected as that day's mental state allows."

Witnessing a parent's mental decline is wrenching for a host of reasons. First, of course, is the sadness precipitated by watching a familiar and beloved personality gradually disappear. For adult children, there's also the worrisome possibility that this same decline will be in store for them. Bob, witnessing his father's slide into Alzheimer's, says, "I find it almost incomprehensible that a lifetime of memories, emotions, relationships, and personal achievement can be completely obliterated. It's like building a beautiful and intricate sandcastle on the beach, only to have the incoming tide destroy it piece by piece until nothing remains."

For now, the castle of his father's mind is still mostly intact. But Bob knows what is to come, and that foreknowledge has changed him in one positive way: "It makes me more aware of living every single moment as fully as I can."

Resources | The Brain

BOOKS

DeBaggio, Thomas. *Losing My Mind: An Intimate Look at Life with Alzheimer's.* New York, The Free Press, 2002. Account by a former journalist of his personal struggle against the disease

Restak, Richard. *Older & Wiser: How to Maintain Peak Mental Ability for As Long as You Live.* New York, Simon and Schuster, 1997. Easy-to-read general discussion of how aging affects the brain.

Shenk, David. *The Forgetting. Alzheimer's: Portrait of an Epidemic.* New York, Doubleday, 2001. Good general overview of Alzheimer's.

ORGANIZATIONS

Alzheimer's Association
800-272-3900 / *www.alz.org*
Up-to-date information on research, treatment options, and help for caregivers.

Alzheimer's Disease Education and Referral Center (ADEAR)
800-438-4380 / *www.alzheimers.org*
Fact sheets, the latest in research and treatment, and help for caregivers.

American Association for Geriatric Psychiatry
301-654-7850 / *www.aagponline.org/*
Resources to help older people with mental disorders.

American Society on Aging
800-537-9728 / *www.asaing.org*
Professionals concerned with various aspects of aging, including the physical, emotional, economic, and spiritual.

American Stroke Association
888-478-7653 / *www.strokeassociation.org*
Information on stroke and treatment options, reducing risks, and support.

Huntington's Disease Society of America
800-345-4372 / *www.hdsa.org*
Information for patients and caregivers.

The Internet Stroke Center at Washington University, St. Louis, Missouri
www.strokecenter.org
Offers a detailed discussion of stroke and explains the various treatment options.

National Institute on Aging
301-496-1752 / *www.nia.nih.gov*
Federally funded, comprehensive resource concerning all aspects of aging.

Parkinson's Disease Foundation
800-457-6676 / *www.pdf.org*
News on research and treatment, help for patients and caregivers.

DRIVING

AAA Safe Driving for Mature Operators
www.aaapublicaffairs.com/
Program designed to improve driving skills and knowledge related to the effects of aging.

AARP Driver Safety Program
www.aarp.org/drive/
Defensive driving techniques and information on age-related cognitive and physical changes that affect driving.

"At the Crossroads: A Guide to Alzheimer's Disease, Dementia & Driving." The Hartford.
www.thehartford.com/alzheimers/ brochure.html
For those facing decisions about the continued driving of persons with dementia.

6 The Medicare Maze

I have firmly decided to bite the dust with a minimum of medical assistance when my time comes, and up to then to sin to my wicked heart's content.

—ALBERT EINSTEIN

ALL OF US HOPE to live out our lives in the best health possible. Despite the playful course charted by Albert Einstein above, that's not the way it turns out for most of us. It's therefore a comfort to know that when necessary, Medicare is there for more than 40 million older and disabled Americans. The system isn't perfect, but it does ensure that beneficiaries can get medical care without shouldering all of the costs.

A cornerstone of the nation's commitment to our aging population, Medicare has been in existence since 1965, when the administration of President Lyndon Johnson established it as part of the ambitious social agenda dubbed The Great Society. Four decades later, one of Medicare's biggest challenges—especially for those newly entering the system—is its complexity. There is so much information to digest about Medicare that this chapter aspires to present "just the facts." Still, these should give you a basic education in the program—enough, that is, to help your parents make the choices that are right for them. (See Chapter 1, "Bringing Up the Subject" and Chapter 2, "Your Parent's Best Advocate" for more guidance on discussing health care with your parents.)

Before your parents make any decisions, however, consult some of the other sources mentioned here—to find out, for example, whether your state has any special requirements that will affect your parents' specific circumstances.

First of all, be sure to check Medicare's own website (www.medicare.gov). Not only does it detail Medicare's features, it also gives you specifics about the costs and availability of plans such as HMOs (health maintenance organizations) and PPOs (preferred provider organizations) that provide Medicare benefits in your parents' home state. The Medicare website also lets you compare one plan against another.

Each state also has an office known as the State Health Insurance Assistance Program, or SHIP, which provides free health insurance counseling and can answer questions about Medicare coverage and sources of additional help. Contact information for these SHIPs is yet another offering of the Medicare website; click on "Search Tools," then "Helpful Contacts," then "Related Websites." (You can always try directory assistance as well, of course.)

The AARP website (www.aarp.org) is another invaluable resource. It provides up-to-date information on Medicare basics, tracking all the key changes in the program that affect beneficiaries. Click on "Legislation and Elections" for links to Medicare information.

Finally, your parents—and you, if you're helping them navigate this program—will need to stay on top of the statements sent by Medicare (page 115, "How to Decipher a Summary Notice") to make sure they are accurate—and to file appeals if they are not.

The ABCDs of Medicare

Medicare is a federal government insurance program for Americans 65 years of age and older (as well as younger Americans with certain disabilities and medical conditions). The program provides coverage for hospitalization, other medical services including doctor visits, and some health screenings.

Age 65 remains the starting date for Medicare eligibility if your parent has paid into Social Security for at least 10 years or is eligible to receive Social Security benefits on a spouse's earnings. If your parent does not meet these requirements, she may still be able to get Medicare by paying a monthly premium.

Are Your Parents Covered?

IF YOUR PARENT doesn't know the details of his current Medicare coverage, you can call 800-633-4227 with your parent on the line and ask. If your parent isn't able to do this, you'll need to have written authorization already on file or the customer service representative (CSR) cannot give out any information. Ask the CSR how to file proper authorization.

The following people can enroll in Medicare before age 65: Those who are permanently disabled and have received Social Security disability insurance payments for at least two years; patients with end-stage renal disease; and people with Amyotrophic Lateral Sclerosis.

There are four main parts to Medicare, labeled A, B, C, and D. There are also private supplemental insurance options—such as through a former employer or individually purchased policies called Medigap—that pay some of the costs not covered by Medicare (see page 120). It is important to understand all the options and compare them to make the selections that will work best for your parents. If your father is still working, for instance, should he enroll in Medicare? What plan will work best for your mother? If she is retired, does she have medical insurance from her former employer?

You can help by laying out these issues for your parents in straightforward terms, based on what you learn from this chapter and from other sources such the Medicare or AARP websites. (Again, check both websites regularly for updates on such things as coverage and eligibility.)

Names & Numbers You'll Need

EQUIPPING YOURSELF with some of the basic facts regarding your parents' health needs and available Medicare benefits will make it much easier for you to help your parents make decisions concerning their insurance coverage and costs. Here's a list of basic, important information about each of your parents that you should collect and keep in a safe location:

☐ Social Security Number

☐ Medicare number

☐ Name, address, phone number, and policy number for any other insurance

☐ Contact information for doctors, specialists, and pharmacies

☐ Current list of prescription medications

☐ List of present health conditions

☐ History of past health conditions

☐ List of any allergies to foods or medicines

Medicare Part A: Hospital Insurance

Part A of the Medicare system is hospital insurance. Enrollment is automatic at age 65 for people who are starting to receive Social Security or Railroad Retirement payments. If you are close to age 65 and are not yet getting Social Security or Railroad Retirement benefits, you must apply for Part A.

What it covers. Part A covers a percentage of the cost of hospital care, including a semi-private room, meals, nursing care, hospital supplies, and other hospital services. It also sometimes covers brief periods of nursing-home care or home health care after a stay in the hospital, and it pays for hospice care. See www.medicare.gov for specifics.

What it costs. For most people, there is no monthly premium for Part A coverage. There is a deductible ($912 in 2005) that the participant must pay for each benefit period. A benefit period is defined as beginning when a beneficiary enters a hospital and ends when the person has not received any skilled care in a nursing home or hospital for 60 days in a row. Once the patient has paid the deductible, Medicare will pay all covered costs during the first 60 days in the hospital. See the Medicare website for specifics about costs beyond the first 60 days of hospitalization.

If skilled nursing-home care follows a hospitalization of at least three days,

Check List of Choices

IN ADDITION TO THE FOLLOWING options, some people are enrolled in both Medicare and retiree health plans. For more information on how retiree health coverage relates to Medicare, see the Medicare website.

☐ *Original Medicare.* This is the traditional fee-for-service plan and consists of Parts A and B (hospital and medical insurance). Everyone who qualifies gets Part A upon turning 65 or, if younger than 65, if he or she meets Medicare's disability requirements. Part B is optional: People who are still working and covered by group insurance at their place of employment may not need it. Enrolling later may result in a penalty if the delay is for a reason other than having group health coverage.

☐ *Medicare Advantage (formerly Medicare+Choice).* These are Medicare's managed care and private fee-for-service plans. They can offer cost advantages over Original Medicare and possibly

some added benefits, but may also have some restrictions on choice of hospitals and doctors. In 2004, fewer than 15 percent of Medicare beneficiaries were enrolled in a Medicare Advantage plan.

☐ *Original Medicare plus drug coverage (starting in 2006).* Participants can supplement the basic Original Medicare coverage with the Part D prescription drug benefit starting in 2006. Because some people may already have drug coverage, beneficiaries may choose not to enroll in a Part D plan.

☐ *Medicare Advantage plus drug coverage (starting in 2006).* If the participant's Medicare Advantage plan doesn't cover drug costs, it can be supplemented with a separate Medicare prescription drug plan. Note: You do not need Medigap if you're in a Medicare Advantage plan; in fact, it's illegal for an insurance carrier to sell you Medigap insurance if you have Medicare Advantage coverage.

Medicare pays all covered costs with no copayment for the first 20 days of the nursing-home stay. For days 21 to 100, the beneficiary must pay a $114 per day co-pay in 2005. After the 100th day of a Medicare-covered stay in a skilled nursing home, Medicare will no longer cover skilled nursing home care for that benefit period. (Medicare will, however, still cover Part B services for a Medicare beneficiary in a nursing home.) For hospice care, Medicare pays all covered costs if the beneficiary meets

> *Any sufficiently advanced bureaucracy is indistinguishable from molasses.* —Unknown

eligibility requirements; there is cost sharing for outpatient prescription drugs and inpatient respite care under the hospice-care benefit. Check the AARP or Medicare websites for more information.

The fine print. Be sure to find out if a particular nursing home or home health care agency has signed an agreement with Medicare to participate. If not, Medicare won't cover any of the costs.

If your parent is in the hospital and is being discharged before you think she is ready, ask the hospital for a copy of its "Notice of Noncoverage." This document explains whether the doctor agrees with the hospital's decision about a discharge date. The patient is supposed to receive this notice three days before the scheduled discharge. During that time, you should work with the hospital discharge planner to set up a plan of care (or appeal the decision if your doctor disagrees with the discharge date).

Medicare Part B: Medical Insurance

Part B of the Medicare system is medical insurance. Together, Parts A and B constitute Original Medicare. Enrollment in Part B is automatic when your parent becomes eligible to receive Medicare. If they have not applied for Social Security, Railroad Retirement benefits, or Medicare Part A and are approaching their 65th birthday, they can sign up at any time during the six-month period that brackets their 65th birthday.

Unlike Part A, Part B is voluntary and requires payment of a monthly premium. So if your parent is still working at 65 or has other coverage through a spouse's employer, he may wish not to enroll in Part B coverage just yet (unless the employer plan requires it). To refuse coverage, your parent should follow the directions on the back of the Medicare card or contact Medicare directly, either by phone or through the Web.

Note, however, that in many cases there is a penalty for signing up for Part B later on. The penalty is an additional premium charge of 10 percent for every year after the year your parent was originally eligible for Medicare. Be sure to check with your parent's local Social Security office before declining Part B to confirm whether he will need to pay a penalty if he signs up later.

What it covers. This part of Medicare covers health care services that include visits to the doctor; the services of a medical lab; X-rays and the use of medical equipment; outpatient hospital care; physical, speech, and occupational therapy; home health care not following a hospital stay and visits over the 100-day Part A limit; and the services of a mental health professional.

Part B also covers an initial "Welcome to Medicare" physical exam within the first six months after enrolling. Some preventive care and screening tests to catch diseases in their early stages are also covered. Encourage your parents to talk to their doctor about which of these simple but potentially life-saving procedures are appropriate:

- Bone density scans to detect osteoporosis
- Colorectal cancer screening
- Tests for glaucoma
- Mammograms
- Pap smears and pelvic exams
- Heart disease and diabetes screening
- Prostate cancer screening
- Vaccinations against flu, pneumonia, and other diseases

What it costs. Part B includes both a monthly premium ($78.20 in 2005) and an annual deductible ($110 in 2005). Although the premium changes yearly for everyone, from 2007 to 2011 it will gradually be adjusted for those with high incomes (the higher the income, the higher the premium will be).

The annual deductible rose from $100 to $110 in 2005, and will continue to go up when the total cost of Part B increases. After the deductible is met, Medicare generally pays 80 percent of covered costs, and the beneficiary is responsible for the other 20 percent.

Part B covers 50 percent of the Medicare-approved amount for mental health services on an outpatient basis by a doctor, clinical psychologist, clinical social worker, clinical nurse specialist, or physician assistant.

The fine print. Medicare calculates an approved amount it will pay doctors for covered services. Doctors are called "participating providers" if they

How to Decipher a Summary Notice

HEALTH CARE PROVIDERS submit medical bills to Medicare, and Medicare sends a Summary Notice to your parent. This notice lists charges, approved amounts, and any balance your parent owes the provider. It is not a bill. Your parent (or you, if you're the appointed health agent for your parent) should scrutinize each notice as soon as it arrives.

Check for correct basic information, such as name, address, and Medicare number. Simple errors can lead to delays in payment and a lengthy process to correct the trouble. Check that there are no fraudulent charges for services not received. If you suspect fraud, call 800-447-8477.

This Medicare Summary Notice is standard for enrollees in Original Medicare. Medicare Advantage enrollees will also receive some sort of written confirmation, but because the plans are administered privately, the forms will look different.

If you disagree with the amount paid, or feel that a service should be covered that isn't, your parent has the right to appeal the claim. Follow the directions on the Summary Notice.

You can also call your State Health Insurance Assistance Program (SHIP) for help. To find the office in your state, go to www.medicare.gov, click on "Search Tools," "Helpful Contacts," and "Related Websites."

"accept assignment," meaning they are not allowed to receive more than Medicare's approved charge for their services.

Be sure to ask doctors in advance whether they take assignment. Medicare will pay the doctor 80 percent of the approved amount; the beneficiary is responsible for paying the remaining 20 percent.

Doctors who don't accept assignment, by contrast, can charge up to 15 percent above Medicare's approved amount. This means your parent will pay no more than the extra 15 percent, plus any required deductible and coinsurance. Some states impose stricter limits on doctors' charges.

Medicare Part C: Medicare Advantage

Once known as Medicare+Choice, Part C allows your parent to elect coverage through a private health care company. Such plans can be less costly and usually offer additional benefits, but they can also limit choice.

Not all companies offer the same benefits in every area of the country. Plan availability can vary county by county, and at the end of each year a company may decide to change where its plan is offered—or withdraw from Medicare altogether. By the same token, your parent, too, has an opportunity, once a year, to stay with the plan, switch to another, or return to Original Medicare. The following types of private plans can offer Medicare benefits:

- Health Maintenance Organizations, or HMOs
- Preferred Provider Organizations, or PPOs
- Private Fee-for-Service (PFFS) plans

What it covers. Every plan is different, so your parents will need to check on those available where they live. This task is simplified by the Medicare website's "Personal Plan Finder," which allows users to compare plans. All private plans must cover the same services as Original Medicare, but typically they have lower cost sharing or may cover additional benefits. In 2005 these benefits could include routine check-ups, vision care, hearing aids, and prescription drugs (the latter will be more widely available under Medicare starting in 2006).

> *Money is always there but the pockets change; it is not in the same pockets after a change, and that's all there is to say about money.* —GERTRUDE STEIN

Managed care plans, though, tend to limit sources of care: Except in emergencies, only plan-approved hospitals or doctors are covered. HMOs tend to restrict choice to the doctors and hospitals that are in their network, but some HMOs offer a point-of-service (POS) option that allows the beneficiary to go outside the network at additional cost.

PPOs work much the same way, covering the cost of services provided within the network and permitting the beneficiary to go outside the network at additional cost. Private fee-for-service (PFFS) plans allow more choice: Beneficiaries can use any doctor or hospital that accepts the plan's fees (but see "What it costs," below).

What it costs. Each beneficiary still has to pay her Part B premium and may have to pay an additional premium for the Medicare Advantage plan. Overall, though, these plans tend to cost enrollees less than Original Medicare. Rather than paying 20 percent of the cost of each office visit, for example, a patient might pay only $10 to $20 per visit. (There may also be co-payments for hospital and other services.) Because Medicare Advantage plans typically provide benefits that fill some of the same holes covered by Medigap supplementary insurance (see page 120), there's no need for Medigap if your parent is in a Medicare Advantage plan.

Even though your parent is still in the Medicare system, the private company—not Medicare—decides how much it will pay the physician (or other health-care provider) and what premium it will charge for the services your parent receives. PFFS plans are different. Like Original Medicare, the plan pays a percentage of the cost of covered services and the participant pays the rest (the percentage varies with the specific PFFS plan).

The fine print. Your parent must already have Medicare Part A and Part B in order to sign up for a Medicare Advantage plan that provides service in their area. If your parent moves out of the service area—to move in with you, perhaps, or into an assisted living facility—she will probably need to choose another plan. Also, any plan's premiums, copays, deductibles, and benefits can change each year.

Medicare Part D: Prescription Drug Benefit

Medicare's biggest recent changes involve prescription drug assistance, which is being introduced in two stages. The first stage, running from June 2004 to the end of 2005, offers savings on prescription medications through Medicare-approved drug discount cards, available from private companies. The second stage, a new drug benefit, begins in January 2006 and works more like other parts of Medicare by paying part of the costs incurred by beneficiaries.

The drug benefit plan: how it works and what it costs. The Medicare prescription drug benefit, available in January 2006, is voluntary and will be offered by private plans approved by Medicare. Beneficiaries can secure Medicare drug coverage in one of two main ways:

1) They can choose Original (fee-for-service) Medicare and enroll in a private, Medicare-approved Prescription Drug Plan (PDP) offered in their area. Beneficiaries will probably have a choice of several PDPs, but every beneficiary is guaranteed access to at least one.

2) They can enroll in a Medicare Advantage plan that offers drug benefits. (If the MA plan does not include drug benefits, they can also enroll in a PDP.)

Each plan can charge different premiums, cover different drugs, and offer different benefits as long as the overall value of the benefits is the same as the "standard benefit." It is too early to know for certain what the premiums will be; in the meantime, the monthly premium for the standard benefit is estimated at $35 in 2006. Coverage and copayments under the standard benefit after a $250 annual deductible are as follows in 2006:

- Medicare pays 75 percent of costs between $250 and $2,250 in total drug spending annually. Thus, after paying the deductible, the beneficiary pays up to $500 annually (25 percent of $2,000).
- The participant pays all drug costs from $2,250 in total drug costs to $3,600 in out-of-pocket drug costs annually. Medicare beneficiaries without any other source of drug coverage will reach $3,600 in out-of-pocket drug costs when their total drug spending reaches $5,100.
- The plan pays up to 95 percent of drug costs above the $3,600 annual out-of-pocket drug spending level. The beneficiary pays a $2 copayment for generic drugs ($5 for brand names) or 5 percent of the prescription drug cost, whichever is greater.

Though the plans will vary, some elements are standard. Plans cannot have a deductible of more than $250 in the first year. Nor can their "catastrophic limit" exceed $3,600 in out-of-pocket drug costs. In addition, some plans may offer better drug benefits—but this will generally mean a higher premium.

Finally, deductibles and coverage limits in the standard benefit are pegged to the annual growth of drug costs under the Medicare benefit. As an example, if drug costs go up 10 percent, the standard benefit amounts will be 10 percent higher the next year as well.

Low-income assistance. Medicare will provide additional assistance to beneficiaries whose incomes are at or below 150 percent of the poverty level (in 2006, this will be about $14,000 for an individual) and who have few financial resources. Beneficiaries with the lowest incomes will not have to pay a premium or a deductible and in 2006 will pay either a $1 or $2 copayment for a generic drug prescription and either a $3 or $5 copayment for a brand-name prescription. For beneficiaries with slightly higher incomes or assets, premiums will be based on a sliding scale, the annual deductible will be $50, and co-insurance will be 15 percent until out-of-pocket spending reaches $3,600 per year; above that threshold, the copayment is $2 for generic drugs and $3 for brand-name drugs. All of these amounts will increase each year.

Your parents can sign up for this new drug coverage starting in the fall of 2005. Here are some factors they should consider before enrolling:

- What their prescription drug costs are now
- What their prescription drug costs may be in the future
- What the premiums and cost sharing are for the different plans they are considering

Who You Gonna Call?

WHAT IF YOU HAVE Medicare and think you've received poor-quality care? David Shipp, a retired textbook salesman from Louisville, learned the answer to that question in 1999. His wife, Doris, 70, was misdiagnosed with a bladder abnormality, and wound up dying of colon cancer.

As reported by Trudy Lieberman in the *AARP Bulletin,* Shipp asked a Quality Improvement Organization (QIO) to examine the case. QIOs (once known as Peer Review Organizations) are statewide groups of doctors and other health experts paid by the U.S. government to monitor and improve the care given to Medicare beneficiaries. Because of the rules then in effect, the QIO could not disclose its medical findings about the care provided by the two doctors involved in Shipp's complaint. Shipp got a letter saying only that the QIO would take action if warranted.

Allying himself with the consumer advocacy group Public Citizen—and aided by AARP Foundation lawyers—Shipp successfully challenged Medicare's policy that kept QIOs from disclosing the findings of a quality-of-care investigation. In a victory for Medicare patients, the final court ruling on the case required QIOs to notify complainants of the results of its reviews.

If you have a Medicare-related clinical quality-of-care concern, you can file a written complaint with your state QIO. (A letter is fine, or you can download a form from your QIO's website.) If the QIO decides to pursue your complaint, it will search for clinical problems in your medical records. Note:

A QIO can assess only that part of the care paid for by Medicare.

After investigating your complaint, if the facts warrant it, a QIO can require a doctor or hospital to take steps to prevent recurrence of the flawed treatment or diagnosis. In rare cases, a QIO can initiate legal proceedings to remove the provider or practitioner from Medicare.

If your complaint concerns a service issue (long waiting times, bad food, an unclean room) rather than a clinical quality-of-care issue (receiving the wrong medication, wrong-side surgery), the QIO may refer your complaint to another agency—but it needs your permission to do so. Or you may file an appeal on your own without the QIO's involvement. The QIO may invite you and your doctor (or provider) to sit down and discuss your concerns. This mediation option, as it is known, is available only when all parties agree to take part.

A QIO can also help you appeal a premature discharge or termination of services from a hospital, nursing home, home health agency, hospice provider, or "comprehensive outpatient rehabilitation facility." These appeal rights are currently available to enrollees in Medicare-managed care plans; beneficiaries in Original Medicare will qualify for them in July 2005.

To file a complaint or appeal, first contact Medicare at 1-800-633-4227 or medicare.gov; a representative will direct you to your state QIO. To reach your state QIO directly, visit www.ahqa.org; click on "QIO Locator," then click on your state.

- What other health care costs they may have in the future
- Whether they have other drug coverage

The fine print. As is the case with Medicare Part B enrollment, your parents will be penalized for not enrolling in the drug benefit plan within the first six months they are eligible to do so. The penalty amounts to one per cent of the premium for each month they delay. If your parent involuntarily loses drug coverage from another source once the Medicare drug benefit takes effect, the penalty doesn't apply so long as that coverage was at least as good as the Medicare standard benefit and your parent enrolls within a specified time period (usually 63 days from the last day of coverage).

More fine print. When it comes to Medigap drug coverage and the new Medicare drug benefit, it's one or the other, but not both. Although Medigap plans H, I, and J now include a drug benefit, your parents cannot have both Medigap drug coverage and a Medicare prescription drug plan.

Starting in 2006, they will be unable to buy a new Medigap policy with a drug benefit. If they already have Medigap with drug coverage, they can choose to keep it; but if later on they decide they want to switch to the Medicare benefit, they may have to pay a late-enrollment penalty. If your parent has an H, I, or J Medigap policy and wants to keep some Medigap coverage, this means he will have to choose one of the following three courses of action:

- stay with the old Medigap plan with drug coverage, and not enroll in the Medicare drug benefit;
- stay with the old Medigap plan but drop the drug coverage and sign up for the new Medicare drug benefit; or
- switch to another Medigap plan without drug coverage, and sign up for the new Medicare drug benefit.

Filling the (Medi)Gap

As you've seen, in most cases Medicare covers only a portion of medical costs. Other health insurance can help pay for these costs or provide benefits not covered by Medicare. Some of the main types of medical coverage used to supplement Medicare are retiree health benefits from former employers or unions, TriCare for military retirees, and Medicaid for those with low incomes.

Medicare supplemental insurance, known as *Medigap,* is offered by private health insurance companies and is specifically designed to fill certain gaps and cover out-of-pocket expenses for those with Original Medicare.

Medigap enrollment. The best time for your parent to sign up for Medigap coverage is during the six months after she turns 65 and enrolls in Medicare Parts A and B. As of early 2005, Medigap insurers could *not* refuse coverage or charge a higher premium because of her health conditions, and they are limited in their ability to restrict coverage for preexisting conditions.

Federal law does not require Medigap insurers to sell coverage to Medicare beneficiaries under age 65. However, some states do require insurers to offer at least some plans to disabled Medicare

> *The rule is jam tomorrow and jam yesterday—but never jam today.*
> — LEWIS CARROLL

beneficiaries under 65. Check with your parents' state SHIP office on the state's requirements with regard to coverage for younger persons with disabilities.

What it covers. There are 10 standard Medigap plans, lettered A through J, from most basic to most comprehensive. (Massachusetts, Minnesota, and Wisconsin have different plans; check with the state SHIP for these states. Also, once the Medicare drug benefit begins in 2006, new Medigap policies with drug benefits cannot be sold.) All plans cover these basic benefits:

- Co-insurance for hospital days 61 to 150. In 2005, these costs were $228 per day for days 61 to 90 and $456 per day for days 91 to 150.
- The cost of 365 more hospital days in the beneficiary's lifetime once all other Medicare hospital benefits have been used.
- The co-insurance component of Medicare Part B; this is typically 20 percent of doctor bills and 50 percent of outpatient mental health services.
- The cost of the first three pints of blood.

Beyond these basic benefits, different Medigap plans cover additional costs under Medicare—foreign travel emergencies, for example, or the skilled nursing facility co-insurance. Plan B, for instance, covers the deductible for a hospital stay ($912 in 2005). Go to the Medicare Web site and click on "Personal Plan Finder" to learn all the specific details about each of the 10 plans. Not every insurer offers all Medigap plans; they only have to offer Plan A.

What it costs. Each of the Medigap plans costs a different amount, and different insurers may charge different premiums for the same plan. They all involve a monthly premium (separate from the Part B premium). You'll find the range of premium costs at the "Personal Plan Finder" page on Medicare's website, but be sure to check with individual companies for the exact premium they would charge.

The fine print. Providers base their premiums on three different methods: attained age, issue age, and community rating.

Attained-age premiums are initially lower; as the participant ages, however, their costs are likely to escalate faster than policies calculated by the other methods. Issue-age premiums (determined by the participant's age at the time of original enrollment) and community-rated premiums (all beneficiaries in a geographic area pay the same premium regardless of age) are initially higher than attained-age premiums, but they do not increase just because the beneficiary ages. Nevertheless, under every method, premiums will go up over time as medical costs increase.

More fine print. There's another form of Medigap, called Medicare SELECT, that's available in some states. It can cost less but may restrict choice of doctors and hospitals. Check with the SHIP in your parents' state. In addition, two more standardized plans have been created and could be available as early as 2006, depending on the state you live in. In general, these two plans cover similar services as the current 10 plans. In contrast to those 10 plans, the two new plans cover less of your initial Medicare spending but limit how much you would pay in total in a year for Medicare-covered services.

Blinded by the Fine Print

As detailed above, dealing with the Medicare system on behalf of your parents requires careful record keeping, attention to detail, and persistence. If you are among the many caregivers who are fully employed, raising families, and trying to keep their heads above their own paperwork, this can be a daunting challenge. For starters, though, you can short-cut the frustration by having your parent (or parent-in-law, as the case may be) file written authorization with Medicare naming you as his representative. Otherwise, Medicare workers are not allowed to access your parent's records and can answer your questions only in a general way.

If you have regular Internet access, bookmark the Medicare website and post the toll-free number beside the phone. When you need to file a claim, check the website first to see what is required; check even if you think you know what's needed in case requirements have changed. Don't hesitate to call the toll-free Medicare hotline (800-633-4227) as often as it takes to get your— and your parents'—questions answered.

Resources | The Medicare Maze

ONLINE RESOURCES

Centers for Medicare and Medicaid Services

Before you or your parents make any decisions about Medicare coverage, check the Medicare website *www.medicare.gov* or call the Medicare number (800-633-4227). To compare the provisions and exceptions in the different plans, click on the "Personal Plan Finder" link.

ONLINE ARTICLES

AARP

http://www.aarp.org/healthcoverage
Check out these articles:

"Choosing the Right Medicare Plan for You"

"Five Steps to Getting Insurance to Supplement Medicare"

"Getting Started with Medicare"

"How to Appeal: What to Do if Your Medicare Plan Won't Pay"

"The Medicare Choices"

"Medicare Comparison Chart: Key Differences among the Plans"

"Medigap Plans: Coverage Listing by Plan"

"Medigap Plans: Medicare Supplemental Insurance Policies"

"Original Medicare: Getting Care in a Hospital, Nursing Home, at Home and with Hospice"

"Understanding Medicare, Medigap and Medicaid"

"Your Rights and Protections with Medigap Plans"

Today's Seniors

http://www.a-guide-for-seniors.com
Website operated by a private financial concern focused on serving retirees.

Medicare Rights Center

http://www.medicarerights.org
Largest independent source of Medicare information and assistance in the United States. Click on:

"Medicare Statistics"
Just about anything quantifiable you'd want to know about the program.

"76 Things You Should Know About the New Medicare Drug Discount Cards"
An exhaustive examination of this new program.

"Interesting Cases"
Some real-life stories of subscribers' troubles with the system.

BROCHURES

"Choosing a Medigap Policy, 2004: A Guide to Health Insurance for People with Medicare," Center for Medicare and Medicaid Services, U.S. Department of Health and Human Services, Washington, D.C., 2004.

"Medicare and You: 2005," Center for Medicare and Medicaid Services, U.S. Department of Health and Human Services, Washington, D.C., 2005.

"Medicare Changes That Could Affect You," AARP, Washington, D.C., 2004.

7 Living Arrangements

A thousand days at home are a pleasure; an hour away from home is a trial. —CHINESE PROVERB

THE PASSAGES OF LIFE, especially in the mobile Western world, are often literally a series of transitions from place to place—from the home of childhood to the college dorm, the apartment of single days, the "starter" house, the family home for the next generation. Despite this seeming uprootedness, most of us still have a deep-seated need for a place to call our own. The changes in where we live may continue as we grow older, sometimes at an accelerated pace. The house may give way to a smaller condominium or apartment, often in a completely different region of the country; or there may be other adjustments—to a retirement community, an assisted living residence, a group home, a nursing home (see "Who Lives Where," page 126).

For older parents facing declining health and diminished abilities, the loss of familiar surroundings can be particularly troubling. And for many older parents, the greatest loss occurs when they must leave their home.

As an adult child, you therefore have two roles to play in helping your parents deal with changes in living arrangements: You need to be able to offer practical advice about the choices available, and you need to be prepared to ease your parents' emotional distress as best you can. You are, in a sense, returning a favor. One of the most valuable things parents do for their children is provide a good home—a place where they are nurtured and feel safe. Helping to provide such an environment for older parents, wherever they live, is one of the best things adult children can do to help their parents maintain as much of their independence as long as possible.

Who Lives Where

- ☐ A little over half of care recipients still live in their own homes.
- ☐ About 20 to 25 percent live in the same household as their caregivers.
- ☐ About 4 percent of care recipients live in assisted living facilities.
- ☐ About 5 percent of recipients are in nursing homes.
- ☐ African Americans and Hispanics are more likely than whites to live in multigenerational households.

You can help in several ways. One is to continue to recognize—and seek to preserve—your parents' independence in whatever new situation arises. If the first transitional step is to adapt their own home to make it safer, they should be as involved as possible in making decisions. If your parents are moving in with you or one of your siblings, it's vitally important that they have their own private space—however small that may be—and that their privacy be fully respected. Transitions to assisted living or retirement homes need to be handled with the same regard for your parents' wishes. Whatever the move, and whatever your parents' capacity, the best psychological support is to encourage them to play a role in building this new "home."

A somewhat subtler way to help is more about attitude than anything else. Remind your parent and yourself—not necessarily in words but in every action you take along this journey—that "home" is not just a particular physical location. It is also the love that made a certain place home—the nurturing and the feeling of security, the sense of self that comes with a feeling of belonging and of being in the right place.

This chapter examines several categories of choices, such as staying in their own home or coming to live with you; shared or assisted living elsewhere; and nursing homes. Beyond these practical considerations, the best thing any of us can do is to make whatever living arrangement is best into a place called home.

Staying Put

If you've been able to make plans ahead of time and are not dealing with a crisis, you may be able to help your parents continue living in their own home. For most older parents, this is far and away the top choice. But you need to be practical about the future, and the fact that their ability to care for themselves may decline. When the time comes, will they be able to afford having paid help come into the home? Do you or one of your siblings live near enough to check in regularly? Is the house capable of being adapted to someone who may eventually become less mobile? These are some of the questions you need to discuss with your parents.

As Lauren's mother, Frances, declared, "I want to stay right here as long as I'm able." In many ways this is an optimal situation, despite Frances's increasing difficulty in walking. Her studio apartment is on a single level in an elevator building with a front desk and a 24-hour attendant. "I called my mother the other day to see if she needed anything from the grocery store," says Lauren. "We've been making a weekly grocery run for my husband's father for about a year now, and just recently the logistics changed so that I pass by my mom's apartment on the way to pick up my husband. I was pleasantly surprised to learn she's had a long-standing arrangement with someone who works in her apartment building. 'Antonio does my shopping every week,' she said. 'So thanks for thinking of me, but I'm fine.'"

> *Happiness is having a large, loving, caring, close-knit family in another city.* —GEORGE BURNS

This kind of established network—of family, friends, neighbors, even hired help—is one of the great advantages of staying put.

The most important consideration is making the home safe. Begin by evaluating each room for potential safety problems. Assess the outside as well. Eyesight and balance often deteriorate with age; falls can easily break fragile bones. The walking paths inside the house therefore need to be made as safe as possible.

The notes on page 128 suggest areas of the home to evaluate and ways to improve your parents' safety. Remember not to make any changes without discussing them first with your parents. You may deem an old area rug a prime candidate for the trash, but it could hold memories your mother or father is not yet ready to abandon; they might prefer to store it somewhere.

If you're not the home-repair type or can't be sure you've covered all the bases, the following sources can supply additional information and assistance:

- Your local Area Agency on Aging may provide referrals for home evaluations within your community, often free of charge.
- A paid occupational therapist can offer skilled suggestions on what to purchase, what to get rid of, and how to provide maximum safety and comfort for seniors.
- A Certified Aging-in-Place Specialist (CAPS) is a professional remodeler

How Safe Is Your Parent's Home?

WHETHER YOUR PARENTS will remain in their own home for a while or you have arranged for them to come live with you, you'll want to make some or all of the following adjustments for their safety and your peace of mind:

☐ *Walking paths.* Adjust lighting to prevent glare and minimize shadows. Move obstacles from hallways such as small tables that could be tripping hazards. Replace old carpeting—especially if it's frayed or can bunch up—with antiskid rugs.

☐ *Stairways.* Have loose steps and loose carpeting secured, or remove carpeting altogether. Install handrails on both sides of steps if they're not already there. Put colored tape on the edge of every step so it's easy to see where each one ends. Good lighting is particularly important on stairs; make sure there are switches at the top and bottom of each staircase.

☐ *Bath.* Most household accidents occur in the bathroom (it's slippery in there!). Install shower seats and handrails in tubs and by the toilet. The bottom of tubs and shower stalls in any home should be lined with nonskid mats or rubber strips. Check the water heater, and lower the setting to 110 degrees F. if it has been set higher. In addition to preventing accidental scalding, this will save money.

☐ *Bedroom.* Make sure nightstands are within easy reach. Consider replacing the present lamp with one that won't tip over and that has a switch on the cord that can be easily turned off from the bed. Install night-lights along the path from bedroom to bathroom.

☐ *Kitchen.* Place frequently used items on the lowest shelves in cabinets and the refrigerator, even if that leaves some upper shelves empty. If it's absolutely necessary to use high cabinet shelves, get a stool with sturdy handrails to hold onto. If your parent's mental functioning is in question, encourage her to use a microwave oven, or get a combination microwave-convection oven to replace a gas or electric stove. Install larger, easy-to-read dials for the burners and oven.

☐ *Alarms.* Install smoke and carbon monoxide detectors in your parents' home—and yours as well. A good rule of thumb is to change the batteries when you reset your clocks in the spring and fall. Look into getting your parent a personal response system, either pendant or bracelet, especially if she is alone.

☐ *Phones.* Consider getting phones with large-print numbers. If your parent has extremely low vision or is blind, purchase a touchtone phone that calls out the number when a key is pressed.

☐ *Outside.* If your parents are still driving, make sure they have easy parking and garage access, that the parking area is well lit, and that there's an automatic garage-door opener. If possible, eliminate steps and replace them with ramps. Whichever you use, however, see to it that all stairs and ramps around the house and yard are equipped with handrails.

or contractor who has been trained through the CAPS program of the National Association of Home Builders (NAHB) in the special needs of older Americans. He or she knows the specifics of aging-in-place modifications, typical remodeling projects, and other solutions to the physical difficulties older Americans may face in their living arrangements.

■ The "Home Design" section of AARP's website walks you through all the things that can be done to make a home safe; go to www.aarp.org, "Care and Family."

The goal in all of this is to enable your parents to remain independent and safe, giving each of you peace of mind. In addition to physical adjustments to the home, such as installing handrails on a staircase or in the bathroom, various assistance tools and gadgets can help. Lauren's father (Frances's exhusband) lives in his own apartment at a veteran's home. A personal response system (see page 73) would have been a godsend when he fell and couldn't get up; as it was, he was not found for several hours. Because of his macular degeneration, Steve's dad, Wally, cannot read written phone numbers. But his talking phone enables him to punch in simple speed-dial codes, which connect him to Steve's house or the security desk at his assisted living residence.

Day-Tripping

Over time, it may not be sufficient to "fix" the home or rely on assistive devices. Your parents may come to the point where they need hands-on care, either in the form of various kinds of community-based care or some type of in-home care.

Even if you live near your parents, you may not be able to help them during the day. Talk with them about what they need and want, but don't hesitate to seek more objective advice about their situation. For a fee, professionals will evaluate your parents' needs and find and coordinate the necessary services.

Individual geriatric care managers—specialists in the field of geriatric care—can help you determine your parents' needs and the support services available in your area. Contact the National Association of Professional Geriatric Care Managers (see Resources, page 141). Discuss fees and philosophy upfront. This type of assistance is particularly valuable if you have not yet prepared for a caregiving role and suddenly find yourself in a crisis situation. As with all professional services, interview the care manager thoroughly—

and don't hesitate to try someone else if you're uncomfortable. If practical, involve your parents in the decision.

If your parents are not at the point of needing in-home care but do need some assistance during the day, investigate various forms of community-based care. You can begin your search by contacting various agencies for free information. One of the best sources is the Eldercare Locator, a public hotline service (see Resources, page 141) that provides information on services for the elderly nationwide, such as locations of adult day services centers, home care, transportation, meal services, and the like.

Volunteer companions. Volunteer companions can be found through organizations such as the local Agency on Aging, local support groups, and churches. Volunteers check in regularly with your parents, keep them company, and may even run errands. Some communities offer additional community services that involve so-called "gatekeepers." For instance, mail carriers in some communities are trained to look out for the elderly and let someone know if it seems that help is needed (mail piling up, for example).

> *The truth is there is only one terminal dignity—love. The story of a love is not important—what is important is that one is capable of love.* —HELEN HAYES

Meal services. Meals on Wheels and other community-based services provide simple meals for seniors, delivered daily. Volunteers who make deliveries sometimes stay and chat to make certain that all is well.

Telephone and companion reassurance services. Churches and volunteer organizations often have volunteers who do telephone check-ins. They offer a friendly voice on the phone. Many are older individuals themselves who can relate to your parents' generation.

Senior centers and adult day services. Senior centers provide entertainment, social hours, a hot midday meal, and many activities. Designed primarily for healthy and alert older adults, they are neither intended nor staffed to meet the needs of those who require supervision. Adult day services centers, by contrast, are geared to seniors who need supervision (and who may require more personal care and assistance as well, with activities such as walking, eating, or using the toilet). Investigate whether the facilities at an adult day services center meet your parents' needs. What staff is there to help? Are the hours of operation convenient?

In-home care. A professional assessment by a geriatric care manager—or your or your parents' own assessment of their needs—may indicate that it's time for a more involved level of assistance in the home. In-home aides are trained in providing personal-care services—everything from simple cooking, cleaning and other chores, to bathing, dressing, help with the toilet, and even more health-specific forms of care.

Various home care agencies can provide experienced caregivers. You can also get referrals for some types of aides from support groups such as those for Alzheimer's or Parkinson's. If your parent has been hospitalized, consult the social workers at the hospital for information.

Here are some additional tips on finding, hiring, and evaluating aides:

- Call the local Area Agency on Aging or your family physician. They may keep a roster of health aides, licensed practical nurses, and others who can come into your parents' home. Check your parents' insurance policy for what will be covered and what must be paid out of pocket. Insurance typically will not cover an aide you hire independently—another important reason to seek a professional assessment.
- Usually the services of an aide will be part of a complete care plan that the home care agency develops after an initial assessment. Such a plan typically outlines the specific tasks to be done by the aide. Alternatively, you can draw up your own list of expectations and needs for in-home caregivers—and have your parents do the same—before hiring someone. Don't hesitate to ask questions. For instance, what kind of training does a health care aide have? Does he or she have references? In addition to listing chores and duties, consider character traits that will make the relationship compatible. Would your parent appreciate someone talkative or more reserved? What about pets? If your parent has a pet, the caregiver will need to be pet friendly. Another good idea is to draw up a daily check list that the aide must refer to and check off as each chore is accomplished. Monitor care. Make surprise "spot" checks and visits.
- Evaluate both the aide and the agency. In addition to getting references, ascertain whether the care provider or agency is bonded. Ask for proof of worker's compensation insurance. Be sure the agency will provide a substitute aide if the regular care provider is unavailable on a given day.
- You'll get a good sense of the caregiver's "fit" with your parent by asking questions such as, What is your favorite duty in caring for a client? What is your least favorite? You can even ask them to rate their own

performance on a scale of 1 to 10 on such tasks as cooking, housekeeping, personal care, flexibility, and willingness to work with other family members who may be providing assistance.

Making Room for Mom or Dad

There are a host of reasons why having your parent or parents come to live with you can be a good idea—and a host of reasons why it might not. In many cultures, of course, adult children fully expect their parents to live with them eventually. No matter what your background, though, if you regard this circumstance as an onerous obligation, the situation will start badly, with the potential to get worse.

Many people have found that, for all its challenges, having their parents in their home turned out to be an enriching experience for the entire family. Not only does it give grandchildren a chance to know and learn from their grandparents, it gives adult children the satisfaction of repaying the care and nurture they received as children.

A few years ago, Ethelinn brought her 78-year-old father, then in the early stages of Alzheimer's, to live with her and her teenage son. "At first I was upset, because this should have been a time in my life to spend with my son," says Ethelinn. "But there are so many positives in having my father with us. He is safe and comfortable. He is surrounded by his books and portraits of my mother. He whistles, he laughs, he feels loved and respected. Every night he says, 'Thank you,' and I know this is the least I can do for him. My father was always there for me, and he is always there for my son, who is learning patience, compassion, and acceptance. Is there any other way this could be?"

As with so many aspects of providing care for older parents, it is crucial to approach this living arrangement with open eyes. There may be myriad issues involved, including the feelings of your siblings; sensitivities in the family from years past are likely to resurface.

If you have the luxury of addressing these well ahead of time, while your parents are in good health, discuss the situation with everyone concerned. Consider not just the practical aspects, but the psychological ones as well. Will you have to modify your home for accessibility and safety? Will extra space be needed? What kind of medical and personal care might be required?

Family dynamics. Adding another adult to any family, no matter how close the relationships are, changes the existing family dynamics, as Yuki discovered in caring for her mother (page 135). Consider the issues:

■ How will the move affect your spouse, your children, and other family members? Do unresolved tensions exist between your spouse and your mother or father? Will any of your siblings be resentful? Will they be able to chip in to help with care if they are in the area? How will you feel about a brother or sister having such access to your home? How will you feel if they *don't* offer to help?

■ Should part of your parents' income be paid to you as rent? For groceries or other monthly expenses? Should siblings contribute to expenses?

■ Is your lifestyle compatible with that of your parents? If you and your family like to take vacations, participate in local sports or go to museums and movies, how will your parents' presence in your home affect your ability to do these things together as a family? Will you need to arrange for their care if you are away from home for extended periods?

> *We rarely think people have good sense unless they agree with us.*
> —FRANÇOIS DE LA ROCHEFOUCAULD

■ How will your parents feel about the move? Consider what will be difficult and what will be relatively easy. Is smoking or alcohol use an issue? (If so, address this immediately.)

■ Are pets involved? Will there be allergy issues or fear-based problems?

■ Will you have to cut back on work to provide care at home? Can your family afford it?

■ How will everyone in the family find time and privacy for themselves? If grandma takes over your daughter's room, how will you remedy the loss of privacy? Will there be hard feelings? Again, communication among family members is vital.

Space. If your house seems too small to accommodate another person, you might want to explore building an addition. Make sure this solution works not only for your parent but for you as well, and the future you plan for this home. The best solution may be to convert space, such as a garage, into an "in-law" suite.

Some people have built separate homes next to their own to offer maximum privacy and independence. A less-expensive alternative is an ECHO unit (Elder Cottage Housing Opportunities), also known as an ADU, or Accessory Dwelling Unit. This prefab unit attaches to the existing house or sits apart from it in the yard. Check housing codes for restrictions.

Available services. Local services need to be factored into your decision to have a parent move into your home. Whether your parents are moving across town, across states, or across the country, they are leaving well-known places for shopping, car repair, social clubs, and so on. Locate services and stores in your neighborhood that will be comfortable for your parents. On a free day or evening, give your parents a tour of what's available in terms of shopping, banking, recreation, and religious services.

Independent Living 101

Your parents may decide to leave their old home while they're still able to live without a great deal of assistance. Some living arrangements can provide a modicum of support services while allowing your parents to maintain maximum independence. These choices typically require a good deal of advance planning.

Homesharing. Two or more unrelated people share a house or an apartment. Sometimes one friend moves into the other's house. In other cases, friends arrange early in their retirement planning to purchase or rent together. Many widowed, divorced, or single women find homesharing attractive for its companionship, its help with everyday tasks, and its reciprocal caregiving.

Senior apartments. These age-restricted apartments are offered to people 55 and older. Although some are luxury apartments with a high price tag, many are priced at market rates or below. Some are built specifically for low-income older people.

Because these buildings are constructed for the elderly, they are designed to be accessible and often include transportation services. Many offer recreational or social services. Bear in mind, however, that these apartments are geared for those who do not need assistance. If your parents cannot manage on their own, a senior apartment is not the answer.

Retirement communities. Many parents, frequently at a very early stage in their retirement planning, opt to buy into a retirement community. They purchase a house or condominium within a complex, essentially as you would in the workaday real estate market. Meal plans may be offered, and post offices, swimming pools, and health spas are often part of the physical plant.

Maintaining their independence may rank high on your parents' wish list,

Tradition vs. Reality

Yuki's mother, 91, is in the early stages of Alzheimer's. She has lived with Yuki, 66, and her husband, Ken, 70, since 1991. Yuki is the second of five children and the eldest daughter. Her older brother is the eldest son—in Japanese, the niisan.

WHEN MY FATHER DIED, in 1975, he and my mother had been living in one half of a duplex that my husband and I had bought for them. In traditional Japanese culture, the *niisan* is supposed to be responsible for his younger siblings and his parents, but my eldest brother had not taken on any of those responsibilities. About a year later, though, he said he wanted to buy the duplex. We sold it to him on the condition that my mother could continue to live there, and that he would help take care of her.

After my father died, I enrolled my mother in weekly lunch meetings with other Japanese ladies and in other senior programs. She learned to take the bus, met people, and had more independence than when my father was alive. She went on day trips and overnight trips. She got to do all kinds of things she'd never done before.

After a few years, however, due to the influence of my brother's wife, my mother really did not feel comfortable living in the duplex. She asked to live with my husband and me, but we still had children coming home from college. I told her that as soon as one room was available with a private bathroom, she could be with us. We found another rented home for my mother until 1991, when our youngest daughter moved out of the house.

At that point, my mother moved in.

My mother and my brother's wife didn't get along. That was the main problem. Even after my mother moved in with us, my brother continued to be very reluctant to help. Just in the past year, however, I have been strongly insisting that he help us whenever we have to go out of town. He's the *niisan*. He should be doing it. He's been a bit more cooperative since my husband spoke to him very frankly and reminded him that this is his mother, too.

but what if they simply are no longer able to manage on their own, even with home help? If living with you is not possible or is not, for whatever reason, a wise choice for your family, you and your parents still face a wealth of other options:

Assisted living residences. These facilities seek to help people stay as independent as possible while offering needed assistance. They are for people who require personal care and support services but do not need the full-time care of nursing home residents. Most offer, at a minimum, help with the following basic daily activities: bathing, dressing, walking, using the bathroom, medication management, housekeeping and laundry, social and recreational activities, and beauty or barber services.

Assisted living can be expensive. Medicare doesn't cover the cost, so your parents will need to pay out of pocket. Costs typically run between $1,000 and $3,000 a month. Though most residences are licensed, the requirements vary by state. Some states mandate training and certification of the staff.

Be rigorous in evaluating assisted living residences. Read the contract carefully. The monthly payment, for example, may cover only basic services, with additional services offered on an "à la carte" basis. And be sure to ask lots of questions.

Some of the critical points to cover are these:

- To what degree is the privacy of the residents emphasized?
- Are there any restrictions on residents with physical needs? Are activity centers in the facility fully accessible?
- Is the fee determined by the square footage of the unit?
- What rights do residents have? Are resident councils permitted? Do residents maintain full control of their personal finances?
- What is the staff turnover rate? Does the facility have its own training program for staffers? What are the state requirements?

Most assisted living residences provide apartment-style living with hotel-style services. They offer meals, housekeeping, transportation, and some level of security, but only limited assistance with using the bathroom and eating, and no medical services. If their needs change, your parents may not be able to remain in this type of facility.

Board and care housing. This living situation may also be called a residential care home, personal care, adult foster care, or an adult family or group home. Usually located in residential neighborhoods, these are generally smaller, private group residences for ten people or fewer. Structured to re-create a homelike setting, these living arrangements often offer simple services such as laundry and cooking, as well as opportunities for social interaction and recreational activities. All have 24-hour services to respond to emergencies.

Continuing care retirement communities (CCRCs). If your parents don't relish making transitions or moving from place to place, a CCRC may be just the right fit. These facilities feature independent-living apartments and homes and the various social, recreational, and cultural activities of other retirement communities. But they also have assisted-living and nursing-home care. In this continuum-of-care system, as it is called, a resident can move from the independent-living tier to the assisted-living tier if his or her health begins to decline. If nursing-home care becomes necessary, the resident moves to yet another tier. Moves can be temporary; the most important feature of continuing care is that core needs are met. Some facilities have Alzheimer's units and orthopedic or physical-therapy treatments. If one spouse remains in good health, he or she can stay in the independent side of the community, free to visit the spouse in frailer health.

A few CCRCs are beginning to offer units dedicated to those with vision impairment. This specialized tier of care provides reading machines, special lighting, and color-coded hallways. Some CCRCs have specialized units for cognitively impaired residents, which provide "wander-inhibiting devices" to keep residents from getting lost.

When a Nursing Home Makes Sense

If your parent needs round-the-clock care, including skilled nursing, a nursing home may be the appropriate option. That's what Emma found. A 60-year-old retired newspaper editor living in Savannah, Emma is an only child who assumed responsibility for both her elderly parents, then living eight hours away in Atlanta. Her father was 88 and her mother 84 when they suddenly became unable to live on their own.

"I've thought about this a lot," Emma says. "I think there's some sort of cultural reflex that leads people to proclaim that they'd never put their sainted parents in a nursing home. Some honor that promise, trying to care for their elderly kin at home—and doubtless that works out in some cases. But I believe a great many elderly are far better off in nursing homes—cared for by professionals and afforded the company of peers and activities suitable to their age and interests.

"That's easy to say, of course. The trick is to find the right home."

Indeed, the process of choosing the right home involves many steps. It starts with making a list of homes in the area; finding out their quality of care ratings; and visiting the homes. This last step is critical, and it cannot be overemphasized: Your visits need to continue even after the choice is made.

Making a list. Here's where your research begins. Location is often an important factor, but it should not be the only one. You can start by looking

Sister Donna

SISTER DONNA ZIELINSKA, a Polish émigré, is the Director of Social Services at Sacred Heart Nursing Home in Hyattsville, Maryland. Sacred Heart has 100 female residents, 80 percent of whom suffer from Alzheimer's disease or other forms of dementia. The staff consists largely of foreign caregivers, mostly from Africa. As Sister Donna says, "They have good, strong values and respect for the elderly. In caring for them, they grow very fond of the residents."

Sister Donna's main mission is caring for the residents, but she makes a point of reaching out to visitors and their families, too. She cares about the role they play—and sometimes don't play—in this stage of their parent's life.

"Some people have good coping skills," she says, "but many do not. Many feel guilty because they live separately from their parents and depend on the calls of neighbors regarding their parents' situation. Some children were never close. Daughters are mostly the caregivers. The small numbers of men don't tend to share their emotions; they are interested in the practical things."

When a family decides that Sacred Heart is the right place, Sister Donna meets with them to discuss the care. "People become very emotional, especially when they have to break the promise they made to their parent that they will never put them into a home. I give them support, telling them that they kept their promise as much as they could, but now their parent needs specialized care."

Residents often long for their old lives. "Independence is the highest value, and residents guard it, even to the end. One resident rejected help even when it meant that she could fall and break a hip. Many residents would give everything to be with their family, even if it shortens their life or if they have to live under poorer conditions."

The transformations Sister Donna sees in the residents are predictable—and, in physical terms, not for the best. But occasionally she witnesses a transformation of another kind. "One resident's daughter wanted to be closer to her mother. The mother had always ordered everyone around. The daughter learned a great deal about her mother from conversations she had with her at the home. She could see her mother as being more human, not so austere. And the mother became more loving toward her daughter. The mother had nothing to control anymore, and the daughter saw her mother's helplessness—a new side of her. She wished that she had gotten closer earlier."

In her experience, the best situations involve families for whom caregiving itself is not a new thing. "If people have cared for their loved one at home, they have more understanding of what's happening at the nursing home. For those who did not care for them at home, it's a learning process."

The rewards for Sister Donna are ongoing. And for her, too, it can be a learning experience. "One resident, a Korean woman, came directly from the hospital. The family came every day because they thought she would soon pass. Then the woman miraculously recovered and the family wanted to take her home. But she refused, saying, 'Now this is my home.'"

at facilities you can visit easily. Then, if need be, widen the region you'll consider. Consult several sources of information. Speak with a social worker or a geriatric care manager.

Also check Medicare's website (www.medicare.gov). Its "Nursing Home Compare" page allows you to assess nursing homes on a variety of measures, such as percentage of residents with loss of ability in basic daily tasks, severe pain, bedsores, and infections. Keep in mind that the measures come from surveys, and that those represent only a snapshot in time—just one of many tools to use in evaluating a nursing home. If your parent is about to be discharged from the hospital, talk with the discharge planner or social worker.

And, of course, consult your local Area Agency on Aging, as well as doctors, family members, friends, and neighbors you trust. A good source of information is your state or local long-term-care ombudsman. Long-term-care ombudsmen advocate for residents of nursing homes, board and care homes, and assisted living facilities; they are trained to resolve problems. Under the federal Older Americans Act, every state is required to have an ombudsman program; most are housed in the state's unit on aging. Ask your Area Agency on Aging for more information about this important service.

> *No matter how old a mother is, she watches her middle-aged children for signs of improvement.*
> —FLORIDA SCOTT-MAXWELL

In Emma's case, there was a fine nursing home just across the street from her house in Savannah. The home had a rule against admitting out-of-city residents, so Emma had to become a strong advocate to persuade them to take her mother, who had fallen and fractured a hip. Her father, meanwhile, had developed a rare blood disorder and was also hospitalized.

For a period of two or three weeks, with both of her parents in an Atlanta hospital, Emma spent a lot of time on the road. She had so much to organize in both places that she relied heavily not only on her own circle of friends but also on that of her parents—especially when it came to clearing the home her folks had lived in for 50 years. "I had to get the house ready for an estate sale and then for a house sale," Emma says. "My parents' friends and neighbors were wonderful through it all." The Atlanta grapevine led her to a geriatric consultant whose help was invaluable. Also supportive was the family accountant, who had a firm grasp of the myriad tasks to be accomplished— and, as a longtime friend, was willing to do a lot of them himself.

Because only one room was available in the Savannah nursing home, Emma had to prepare her own house for her father to live in temporarily. "This meant making the house safe in general, and installing a chairlift," Emma says. Meanwhile, back in Atlanta, the geriatric consultant was proving his worth, dealing with complicated Medicare issues at the hospital.

Finding quality care. According to the Centers for Medicare and Medicaid Services (CMS): "Quality care means doing the right thing, at the right time, in the right way for the right person, and having the best possible results." State inspection reports, resident characteristics, and staffing levels are among the issues you should look into. To find this information, consult your long-term-care ombudsman office to discuss survey results. You can also talk to the state health department, or to friends and others who have personal knowledge of a home.

> *Challenges are gifts that force us to search for a new center of gravity. Don't fight them. Just find a different way to stand.* —OPRAH WINFREY

Research visits. Once you have identified some likely prospects—homes that seem to offer quality care—visit each one several times. Multiple visits should include days, evenings, and weekends—scheduled and unscheduled. Ask for the administrator, and request a tour. Use the check list on pages 208-209 to evaluate the place, and never hesitate to ask questions. If you meet resistance, move on.

The care you show in selecting a nursing home is important, not just in picking the right situation but in demonstrating your commitment to your parents. And once they're in the home, the single most important thing you can do is visit. Visit often; visit unexpectedly. Stay involved with your parents and with those providing their day-to-day care.

Emma was lucky in the nursing home she found for her parents. "Mother was well cared for," she says. "To the extent that she was mindful of much—there was progressive dementia and also lung cancer—she was happy. She had a pretty room and lots of attention, which she loved. After about two years, she died, drifting off in a comfortable morphine haze. She never knew she was ill."

When Emma's husband became critically ill during this time, the same nursing home took her father temporarily—then, a little while later, permanently. Her father is content: "Instead of being rather isolated at my house," says Emma, "he's among people again. He plays the harmonica at their church services, and enlists the help of guitarists to liven things up. A worker at the house said to me once, 'You know, I hope I live long enough to someday become the gentleman your father is.'"

The best thing, from Emma's standpoint: Her father is just across the street. "I can throw birthday parties for him, take him out to jazz concerts. He has new friends around. I've never felt the slightest regret at putting my parents in the Savannah home. Of course, I do have the luxury of dropping in, dog in tow, whenever I feel the urge. So I'm able to avoid the horrible thought that my father might feel abandoned—I was very lucky."

Resources | Living Arrangements

ORGANIZATIONS

Eldercare Locator
Administration on Aging
800-677-1116
www.eldercare.gov/
Eldercare/Public/Home.asp
A first stop for information on services for the elderly.

Family Caregiver Alliance
(National Center on Caregiving)
800-445-8106
http://www.caregiver.org
Provides online fact sheets and a downloadable handbook for long-distance caregivers. Fact sheets also available in Spanish and Chinese.

Meals on Wheels Association
of America
703-548-5558
www.mowaa.org
An association of programs that provide home-delivered and congregate meals.

National Association of Area Agencies
on Aging
www.n4a.org
The single best source of information on living arrangements for the elderly is your local Area Agency on Aging. Contact the National Association for more information.

National Association of Professional
Geriatric Care Managers
http://www.caremanager.org
Website explains the role of care managers and points caregivers to local resources.

8 Caring for the Caregiver

In the event the oxygen masks deploy due to loss of cabin pressure, put on your own mask first, then assist others. —AIRLINE SAFETY INSTRUCTIONS

"THE FIRST THING I did, when I realized the enormity of what I was faced with—that I would be on call 24 hours a day—was to cut my hair," says Isabel. "Very, very short. It helped me focus. I think it was emblematic of my mental state, but it also helped me physically as it was one less thing to be concerned about. Though it may seem obvious, there is no way to prepare for the events that happen to your parents. When they happen, you have to react. Taking care of yourself isn't something you think about at the time."

Isabel, single and 56, took care of her father during an illness and her mother after an injury. When she thinks back on those times, she realizes how much she learned about herself and her relationship with her parents. "I know that experience teaches," she says. "This past year has been a year of discoveries." For her, the biggest reward lay in doing the job "without adopting the mantle of victim or self-sacrificing martyr or the good daughter. Just meeting the challenge in the best possible way."

Physically, emotionally, and psychologically, caring for an aging parent may be the most difficult thing you have ever done. The demands on your time and energy may be compounded by feelings of sorrow, guilt, or anger. Long-buried disputes with parents and siblings can surge back to life. If you are a typical caregiver, you may feel that it's your responsibility to shoulder all the work, proving to yourself—and the world—that you are fulfilling your duty to your parents.

You won't be able to care for your parent, however, if you don't take care of yourself as well. Even though self-care may seem like one more burden to carry, heed the advice of those who have been there: Make your own well-being a high priority.

In some ways, boomers are better equipped to do this than their parents. "Our approach to caring for our parents differs from our parents' generation," says Lucy Mikulak, a psychotherapist who works with families, "in that we're more resourceful—we seek out and talk with friends, coworkers, and professionals. We talk about personal matters that would have embarrassed our parents. And we're more likely to try self-help. We grew up knowing that anything was possible for both men and women."

The Hidden Patients

Although many men are caregivers, women spend far more time at the task, and they are the ones most likely to be providing the truly labor-intensive care. A 1999 study found that one-third of women caregivers decreased their working hours and almost 30 percent passed up a promotion or assignment because of caretaking demands. About one-fifth took a leave of absence or switched to part-time work; 16 percent quit altogether. This curtailed working time has long-term consequences for women: It results in lower wages, fewer benefits, and reduced retirement savings. Male caretakers typically take a different road, deferring their own retirement in order to pay for long-term care for a parent.

Never believe that a few caring people can't change the world. For, indeed, that's all who ever have.

—MARGARET MEAD

Parents might not realize that their expectations put stress on their working children. "My mother feels that children should put aside their lives to take care of their parents," says Susan, a professor of health and nursing. "But her children don't do that. It has taken years of resentment and complaining for her to finally realize that her daughters do care for her, even if we don't drop everything for her. In fact, my sister frequently responds to her calls for assistance, even in the middle of the night—but what any of us does never really meets her hopes and expectations."

These demands on the caregiver's time and psychic energy often affect emotional health. Indeed, as many studies have shown, women who care for ill

Take a Breath

AUTHOR AND STRESS REDUCTION expert Jon Kabat-Zinn teaches mindfulness meditation to patients at the University of Massachusetts Medical Center. The following is a simple meditation exercise he suggests practicing for several minutes each day.

Find a place where you will not be disturbed, and assume a comfortable posture lying on your back or sitting. If sitting, keep the spine straight and let your shoulders droop.

Close your eyes if that's comfortable.

Bring your attention to your abdomen, feeling it rise or expand gently on the in-breath and fall or recede on the out-breath. Focus on "being with" each in-breath. Every time your mind wanders off the breath, note what it was that took you away. Then gently bring your attention back to your abdomen and the feeling of the breath going in and out. Should your mind wander away again, your "job" is simply to bring it back to the breath every time—no matter what it may have become preoccupied with.

Practice this exercise for 15 minutes every day for a week, whether you feel like it or not, and see how it feels to incorporate a disciplined meditation practice into your life. Be aware of how it feels to spend time each day just being with your breath without having to do anything.

parents are twice as likely to suffer from depression and anxiety as noncaregivers; they have higher levels of stress, hostility, and self-criticism than the general public. Small surprise, then, that the American Medical Association refers to caregivers as "the hidden patients."

Yet few caregivers regret taking on the task. Women who are called upon to be the family's emotional mainstays find it to be among the most rewarding aspects of caregiving. "I cared for, loved, and respected my parents" says Joyce, who lives in the United States while her elderly father is in Puerto Rico. "I do not ever regret my dealings with them. After my mother died, I 'replaced' her—so now my father consults me for everything. Each time he has had a physical or emotional crisis, he has called me here for help." Her connection to her father was also a welcome connection to her cultural roots. "He is my direct link to my people, language, and traditions."

The Stress Factor

Caring for an aging parent brings a host of pressures to bear on your time, finances, emotions, and relationships. Many people regard caregiving as yet another task to master. They set up the same high expectations that they have brought to other life challenges, such as tackling new jobs or raising children. Then they fall short of those expectations, over and over again, adding guilt and frustration to the sense that they are butting their heads against a whole series of walls.

It's important to recognize that stress usually results from the attempt to control a situation that is beyond your control. Step back and accept it: You are not in charge of life. You won't be the perfect caregiver. You cannot handle every detail. You can't cure your parent's illnesses. You won't be able to change other people's personalities, their ingrained habits, their fixed prejudices. You are not going to become a saint who forgives all old wrongs and never speaks a harsh word. And that's okay. Just do what you can reasonably manage and accept that the rest of life, for better or worse, is going to flow past you. It really isn't up to you to make it all better.

You may not be able to control life, but you *can* control how you react to it. Changing your reactions can do a lot to reduce your stress. The first trick is to listen to your body and recognize the physical symptoms of stress: shortness of breath, headaches, tense muscles in the shoulders or face, stomach or

---

Rewrite Your Inner Script

IF YOU'VE SPENT much time with a teenager, you probably recognize these kinds of over-dramatic responses:

"You never take my side!"

"Everyone hates me."

"I just know she won't go out with me —it's not worth asking."

But do you recognize them in yourself? Negative thinking is natural in the stressful life of a caregiver, but it is also a barrier to solving your problems and reducing your anxiety. Be on the alert for your own negative responses and try to replace them with more positive statements. Some examples:

Generalizing: "Dad never listens to me. He never takes my advice." *Instead:* "Dad hears what I'm saying, but it's hard for him to accept one of his children as a knowledgeable adult."

Ignoring the positive: "Sure, the medicine is helping Dad right now, but eventually he'll go downhill again." *Instead:* "It's great that this medicine is helping now. It will give Dad some quality time that he wouldn't have had otherwise."

Jumping to conclusions: "Why bother taking Mom to day care? I'm sure she'll just hate it." *Instead:* "I can't read Mom's mind. There's no harm in trying."

Labeling: "I'm so selfish. I should be helping my sister more. *Instead:* "I'm not selfish; I'm trying to balance my own life with caregiving, and it's not easy."

intestinal cramps, a knot in the throat. Calm your on-the-spot frustrations with a quick time-out. Leave the room (you can say you need to use the bathroom) and count slowly to 10; take deep breaths; consciously relax each tense muscle from your toes to your forehead. When you have a few more minutes, practicing some basic relaxation and meditation techniques can help restore your equilibrium (see "Take a Breath," page 145).

Be alert to unhelpful thought patterns that increase your stress—for instance, "shoulda-woulda-coulda" statements. Any sentence that begins "I really should" is a sign of internal conflict. Finish those "I really should..." statements, at least in your head, with a "but..." and a "because...." "I really should call my mother today, but I don't want to because I feel guilty when I talk

> *I can feel guilty about the past, apprehensive about the future, but only in the present can I act.*
> —ABRAHAM MASLOW

to her." Or, "I really should tackle those hospital bills, but I can't do it before Friday because I have to meet a deadline at work." Doing this won't solve your problems, but it will put you on the road to defining your conflict so that you can deal with it (see "Rewrite Your Inner Script," opposite page.)

Some people tend to obsess about small problems, adding to their own stress by rehashing minor mistakes or worrying continuously about an upcoming event. Others are more likely to have the opposite reaction, blocking out unpleasant thoughts to the point where they haven't dealt with them at all. Caregivers of either tendency can benefit by recognizing the stressful thoughts and setting them aside for later consideration—say, during 10 minutes in the afternoon when they have a cup of tea or, even better, when they can discuss them with a friend. Until that designated "worry time," try to put the obsessive thoughts on a mental shelf—and reshelve them whenever they threaten to intrude on your day.

Making Yourself a Priority

"I have found that it is very important for caregivers to have a good sense of self. They have to value themselves," says psychotherapist Mikulak. "Writing in a journal is helpful. I encourage my clients to begin one if they haven't already. I also encourage them to look at 'little successes'—renewing their driver's license on time, shopping for a new pair of shoes they need."

Just because your parents are important, and their needs are many, does not mean that your needs should be ignored. You deserve your own time—time to go to a movie or a concert, to visit a museum or a garden. Mikulak advises caregivers to look at their old interests and ask themselves, "What did I used to enjoy doing?" Yuki, the primary caregiver for her 91-year-old mother, who has Alzheimer's, cultivates her pleasurable times. "When I have to be out of the house, my husband will give my mother her pills with meals or take her to a doctor's appointment," Yuki says. "But I prepare the meals and mostly care for my mother by myself. Still, I make time for other things. I am the Buddhist representative for a hospital chaplaincy program and I also sing with my church. When I'm singing, I forget everything!"

If you want others to be happy, practice compassion. If you want to be happy, practice compassion. —THE DALAI LAMA

Depression. For some caregivers, the emotional fallout from caring for ailing parents goes beyond stress and into the realm of depression. This is particularly true for women, who are more prone to the illness, and for those who are caring for someone with dementia. You might already be on the alert for symptoms of depression in your ailing parents (see page 94). Watch for them in yourself, as well. Insomnia—which can lead to fatigue, which can lead to difficulty concentrating—may seem like it goes with the territory. But if the sleeplessness and spaciness persist—especially in tandem with other unrelenting symptoms, such as feelings of hopelessness and a loss of pleasure in once-enjoyable activities—you must get help. Depression is a treatable illness. Tell your doctor how you are feeling and request a physical exam to rule out medical causes for the symptoms; at the same time, ask him or someone else you trust for a referral to a mental health professional, such as a psychiatrist, a psychologist, or a social worker.

Be good to your body. As busy as you may be tending to your parent's body, don't give up on your own. A decent diet and some regular exercise will boost your energy and your spirits far more, in the long run, than junk food wolfed down in the car. Now more than ever, try to eat regular, light meals that feature whole grains, fruits and vegetables, and low-fat meats and cheeses. Limit your intake of saturated fats and sugars. Be particularly careful about self-medicating with too much alcohol and coffee.

Exercise not only helps your body, it improves your mood. Studies have shown that regular exercise affects your brain chemistry and can be as effective as medication in combating mild depression. If you haven't been exercising regularly, don't start a regimen that is too strenuous to maintain. Choose an easy routine such as daily walks around the neighborhood or a swim at the local pool three times a week. You can combine your activity with errands such as a walk to the neighborhood store or a session in your mother's garden. For extra benefits, exercise with a friend. You are more likely to keep it up and will probably be cheered by the emotional support as well.

Lightening the Load

The burden of caregiving usually falls most heavily on one person, typically a daughter or daughter-in-law who lives nearby. Susan's younger sister, who lives closest to their mother, is their mother's primary caretaker. "She takes care of crises for our mother, who is a high-maintenance personality, and I took care of my father—seemed like I got the better deal there."

Indeed, the issue of who got "the better deal" is often a bitter one among siblings. When Susan's father began to show signs of Alzheimer's disease, her stepsister was caring for him as well as for her young family. Eventually she announced that she couldn't cope with him any more. "She really resented that nobody else was pitching in," says Susan. Their father went to live with her stepbrother, then with Susan before moving into an Alzheimer's residence.

Share the Care

In March 1998, a dozen women received a call to attend a meeting devoted to finding a way to help their friend Susan, a divorced mother of two whose cancer was growing worse. Many of the women—Susan's friends, co-workers, and neighbors—were strangers to one another. But over the next three and a half years, they coalesced into a tight-knit group that handled everything from daily cooking and shopping to taking Susan to doctor's appointments, keeping track of her medications, and checking her in and out of hospitals. They even organized her daughter's wedding six months before Susan died.

A few months later they helped someone else form a similar group for another woman battling cancer. Watching that "family" swing into action again inspired the originators of the method to capture their caregiving system in a book, *Share the Care: How to Organize a Group to Care for Someone Who Is Seriously Ill.* The system has become a model for groups nationwide. Visit www.sharethecare.org to learn how to start a caregiving group of your own.

Too often, the primary caregiver soldiers on alone, waiting for siblings to read her mind and come forward to volunteer—or even turns them down when they do offer, wanting to be the "good one." This can set up a destructive cycle of guilt and recrimination among family members. The primary caregiver is exhausted and resentful. Siblings and spouses feel guilty and angry. None of this helps the parent.

Caregiving is not a one-person job. You deserve help, and you should ask for it—from family, from friends and neighbors, from community services.

> *I cannot give you the formula for success, but I can give you the formula for failure, which is—try to please everybody.* —HERBERT BAYARD SWOPE

With your family, do it in person if possible, or by phone if necessary, but don't wait until you're angry and worn out after months of care. If your relationships with your siblings are strained and you don't think you'll communicate well, consider meeting with a mediator such as a social worker. An outside party can work wonders in defusing an emotional situation.

If you've somehow fallen into the role of primary caregiver without a prior discussion with other members of your family, see Chapter 1 for suggestions about conducting this meeting and the types of issues to discuss. If your family is already involved, to whatever degree, it may be time to restructure some roles and expectations. Before the meeting, draw up a list of tasks that need doing. At the meeting, discuss these tasks with your family and ask them what other jobs they can think of. Tell them what you can and cannot do yourself. Then find someone—inside or outside the family—to tackle the other jobs.

Nearby siblings and grandchildren can, for instance, make regular visits to a parent, bring prepared meals for the week, do grocery shopping or lawn care, or drive a parent to the doctor's office or the library. Distant brothers or sisters could pay bills, make regular phone calls, and visit to give you a respite.

Learn to say "Yes." Friends and neighbors will often ask what they can do to help. This is not the time to turn them down politely. Practice saying "Yes." As in, "Yes, a visit once a week would cheer up my mother tremendously," or "Yes, you could help me find her a good doctor," or "Yes, I'd love to know that someone is shoveling her walk this winter."

Talk to others. When Peter began to take over his mother's affairs after his father's death, he turned to friends for relief and support. "The most important thing is to have support from friends and family. It's vital. Nothing is more important than having a circle of people in your life whom you care about—and making sure you maintain those relationships."

For the overworked caregiver, an evening out is a necessary mental vacation, a time of laughter and friendly encouragement. Make sure that, no matter how tight your schedule becomes, you make time to talk to friends. Find a sitter for your parent, if necessary, or host a potluck dinner at your house. Get on the phone or go for a walk with a buddy.

In addition to talking with friends, consider joining a support group. Almost every town has one or more, and online groups are as close as the nearest computer. Some are specific to those caring for people with particular ailments, such as Alzheimer's disease. Look for a group that most closely fits your own situation. Groups that meet often and have a leader, or moderator, are the most likely to be cohesive and organized, but your best bet is to visit a few to find the one that works for you.

Spiritual and religious organizations can also be a great source of guidance. When Susan was debating whether to bring her ailing father to live with

---

LIFE STORY

The Art of Self-Preservation

As THE FOLLOWING STORIES REVEAL, everyone finds their own way to relieve the stress of caring for their parents. Look for methods that work for you.

Isabel: The best thing is when another family member takes my mother out of the house for a meal, and to visit their family. It breaks up whatever tension may have developed in our house. People get cranky if they don't leave the house occasionally. It's the best possible thing for my mother—and for us. It lets her get out into the world. And it gives us the chance to relax in our own home—a chance to talk openly and to have uninterrupted quiet and privacy.

Jane: I live near my dad, who has Alzheimer's but still lives on his own. I walk the dogs by there every morning and can check to be sure everything is okay. But it's hard always being on guard, never knowing when something's going to go haywire. I do a yoga class once a week and am now looking into returning to the divinity studies I gave up years ago.

Hannah: My parents are in a retirement home, where my 90-year-old father is caring for my mother, who has Alzheimer's. I go over there every day. For my own sanity, I go and get a massage every two weeks. I also make sure I go out with friends every couple of weeks. And I've hired someone to come in for an hour or two a couple of times a week so my dad can have some time for himself as well.

Finding Clarity

AS YOU WEIGH important decisions in life, the power of having others listen to you in a nonjudgmental way while asking positive questions can help you find your own answers. The clearness committee, created by Quaker religious groups in the 1660s, is a gathering of impartial individuals whose function is not to give advice or to "fix" people but to remove the interference so that people have a chance to discover their own wisdom.

The clearness committee is grounded in three core beliefs:

People are not problems to be solved, but mysteries to be embraced.

Each of us has an "inner teacher" that offers the guidance and power we need to deal with life's challenges and dilemmas.

By sharing our dilemmas with good listeners, we learn how to find our own answers to life's most difficult questions.

---

her, she turned to her Quaker "clearness committee" to help her through the decision. "They asked questions like, 'How would you feel six months from now if you didn't bring him to live with you? How would you feel if you did? Who else in your family needs to be part of this decision?'"

Your Area Agency on Aging and national organizations such as the Alzheimer's Association can direct you to support groups as well as online groups and message boards (see Resources, page 155).

Give the Pros a Chance

No matter how committed you may be to taking care of your parents by yourself, give serious consideration to programs outside the home, such as those provided by senior centers, adult day centers, and respite care. Getting older can be isolating, and these outside programs can give your parents vital social stimulation while giving you a much-needed break. But don't be surprised if your parent is reluctant to try a new place, or is slow to warm up to it. We all know how intimidating it can be to break into a new social group; for those who have been by themselves for a while, it can be doubly difficult. Don't give up before you've given it some time.

Senior centers. Almost every community has one or more senior centers—local organizations that provide classes, exercise, games, and other recreation, from bridge clubs to Internet training, for older adults. The centers are typically open on weekdays, and they may serve lunch and provide transportation to and from your parent's home. Senior centers serve a wide variety of older people, but they are best for those who do not have serious physical or mental problems, because their staffers are usually not trained to deal with heavy-duty care.

Adult day centers. If your parent needs more intensive care, adult day center programs can step in. These programs are often affiliated with hospitals, nursing homes, religious organizations, and other nonprofit organizations. They are designed to provide daytime care, including rehab, meals, therapeutic activities, and counseling for people with some degree of mental or physical impairment. You'll pay a daily fee for the services—typically much less than you would have to pay for in-home care. Your local agency on aging or the Eldercare Locator can help you find one.

Shop around for the program that suits your parent best. If she is in good shape mentally but most of the other participants have dementia, she won't be happy; nor will she fare well if she needs intense care from a staff that is

Choosing Adult Day Center Programs

ALTHOUGH RULES REGULATING adult day center programs and staff vary from state to state, good adult day centers should provide your parent with stimulation and community, not just a place to sit for a day. The National Institute on Adult Day Care recommends that you look for a center that:

☐ Assesses your parent's abilities and needs before admission

☐ Has a range of services, such as transportation, health screening, personal care, meals, and counseling

☐ Provides an active, individualized program that meets your parent's social, recreational, and rehabilitative needs

☐ Provides referrals to other community services for older adults

☐ Has well-trained, well-qualified staff and volunteers

☐ Meets or exceeds existing state guidelines

☐ Has clear criteria for terminating services

Look as well for signs that the center is comfortable and welcoming:

☐ Is the facility clean?

☐ Is there a chemical odor masking urine or other smells?

☐ Does it have sturdy, comfortable furniture?

☐ Did the staff spend time with you?

☐ Were there smiles on their faces as they cared for their participants?

☐ Do they involve the participants in decisions?

accustomed to healthier clients. Visit the centers and talk to the administrators about their programs and about which people do best there. Good adult day centers may have a waiting list, so try to visit them before your need becomes critical.

Respite care. Although respite care can include an adult day center, it typically refers to temporary relief (either in your parent's home or in another setting) that allows you to take a complete break—to take a vacation, to visit family, or simply to have some mental health time off.

Depending on your parent's health, you can hire companions, homemakers, or trained health-care workers to stay with him in his home while you are away. If possible, have them meet with your parent before you leave. Discuss his daily routine and care, and leave a detailed list of his medications and the phone numbers of doctors, neighbors, and friends.

Nursing homes, assisted living facilities, VA hospitals, and similar institutions sometimes provide respite care away from home. As with in-home care, do a little prep work if you are taking your parent to such a facility. The facility will have its own requirements, but you'll want to give the staff the relevant phone numbers, medications list, and so on. You may also want to provide some personal information about your parent: his background, profession, favorite hobbies, topics of conversation.

The cost of respite care ranges from zero (if you are lucky enough to find a volunteer through local religious or service organizations) to high (for care in a facility). But it's likely that most of the costs will come out of your own pocket. Your area agency on aging, department of social services, or your parent's doctor may be able to make referrals. In addition, the Eldercare Locator can identify local respite services.

The primary reason caregivers often put off finding respite care is guilt. Taking an ailing, dependent parent to an unfamiliar place and leaving him for a week may feel even more wrenching than the first time you left your wailing three-year-old at preschool. But those who have used respite care will tell you that it is a godsend—a vital sanctuary in time for those who bear the heaviest burden of care. Some caregivers have a weekly arrangement for an afternoon of respite care, which they capitalize on to go shopping, visit the hairdresser, or just take a long walk, at ease in the knowledge that their parent is being well cared for.

Resources | Caring for the Caregiver

BOOKS

Abramson, Alexis. *The Caregiver's Survival Handbook: How to Care for Your Aging Parent without Losing Yourself.* New York: Perigee Books, 2004.

Berman, Claire. *Caring for Yourself While Caring for Your Aging Parents.* New York: Henry Holt and Co., 1996.

Capossela, Cappy, and Sheila Warnock. *Share the Care: How to Organize a Group to Care for Someone Who Is Seriously Ill.* New York: Fireside, 1995.

Carter, Rosalynn. *Helping Yourself Help Others: A Book for Caregivers.* New York: Random House, 1994.

Loverde, Joy. *Complete Eldercare Planner: Where to Start, Which Questions to Ask, and How to Find Help.* New York: Times Books, 2000.

Morris, Virginia. *How to Care for Aging Parents.* New York: Workman Publishing, 2004.

ONLINE ARTICLES

"Adult Daycare"
University of Texas Medical Branch
www.utmb.edu/aging/outreach/archive/adacare.htm

"Community Services That Help with Caregiving"
www.aarp.org/Articles/a2003-10-27-caregiving-communityservices.html

"Plain Talk about Handling Stress"
National Institute of Mental Health
www.thebody.com/nimh/stress.html

"Women and Stress"
Baylor College of Medicine
www.bcm.edu/we_care/womenstress.htm

ORGANIZATIONS

Administration on Aging
Eldercare Locator
800-677-1116
www.aoa.dhhs.gov
www.eldercare.gov/Eldercare/Public/Home.asp

Children of Aging Parents
800-227-7294
www.caps4caregivers.org/links.htm

Family Caregiver Alliance
415-434-3388 or 800-445-8106
www.caregiver.org

National Adult Day Services Association, Inc.
800-558-5301 or 703-435-8630
www.nadsa.org

National Association of Area Agencies on Aging
202-872-0888 / *www.n4a.org*

National Association of State Units on Aging
202-898-2578
www.nasua.org

National Family Caregivers Association
800-896-3650
www.nfcacares.org

National Respite Locator Service
919-490-5577
www.respitelocator.org

Share the Care
www.sharethecare.org

9 Saying Good-bye

*As we can live into our old age with consideration
and grace, we can approach death with minimal
distress, meeting it with dignity and deference.*

—Helen Nearing

Margaret's life was not without sorrows, and her fortunes were far from grand, but in the end she was an exceptionally lucky person. Born near Glasgow, Scotland, in 1899, she lived her entire adult life in a small village, where she raised three sons and a daughter. Margaret's husband, a handyman, died of a heart attack at the age of 56. Her youngest son underwent a decades-long roller-coaster ride with alcohol. Yet Margaret always had a twinkle in her eye. She loved pulling surprises. At the age of 85, with the help of her two American grandchildren, she flew from Scotland to Philadelphia to "drop in" on her daughter, Nan, on Christmas Eve. It was something she'd dreamed of doing for years. On her 90th birthday, all but four of the 19 people descended from Margaret—children, grandchildren, and great-grandchildren—gathered for a celebration. She was stooped by then, but still spry enough to enjoy it all.

A year and a half later, she had grown frailer. Though still relatively healthy, she talked through the summer about being "ready to go." Nan made arrangements to fly to Scotland to stay with her that fall. In November, Margaret simply decided not to eat anymore. Nan didn't object, but she made sure her mother got plenty of fluids.

By the middle of the month, Margaret was much weaker. One morning she said, "Nan, I think it's going to be today. Can you get me ready?" Nan dressed her in her prettiest nightgown, trimmed her nails, and combed her hair. Not long after that, as Nan sat beside the bed, she heard her mother chuckle. "I don't think it's going to be today after all." They both laughed, then carried on reminiscing, as they'd been doing whenever Margaret was awake.

Three days later, Nan noticed that her mother's breathing was rapid and shallow, and that she wasn't responding. She called her son, Bob, and said, "I don't know if she can hear you, but I'm going to put the phone next to her ear." Bob told Margaret that he loved her, and said good-bye. When Nan returned to the phone, she said, "Her breathing's much calmer now. I think she must have heard you."

> *Dying is not primarily a medical condition, but a personally experienced, lived condition.*
>
> —WILLIAM BARTHOLME, M.D.

As other family members dropped by the house, Nan took the opportunity to go down to the shops while her niece Fiona sat with Margaret. When Nan returned half an hour later, her mother had died. Fiona told her, "She just slipped away."

Margaret was about as lucky as you can be. Bright and sharp right up to the last, she died with dignity, in her own home. And she got to say good-bye.

For many caregivers and their families, the days and weeks preceding a parent's death can be the most difficult part of the journey. Not only does it represent the end of the caregiving relationship, it means the end of the parent-child relationship as well. And it is often handled poorly by medical professionals, many of whom want to extend life at all costs. In today's world, death rarely occurs at home, amidst familiar surroundings. All too often it occurs in a hospital, behind a curtain. Despite these difficult realities, there are many things we can do to enable our parents to die a "good death," and to find closure for family members.

A New Intimacy

For both the parent and the child, it's important to make farewells in whatever way is available, and to prepare for that time as best as possible. The kind of emotional intimacy that adult children can experience with their parents in these final moments does not come easy if such intimacy has not been a lifelong norm; indeed, developing a truly intimate relationship is difficult even during times of good health. When a caregiver is providing constant physical care, either party may feel guilt or shame at having emotional needs. To try to maintain an emotionally intimate relationship with a parent who is terminally ill, counselors advise caregivers to remember the three A's: acknowledgment, attention, and affection:

Acknowledgment. The essential ingredient here is good communication. Remember the "And Stance" (see page 14). Accept your differences and listen to your parent's opinions. It's not about one or the other of you being "right"; it's about both your stories being worthy. Try not to close the door on sensitive subjects. If your parent wants to discuss his thoughts about death, invite discussion whenever possible and acknowledge his feelings.

Also be prepared to acknowledge your parent's efforts to acknowledge you. Charlotte did this as her mother fought a losing battle with bone cancer. "My mother hated to ask for help at first," says Charlotte. "When her despair was at its worst, she barked at me one morning—I didn't have her dress ready. I ironed it and brought it to her, and she said through her teeth, 'You know, we really appreciate all that you do.' I knew she wasn't feeling that at that moment, and she couldn't apologize. But she was determined to do what was right. I gave her a kiss and she teared up."

Managing Pain

THERE IS NO REASON for your parent to be in pain at the end of life. If your parent is under hospice care—at home or in a care facility—caregivers will make the patient's comfort a priority. Educate yourself about pain management and ways you can make a difference:

☐ Learn the types of medications your parent might take to alleviate pain. Help him to understand that pain is much easier to prevent than to treat once it becomes severe.

☐ Be an advocate for your parent. If he isn't assertive enough to tell a doctor or nurse about severe pain, do that for him.

☐ Help your parent and his caregivers by keeping a record of the time, location and severity of the pain and the medication that relieved it. Give this to the hospice-care nurse during each visit.

☐ Understand the dosage that is appropriate for your parent. If you have questions about the dosage, ask. Be sure to have names and phone numbers of doctors and health care workers at hand.

☐ Arrange for your parent to have enough pain medication to tide him over weekends and holidays.

☐ Learn about the level of pain medication your parent can expect at the end of life; the amount may increase as the body begins to shut down.

Adapted from "Checklist: 11 Ways to Ensure Proper Pain Management." *AARP Bulletin Online.* www.aarp.org/bulletin/yourhealth/Articles/a2003-08-07-11ways.html

Attention. Monitoring your parent's well-being is not all that's involved in paying attention. Listening attentively, including making eye contact, is critically important. Similarly, being aware of your parent's nonverbal communication—including how she holds her body, whether she's full of tension, and whether she is making eye contact—can tell you much about her state of mind. Samuel found another method of nonverbal communication with his mother: "I played the piano for her. Hours and hours, all night. I know it helped my dad, too, because he always loved my mother's playing. She always kept music in the house."

Affection. A kiss on the cheek or forehead and a warm smile go a long way in maintaining emotional intimacy. Other physical gestures—a back rub, brushing your parent's hair—also help.

Theresa, who helped care for her father in the last three years of his life, visited him on what would be the night before he died. "He was very shaky and had to wait a long time before the nurse came to put him in bed," she recalls. "So I rubbed his very bony back because it was something I could do, and because he was agitated and angry. To pass the time, I put on a CD of his favorite opera, *La Bohème.* We both became very silent listening to it, and when Mimi sang '*Si, mi chiamano Mimi*,' my dad looked up at me and whispered, 'Beautiful.' He was truly at peace. We held hands through the whole aria, me kneeling next to his wheelchair, and I will always hear his voice when I listen to that aria. He used to say, 'Your little hand is so cold,' just like Rudolfo. That will always be my father's song, and I really value that last little experience I had with him."

Making Arrangements Ahead of Time

Saying good-bye to a dying parent can be a literal moment, a bedside exchange that distills an entire relationship and that resonates in memory, like Theresa's. Or it can be an accumulation of experiences and times together—even, simply, the acts of discussing and preparing for those last days well in advance. In whatever way it happens, being able to say good-bye represents a turning-point in the lives of adult children.

It deserves thoughtful planning, sometimes in quite specific terms, so that your parent's last wishes can be addressed—and so you can move forward without regrets. One of the most important things you can do for an aging parent is to make certain that her wishes for care and for memorials are fulfilled. It's a good idea to make an effort now to discuss advance directives and funeral arrangements.

There are two main forms of advance directives: a durable power of attorney for health care and a living will. The legal document known as a durable power of attorney for health care (also known as a medical power of attorney) designates someone to make medical decisions for patients in the event they become incapacitated. It can specify treatment options and also gives the proxy party the flexibility to make decisions if circumstances change. A living will—also known as "instructions" or "directive to physicians"—deals more specifically with the patient's wishes about life-sustaining treatments. A living will can, for example, specify that "no heroic measures" be taken to prolong life or that the patient wishes only palliative (or "comfort") care instead of life-prolonging intervention in terminal situations.

Planning a funeral or memorial service in advance may seem morbid, but it can comfort everyone concerned if specific desires are spelled out ahead of time. If your parent has a strong religious affiliation, talk with the appropriate member of the clergy and also offer the option of some other form of remembrance. Some people like to have some kind of observance before they die, as is the tradition in a number of other cultures. In Vietnam, for example, the aged invite family and friends to visit and establish a period of a week or two for remembering their own lives, healing grievances with enemies, and saying good-bye to their loved ones.

Ask your parent about favorite hymns or songs, or poems or prayers, and be guided by her desire to have certain things said or done. But remember this as well: Memorial services are as much for the living as for the dead. If your parent doesn't express any specific interest in planning such an occasion but you feel you would appreciate it, go ahead and plan the event yourself. Don't hesitate to establish your own family's way of remembering (see Chapter 10, "The Alchemy of Sorrow").

Achieving Closure

Beyond the specifics of discussing—and not being afraid to discuss—such things as advance directives and funeral arrangements, it's important to be prepared for the kinds of thoughts and concerns that may surface during the last days of your parent's life. If your parent is still able to communicate, he may want to review his life, psychologically tying up the loose ends of things done and undone. He may express wishes, often in the form of final requests for loved ones to do something. And he may voice remorse. The most helpful thing you can do is listen to and acknowledge these expressions. If a final request seems unreasonable or impossible to fulfill, don't ignore it or challenge it—but don't make false promises either. A good solution is to say something like, "I promise I'll remember what you've asked." Listen to expressions of regret with compassion. Sometimes the most comforting thing you can say is, "I understand."

Despite an adult child's best intentions, it may not always be easy, or even possible, to make peace with a parent if the relationship has long been fraught with tensions. Ron's last visit with his mother happened in June, at her 70th birthday and a few weeks after his 43rd. "She was terribly weak then, and dependent on oxygen," says Ron, "but very pleased by the signs of love, from family and friends, that she received."

She had been ill for decades, since Ron was in high school. Something that had always bothered—even angered—him was her oft-shared fantasy of ending her life by having her sons deposit her a mountainside, there to be anesthetized by martinis and left to die peacefully of hypothermia.

"She had convinced herself that we'd promised we'd do that for her," Ron says. "I had not promised, and in one of the conversations while she was in

Choosing Hospice Care

MANY ORGANIZATIONS PROVIDE hospice care for the terminally ill. Your parent's doctor or hospital should be able to refer you to several of them. You may also want to do some research yourself. Here are some appropriate questions to ask as you make your evaluation:

☐ What services does the agency provide to the patient and family members? Can they be tailored to the patient's specific needs?

☐ Is the agency accredited by a nationally recognized organization? What are their standards for providing quality care?

☐ Does the agency's program meet federal standards? This is important if care will be paid for through Medicare.

☐ What references can the agency provide, both from medical professionals and from families who have taken advantage of their services?

☐ What types of aftercare services does the agency provide? Many organizations, for instance, provide a full year of bereavement services following a family member's death.

the hospital I said so. I had thought of her fantasy or plan as a sign of her longing for death because she was so unhappy with her life, and I did not want to side with that unhappiness."

The Hospice Solution

If your parent's illness has progressed to the end-of-life stage, you may wish to consider hospice care—either at home or in a hospice facility. Your parent's doctor may refer you to hospice care if his or her current life expectancy is six months or less.

The decision to include hospice care during your parent's final weeks and months has both practical and emotional advantages. If your wish is to spend meaningful time with your dying parent and to say good-bye in a way that is satisfying to both of you, the practical support of a hospice team can be invaluable. Going it alone as your parent's caregiver may leave you so exhausted and emotionally drained that such an experience isn't possible.

Hospice focuses on a holistic approach to dying—that is, providing services that relieve physical pain and symptoms and also offer emotional and spiritual support to the patient and the family according to the patient's wishes. The goal is comfort and caring, not curing. "I tell our families that the goal of hospice is to help a patient live—underline *live*—as best they can with their illness," says Debbie Seremelis-Scanlon, hospice liaison for the Fox Chase Cancer Center in Philadelphia.

A typical hospice team might include the patient's primary doctor, a hospice physician, nurses and home health aides who provide regular ongoing care, social workers, clergy members, trained volunteers, and family members. That team generally is available to the patient 24 hours a day.

Whether your parent is at home or in a care facility at the end of life, there will be signs that your parent's body and mind have begun the process of dying. Not all of them will occur with everybody, or in a particular order; hospice organizations note several ways in which the body prepares itself for death (see "As the End Nears," page 166).

One typical sign is that your parent, like Margaret in Scotland, may begin to lose interest in eating or drinking. Don't force food or fluids, but ice chips or frozen juice can keep the mouth moist when swallowing larger amounts of fluids becomes difficult. Your parent may previously have enjoyed lots of family members and other visitors. As she grows weaker and tires more

Letting Go

Rowena, 44, spent two months in her child-hood home helping care for her ailing father. She sent this e-mail to her husband about six weeks before her father died.

IN SOME WAYS, it's hard being around Dad. You come down to his pace and after a while you're seeing his outlook, how life has become old and bothersome. But if life is boring and seems pointless, maybe that's nature's way of making it easier to leave, since death is a part of the flow of all things.

He's making an effort to show he can do more on his own. But what to do all day? He doesn't read anymore. TV bores him. He can't do woodworking because his coordination is shot and his breathing becomes labored if he extends himself in the slightest. Monday someone will deliver portable canisters of oxygen, and then we're going to a place that rents power chairs.

Quite honestly, though, all this arranging to make his life more "independent" is just going through the motions. As he spends more time in his sleep world, I think he'll decide to let go.

I came here with three things in mind: to bring good cheer and a sense of family back into Dad and Mom's life, to spend quality time with Dad and help him feel complete about his life if it's his time to go, and to help him achieve the mobility he always envisioned for himself knowing that post-polio would eventually require the use of a wheelchair. But if he starts spending more time sleeping and less time in the power chair, or if he becomes completely bedrid-den, then hospice will bring in an aide to bathe him and make him as comfortable as possible as he goes through the final stages. If that happens, I would feel at ease about leaving. I don't feel I need to be here for the very end. I would be fine hearing about it on the phone.

The day after Rowena returned home, her father died in his sleep. "I don't know if I'm any braver about my own death now," she says, "but I want to try to savor this relief I feel."

easily, she may still want visitors but may now prefer a calmer environment, with just one or two people around. A slowing metabolism makes dying patients less responsive to activity around them or words spoken to them, and they spend more time sleeping. But because they may still be able to hear or otherwise sense their environment, it's important to be with them as much as possible—if only to hold a hand or talk quietly.

As the circulation of oxygen decreases to the brain and other changes asso-ciated with dying affect the central nervous system, your parent may experi-ence sensory changes and show signs of confusion or restlessness. Many people have said their dying parent began to "see" people or things that didn't physically exist, became easily startled or frightened, or stopped recognizing familiar faces. Physicians characterize the changes as illusions (misperceptions of ordinary sensations), delusions of grandeur (feeling an exalted sense of self) or of persecution (feeling that others are trying to hurt them), and hallucinations, which may be auditory, visual, or tactile. Rather than argue about the reality of what your parent has seen, heard, or felt, focus on reassuring her by talking calmly, touching, or playing soft music.

Persons in a coma may still hear what is said even when they no longer seem to respond. Caregivers, family, and physicians should always act as if the dying patient is aware of what is going on and is able to hear and understand voices.

Frank remembers that when he arrived at his parents' house with his kids, his mother was in a hospital bed in the house, in a coma. "I talked with her, telling her I was back," he says. "I held her hand, told her a few things about what was going on with the grandkids, and so on. She did not open her eyes or otherwise respond. I honestly can't recall if I brought my kids into the room that night to see her; I think I did, and told her they were there with me. Of course she was not able to react."

Frank's mother died in her sleep that night. "I have always strongly believed that sheer force of will kept her alive," he says, "until she knew that all of her children, and all of her grandchildren, were in the house. She had always been like that: She would stay awake until we were home safely from dates or trips, and only then would she let down her guard. I'm sure that's what happened when she died."

Getting Down to 'What Was Good'

It's important to be realistic about how family members will face the end of life. Although you may learn something surprising about your parent, people generally tend to face death in much the same way they approached life. People who have been fretful throughout their lives will likely be anxious as they die, whereas the optimist will tend to remain hopeful.

But dying is also an opportunity to show great courage. The father who was never openly affectionate may now be ready to embrace his children. The mother who was always tentative and overly cautious may face the end with surprising resolve and calm. Acknowledge their courage—and don't hesitate to express your pride in them.

As the End Nears

ALTHOUGH PHYSICAL CHANGES associated with dying will vary greatly depending on the cause of death, your parent's general health, and the medications he is taking, the following physical events are typical:

☐ Activity decreases, with less movement, less communication, and reduced interest in the surroundings.

☐ Interest in food and water diminishes.

☐ Body temperature lowers by as much as a degree or more.

☐ Blood pressure gradually begins to fall.

☐ Circulation to the extremities is diminished so that hands and feet begin to feel cooler than the rest of the body.

☐ Breathing changes from a normal rate and rhythm into a pattern known as Cheyne-Stokes respiration: several rapid exchanges of air followed by a period of no respiration.

☐ Skin color changes to a duller, darker grayish hue.

☐ The fingernail beds become bluish rather than the normal pink.

☐ Speaking decreases. The person ceases to respond to questioning and no longer speaks spontaneously.

☐ Coma ensues and may last from minutes to hours before death occurs.

Adapted from *The Dying Process: A Guide for Caregivers,* Hospice Foundation of America

For many people, a parent's last days can be a time of deep connection. Psychologist Frank Pittman has said that at this time, everyone has a chance to "grow their own souls." Charlotte learned this during her last days with her mother. Throughout Charlotte's life, the relationship with her mother had always been "intense, whether we were affectionate or quarreling." Near the end it was not so much that their relationship changed, says Charlotte, "it was more that we simply discarded the bad bits—the competition, the conflicts, the various defenses—and got down to what was good."

Radiation had driven the cancer into remission for about seven months, but Charlotte happened to be visiting when the pain came back.

"I sat with her at the doctor's, saw the X-rays," Charlotte says. "It gave me a quick dose of reality, I can tell you. She had become hunched over as her bones deteriorated. She didn't complain, but one afternoon, when she was walking down the hall toward her room, she whispered to herself, 'Oh, I wish I could hold my head up!' She didn't know I'd heard her. I was stunned; I ached for her. My proud mother, the hyperactive adult who loved to swim and dance."

As Charlotte returned for visits home over the coming weeks, her mother's condition worsened. And she grew weaker.

"She was terrified that something would happen in her neck and she'd be paralyzed," says Charlotte. "She almost never complained about the pain, but it had to be bad enough to turn her skin gray before she'd agree to take a painkiller. She said she was afraid of getting addicted, for heaven's sake. I think it was that she didn't like feeling drowsy. I wish now we'd had someone there who could have helped manage her pain better."

Her mother did complain, however, about the humiliating side effects from the cancer treatments: Radiation for her neck made her lose her voice

---

FIRST PERSON

'Time to Go to Balfron?'

Bill's father, a Presbyterian minister in Philadelphia, was a month shy of 66 when he suffered a heart attack in 1986.

MY DAD WAS NEVER openly emotional, and he had a hard time telling us what he'd experienced when he'd gone into cardiac arrest. He said he'd seen figures silhouetted in a bright light. My mom asked if they were angels. No. Relatives? No. Messengers? Yes, he said, but he had told them he wasn't ready yet.

Dad had tubes down his throat, so he communicated by writing notes. Over the next 10 days I spent as much time as possible with him, watching TV from a chair next to the bed. It wasn't from any sense of obligation, I just wanted to be with him. On Sunday morning, we were called and told to come in as quickly as possible. As the doctors were about to wheel his bed to the operating room, he wrote a note: "How long do I have? Minutes? Hours?" Then he wrote, "Time to go to Balfron?" Balfron is the village in Scotland where he was first a

minister, where he met my mom, and where he would be buried. I reassured him that everything would be all right. An hour later, a doctor came to tell us that they'd lost him; he had died during the procedure.

I was never troubled that we hadn't been with him when he died. I guess I felt I'd already said my good-bye. Just before they took him away, I had gotten down next to the bed and said, "Dad, I've always been so very proud of you, but I've never been prouder than I have these last few days."

This was a man who *hated* hospitals and doctors, and he had been strong and cheerful and clearly fighting right up to the last two days. I later learned that the damage to his heart had been truly massive—close to 40 percent of the muscle was dead. The doctors had been astounded that he had lasted as long as he did.

It was then I understood that what my dad had said to the messengers had been his way of preparing us all. He hadn't been ready, and we hadn't been ready, for him to go right then. So he hung on until we were.

The Last Details

THE DAYS AND WEEKS AFTER your parent's death will be an emotional time. If you have not already done so (see pages 198-199), you will want to work with your parents and the rest of the caregiving team now to locate the following documents so that they will be on hand when needed:

☐ *Insurance policies.* Your parent may have several types of insurance policies, such as life insurance, mortgage or loan insurance, medical insurance provided by an employer, auto or other accident insurance, or credit card insurance. The proceeds of a life insurance policy are paid directly to the beneficiary named on the policy and can be an important source of income for survivors left with multiple expenses. Consult a lawyer or financial adviser for options in receiving this income.

☐ *Social Security numbers.* Filing for benefits on behalf of yourself or a surviving parent will require the Social Security numbers of the deceased, a surviving spouse, and any dependent children. Notify the Social Security Administration of your parent's death immediately; any checks or deposits received after the death must be returned.

☐ *Military discharge certificate.* If your parent was a veteran and you are filing for burial or survivors' disability benefits, you should have a copy of a certificate of honorable (or other than dishonorable) discharge. If it isn't available, you can request a copy from the National Personnel Record Center, 9700 Page Blvd., St. Louis, MO 63132. Request forms may also be downloaded from www.archives.gov.

☐ *Marriage certificate.* If your surviving parent files for any benefits, he or she will need a copy of the marriage certificate. Copies can be ordered through the county clerk's office where the original license was issued.

☐ *Birth certificates.* If these aren't available for the deceased and any dependent children, copies can be ordered through the county records office where the person was born.

☐ *Will.* Your parent's written will is most likely to be kept in a safe deposit box or among other personal papers. If the will was written with the help of a lawyer or other counsel, contact that person to see if they have a copy as well.

☐ *List of assets.* Compile a complete list of your parent's property and other assets for easy access. The list should include any real estate, stocks, bonds, savings accounts, or other personal property such as automobiles or boats. A copy of your parent's most recent tax return may also be helpful.

A final note. A death certificate is not something you can handle in advance, of course, but it is useful to be aware that a number of agencies will require copies of it. You will need at least a dozen certified copies, purchased from the funeral director or the county health department.

Source: "Final Details," a publication of AARP Grief and Loss Programs. Publication #D14168

and her sense of taste; it also caused miserable mouth infections and cold sores. She endured alternate diarrhea and constipation. Her ankles swelled with edema.

At first, Charlotte's mother hated to ask for help. But then, even as she grew weaker, she slowly began to cheer up and accept help. As she did, Charlotte and her mother grew closer. "Once she said she'd kill for a shower. She was a dainty person—she hated sponge baths as not thorough enough—but she was too weak to get in and out of the bathtub. So I said, 'Of course you can have a shower—and I'll take it with you!' We wheeled her into the bathroom and banished my father. Then I undressed us both and helped her into the shower and showered with her, holding her up. By that time it was easy. She was as small as a child; she weighed about 80 pounds, and she came up to my armpit. When I dried her off, I saw that her spine described a huge *S*, from one side of her back to the other.

> *Those who love deeply never grow old; they may die of old age, but they die young.* —Sir Arthur Pinero

"While I was washing her hair, I remembered how she had washed mine when I was little and I felt waves of tenderness for her, she was so tiny and frail. A feeling like that is a gift in itself. Later I heard her telling her hair-dresser, who came in afterward to do her hair, that her daughter had given her a bath. 'That's right,' said the woman. 'First we bathe them, then they bathe us.' And they both laughed. A wonderful sound."

Charlotte's mother didn't talk much about her own impending death, but she gradually began handing off tasks that she had formerly seen to. "She did worry about Daddy, which I think was her way of warning me it was near. One night after we'd watched a film, she passed me her Christmas-card box and lists and said rather diffidently, 'If I'm not around, maybe you'd feel like doing our cards for Daddy this year.' I said, 'I'm planning on having you around, Mum,' and she said, 'I don't think so, dawlin' (she was very Southern). So I said not to worry, of course I'd do the cards. And I have. Every time I do them, I have images of her."

Charlotte's mother also let her know, indirectly, that she loved her. "She'd tell me things she liked that I'd done that she valued," Charlotte recalls. "And I found myself doing the same thing. All this was in little comments scattered about, not in long conversations. She didn't like sentimentality. But we both knew what we were saying."

At the end of Charlotte's last trip, in July 2000, her mother seemed amazingly improved. She was eating better and asking for favorite dishes. She seemed stronger, too. "My sister, a nurse, told me later that this often happens as dying patients reach the end. One of my sisters came to take over. We gave her a shower the morning I left, all of us laughing like hyenas. As we said good-bye, I told her I'd be back in a few weeks and she said she'd be counting the days—which was totally unlike her. I should have known then. I said I loved her and she said, 'I love you, my dawlin' girl.' We talked on the phone the next day, and the day after that she had the stroke that killed her."

> *The death of any loved parent is an incalculable lasting blow. Because no one ever loves you again like that.*
>
> —BRENDA UELAND

As difficult and grim as those months were, Charlotte says, "they were also a gift from the gods. I had the chance to care for her—a small return for all the care she had given me all my life, and a way to show that whatever our quarrels, I loved her. She had the chance to show me the same. And in letting me care for her she gave me the chance to do something I knew was good. I don't mean that in a self-satisfied way; I mean that most things we're involved in have some ambiguity, some element of the self-serving.

"The illness and its demands were a gift because of the closeness they created. We were able to ditch all that dreary baggage we'd been carrying around. I don't mean that I suddenly developed an idealized picture of my mother—none of us has. But I learned that what was underneath was stronger.

"And I felt—we all felt, as we phoned each other, working out schedules so my parents would never be alone—as if we were going down the path with her as far as we could. And I think she knew that, at the end."

Resources | Saying Good-bye

BOOKS

Byock, Dr. Ira. *Dying Well: Peace and Possibilities at the End of Life.* Riverhead Trade, 1998.

Byock, Dr. Ira. *The Four Things That Matter Most: A Book About Living.* Free Press, 2004.

Doka, Kenneth J. et al. *Living with Grief: Loss in Later Life.* Hospice Foundation of America, 2002.

Caregiving & Loss: Family Needs, Professional Responses. Hospice Foundation of America, 2001.

Lynn, Joanne M.D. and Joan Harrold, M.D. *Handbook for Mortals: Guidance for People Facing Serious Illness.* Oxford University Press, 2001.

Morris, Virginia. *Talking about Death Won't Kill You.* Workman Publishing, 2001.

OTHER RESOURCES

"Planning for Incapacity: A Self-Help Guide," Publication # D14513. AARP and Legal Counsel for the Elderly, Inc. 202-434-2120 / *www.aarp.org/lce* Provides guidance on advance directives, medical powers of attorney, and living wills. The manual is available for all 50 states and the District of Columbia. Available for $5 from LCE, Inc., P.O. Box 96474, Washington, DC 20090.

ORGANIZATIONS

Aging with Dignity
888-594-7437
www.agingwithdignity.org
A nonprofit organization advocating for the care of the elderly nearing the end of life. Its "Five Wishes" advance directive addresses medical needs at the end of life as well as emotional and spiritual needs.

HospiceNet
www.hospicenet.org
Offers resources for caregivers on finding hospice care, arranging time away from work, and handling grief.

National Association for Home Care
202-547-7424
www.nahc.org
Represents home health care agencies, hospices, and organizations that provide home care aides.

National Hospice and Palliative Care Organization
800-658-8898
www.nhpco.org
Offers help locating the hospice programs closest to you, information on Medicare benefits for hospice, and communicating end-of-life wishes.

National Resource Center on Diversity in End-of-Life Care
866-670-6723
www.nrcd.com
Works to improve care for culturally diverse populations, largely by providing training and materials for health-care providers who want to address end-of-life issues in ways appropriate to the cultures they serve.

10 The Alchemy of Sorrow

As I look back upon my life, I see that every part of it was a preparation for the next. The most trivial of incidents fits into the larger pattern like a mosaic in a preconceived design. —Margaret Sanger

When Alice talks about her parents, she remembers their sparkle and glamour, the sheer fun of lives at foreign service posts from England to Egypt, the elegant retirement divided between Greece and Washington. But when she remembers their deaths, which occurred almost a decade ago, there's a deep sadness. Their last couple of years were hard. After strokes and brain infections had battered Alice's mother and left her mind like "torn lace," after congestive heart disease and emphysema had slowed her father, Alice's parents settled in Washington, D.C., near the house she occupied with her husband and two sons.

With the help of a housekeeper, Alice watched over them. She shepherded her mother back and forth to an elder day services center. She took her mother to a favorite garden and to lunch, helped her father organize his legal affairs, cooked, arranged weekly family brunches. "We were just hobbling along," says Alice. "Nothing to sink the boat yet."

Then a massive stroke killed Alice's mother, and three months later, in a "black hole" of despair, Alice's father committed suicide. In the emergency room, Alice says, "I simply collapsed. It was too tough to take. He'd left me a note saying he loved me and my sisters, but that it was too painful to go on."

Almost immediately, though, Alice rallied. "Those first few weeks, I was suspended in space. I remember thinking, *I'm just not going to think about this, not about anything, I'll deal with the guilt later. I'm just going to get through this.* So I did. There were the obituaries. We'd just had a small service for Mom, and then I had a celebration of both their wonderful lives at their country club. There was lots of food, swarms of people—some of whom I hadn't seen since grade school."

Afterward, Alice says, she was assaulted by "all the what-ifs and if-onlys. I was bereft, heartsick I hadn't been with him, as we were with Mom. I was angry, yet there was a certain resolution: The worst had happened. It was a sort of relief."

A parent's suicide brings with it a host of stormy emotions far different from those experienced when, say, a 98-year-old grandfather dies in his sleep after a long, full life. Still, Alice had begun the journey through grief that follows the death of a parent, no matter what the circumstances.

It is a journey like no other.

Your parents are among the few people who have known you all your life. They are part of you: They helped shape your personality and your view of the world. Even if you are solidly in middle age and long independent, even if you are married, with beloved children of your own, your parents' love for you and their significance in your life are unique. They are the ones who remember when you cut your first tooth, said your first word, took your first step. And they provide a kind of bulwark between you and death. When your parents are gone, as one man puts it, you're left on the precipice, "gazing at infinity."

Many circumstances shape how people grieve for their parents: the life-long parent-child relationship, the amount of caregiving the adult child had to do, whether there are siblings with whom to share the grief. But all people do grieve. Like Alice, they find themselves caught in the maelstrom of emotions and physical symptoms that loss evokes. They mourn; they learn to relinquish old ties to their fathers or mothers, and they move on to a new relationship with memory.

Such grief and mourning are natural, even essential parts of life. As psychiatrist Robert Jay Lifton wrote, "There is no love without loss. And there is no moving beyond loss without some experience of mourning. To be unable to mourn is to be unable to enter into the great human life cycle of death and rebirth—to be unable, that is, to love again."

Essential though it may be, grief demands a great deal of the bereaved.

During the internal chaos created by normal grief, it helps to know what to expect, where comfort lies, and how memory may be honored.

The Phases of Grief

Grief was once viewed as a voyage through discrete stages from denial through anger, bargaining, and depression to acceptance. Now, however, experts generally see normal grief as including so many reactions and so much overlap, ebb, and flow that it is better to think of it as gradually shifting phases.

The first phase is avoidance—"I'm just not going to think about this," as Alice succinctly put it. This is the psychic shock that follows the death of a loved one. The bereft person is intellectually aware of what has happened, but the feelings are dulled. It's a protective response: Numbness keeps one from being overwhelmed. It lets people absorb the shock gradually and get on with such necessary business as writing an obituary or planning a funeral.

As the initial shock of death wears off, people move in and out of the second, deepest phase of grief, confrontation. Now

---

When to Seek Help

SOMETIMES GRIEF IS SIMPLY too much to handle. You might need professional counseling and advice, which you'll be able to find through your spiritual advisor, your physician, or one of the organizations listed on page 185. Think about getting help if:

☐ Friends and family repeatedly tell you you need it, or if you yourself think you need it; for instance, if grief seems to be going on too long or is causing physical problems.

☐ Your pastor, rabbi, or doctor thinks you need it.

☐ You feel you have no one to comfort you.

☐ You have a history of emotional problems.

☐ You think seriously about suicide.

☐ You are drinking heavily, smoking, taking drugs, or gaining or losing large amounts of weight.

☐ You indulge in other self-destructive behaviors, such as performing badly at work, going on shopping binges, or damaging your marriage or friendships.

---

they realize the loss not once, but time and again. The world is full of reminders—old letters, photographs, flashes of memory. "I had to clear the house where she had lived for 50 years," says Joan, whose mother died when Joan was in her 60s. "That's when I did most of my crying. I'd see things of mine she had saved, and I'd weep." The same thing happened to Alice and her sisters as they dealt with clearing their parents' apartment.

Emotions during the confrontation phase are chaotic. They may include fear and anxiety, anger and guilt, stabs of sorrow and longing. Mourners may have difficulty concentrating. There may be physical reactions, most importantly exhaustion—grief is draining—but also apathy, lethargy, restlessness, and irritability. "It's really, really hard," Alice says. "You walk along and there are pitfalls, you have troubled times, you think, 'I'm a bad mother, I was a bad daughter . . . '" Confronting loss is demanding. This is one time when reactions that are abnormal in most situations are perfectly normal.

Gradually, with many shifts to and fro, mourners move into the period called the accommodation phase. They still grieve, but they can live with the loss. They don't forget their parents, but the relationship now is with a memory. As Alice puts it, "You just put one foot in front of the other, thinking things will be okay again. After a couple of anniversaries of Daddy's death, I got to the point of thinking, *This was his choice. This was his choice.*"

Variations on a Theme

Describing mourning in terms of its phases gives a fair general picture, but each grief is as unique as every child, every parent. Grief will be affected by the circumstances attending the parent's death. When Alice's mother had her stroke, she came to consciousness just before she died. As Alice describes the experience, "My sister and I held her hands and sang her out to the tune of "Clara" from *Porgy and Bess*. She loved to hear us sing. We sang to her toward the light. It was such a relief to sing her out of her broken body." For Alice, this experience of death was "a wonder." Her father's solitary end was too sad to contemplate.

Middle-aged children have their own lives, careers, and families. They may have lived away from their parents for decades. Yet they will still grieve, whether the relationship was a good one or not.

Some children, though, have cared for their parents for months or years—at a distance, with visits and help, as in Alice's case, or in their own homes or in nursing homes. Even when affection remains strong, there will be relief at the easing of conflicts and demands. "My first thought was, *Her suffering is over*," says Joan, who had been caring for her mother for years. "*She is free. And so am I.*"

It's a natural response, and it usually induces guilt—guilt about disloyalty, guilt about the resentment a parent's demands may have aroused, guilt at any revulsion evoked by the symptoms of aging or illness. This is to be expected. All relationships include ambivalence, and most mourners feel guilty—especially early on, when they tend to remember their moments of neglect rather than their good deeds. In time, a more realistic view prevails.

In some families, the parent-child relationship may have always been troubled. Some mothers or fathers are abusive, others distant, still others manipulative or competitive. The child of such a parent may feel not only relief but grief and guilt over unresolved conflicts. Even good parent-child relationships are fraught with many conflicts over the course of a lifetime, and residual guilt stems from those. In rare instances, the problems may have been bad enough that death actually freed the child from pain. In situations like this, there's simply nothing to grieve for.

> *I measure every Grief I meet*
> *With narrow, probing Eyes—*
> *I wonder if It weighs like Mine—*
> *Or has an Easier size.*
> —EMILY DICKINSON

Consider the case of Emma: Although she was close to her father, she says, "For most of my adult years, I communicated with Mother as little as possible. She was a negative person, not very loving—from my earliest childhood she avoided touching me—and extremely insecure, a closet alcoholic. She shouldn't have had a child."

Nevertheless, when Emma's parents reached their 80s and became too frail and ill to cope with life, Emma stepped in. She moved them into a nursing home and saw that they were comfortable. Her mother, deep in dementia, died from lung cancer two years later, "drifting off without pain. When she died, I was grieved that the strongest feeling I had for her was one so grim as duty. Yet I was content that I'd done that duty as best I could.

"We had said our good-bye a few years ago," Emma adds, "when Mother was first in the hospital. I'd taken her to the smoking area for a cigarette, and she had a lucid moment, maybe the last time she recognized me. She said, 'There's something I want you to know. I may not have been a very good mother to you, but I've always loved you and I've always wanted the best for you.' I remember it vividly. But I'd done my grieving long ago."

Emma is describing what psychiatrists call "anticipatory grief." This happens not only in conflicted emotional situations, but also when a child becomes a caregiver. It deepens during a progressive disease such as Parkinson's or Alzheimer's. When both parent and child know the end is coming, both mourn the past—the strength or skills already lost. They mourn the present—the steady erosions of health and dignity. And they mourn the future—the parent his own death, the child a world without the parent. Anticipatory grief makes caregiving sadder. But it usually eases the mourning after a parent dies.

Yourself and Others

Parts of grief are always solitary, but rarely do people grieve alone. The death of a mother or father affects the whole family. All must share the reality of the death and the experience of grief. All must work out the new roles and relationships that bring the family to a new balance.

It helps to remember that everyone grieves differently, because mourning demands understanding and compromise on almost every issue, from how to comfort a surviving parent (opposite) to how to inform the grandchildren (see box, page 180) to how to face the holidays (see box, page 181).

Life does not cease to be funny when people die any more than it ceases to be serious when people laugh.

—GEORGE BERNARD SHAW

When Marian's mother died in Florida, for instance, she left behind her husband of almost 60 years and her four children—Marian, Brian, Maggie and Charlotte—as well as their spouses and children. Even though they had all helped at the family house during their mother's last six months and were present at her death, they each report going to her funeral in shock, "as if she had died suddenly and we hadn't known about it."

The months that followed, however, were different for each of them. Marian, whose relationship with her mother was one of "mutual incomprehension and prickly affection," remained "protectively numb" for about a month, then began to grieve: "A year after she died," Marian says, "I remember thinking that I wouldn't want to have her back because I didn't want to go through that first year of grieving for her ever again."

Brian, whose feelings for their mother were affectionate but more distanced, says, "My worst grieving was when Mom called to tell us she had bone cancer. I was devastated. I wept for hours. After that, except for a few sad twinges, it was just dealing with it."

Marian's oldest sister Charlotte's feelings for their mother had been intense and ambivalent—a mixture of deep affection and furious quarreling. But Charlotte had spent many weeks caring for her mother in her final illness, and felt they had "come together" (see pages 166-170). Charlotte, numb like

The One Left Behind

WIDOWHOOD IS DIFFICULT. Widowed parents may not complain to you, but they are quite likely to lose appetite and energy. They may be confused and forgetful. They may seek seclusion.

These are all normal reactions. The newly widowed must not only endure overwhelming grief but also deal with practical problems. Your widowed mother may need help handling finances; your father may require help cooking meals. After decades as a couple, it can seem impossible to face life alone. Widowers in particular are at real risk of serious depression and even suicide in the year after their wives' deaths. New widowers' death rates are 40 percent higher than those of married men their age. It is therefore crucial for parents and children to help each other out:

☐ In the first few months after a death, visit, call, and write as much as possible. If your parent uses a computer, you might set up a family e-mail address to which everyone can send notes, keeping your widowed parent in daily touch.

☐ Make sure your parent sees the doctor regularly and takes care of his health.

☐ Social life is important. Encourage your parent to see her friends. Invite her as often as you can to stay with you.

☐ In general, the widowed should put off major decisions until the worst mourning is over—usually about one year.

☐ Don't hover. Your parent is an adult. Your father or mother can learn to survive on his or her own. Love them and be there for them, but don't take over (and try not to get bossy!).

☐ Be aware of anniversaries and birthdays, which are often heartbreaking for the widowed. Offer company to your widowed mother on your father's birthday, on the anniversary of his death, on their wedding anniversary, and during the holidays.

the rest at first, found that her deepest grieving lasted about six months.

Middle sister Maggie, her life deeply intertwined with her mother's, had it much harder. She lived nearby, she visited her mother frequently, and her mother's friendship played a large part in her life. (Maggie was also awaiting hip surgery and unable to work.) "I was fine until I got home and realized I would never see her again," says Maggie. "I just fell apart. I had nightmares where she was lost in the dark and I was holding her poor, frail body."

Only 49, Maggie had a near-fatal heart attack the year after her mother's death. "Nothing went right after Mother died," she says. Several years would pass before Maggie felt she was finally emerging from this tunnel of turmoil.

As Maggie and others have found, unless you take particular care, grief can have a deleterious effect on a survivor's health (see "Grieving Well," page

183). All four children agree that what held them together was their concern for their much-loved, deeply grieving father. Worry for him—and respect for his ideas of civility—helped the usually competitive siblings reach consensus about sharing work and time with him.

Charlotte and Marian took turns visiting their father for six weeks after their mother died, selflessly covering for Maggie, whose hip condition kept her sidelined at home. Six weeks after that, the siblings gathered to celebrate their father's 80th birthday. The house party's liveliness took them by surprise. This reunion, the first of many, was "incredibly comforting," says Marian. "It made us realize we were a unified family, with a shared history and a shared point of view." With their father as fulcrum, the family had made a huge stride forward in the work of grief: They had begun to establish a new pattern.

The Virtue of Ritual

Funerals and memorial services can be enormously important for healthy grieving. They are rituals that embody loss. They are affirmations of a life that was lived. They acknowledge death and point toward ongoing life.

Children and Grief

AS YOU GRIEVE FOR YOUR mother or father, be honest with your children. Even toddlers will sense—and echo—your distress. So explain what has happened—your mother or father has died—and why you are sad.

☐ Don't use euphemisms. Children younger than six are literal minded. The phrase "God took her" could well inspire fear that God will take the child, too. "She's gone to sleep forever" raises unnerving bedtime questions.

☐ If your child is very young, explain that her grandmother's body doesn't work anymore, and that although she is not in pain, she won't be coming back. Let the child know that death is natural. Tell her

that Grandma lives on in your memories, or in heaven, or whatever you believe.

☐ Let the child grieve in her own way. She may simply go on playing. She may ask the same questions about death over and over. She may hold mock funerals for her toys. Let her. She's trying to understand.

☐ Cut your child some slack. If he's grieving for his grandparent, he may act out by misbehaving, getting angry, or withdrawing. Don't overreact. Talk to your child about your feelings. Reassure him that the family will go on—his first concern is his own security—and that the sadness will, in time, fade away.

For most people, the funeral is the typical mourning ritual. Most cultures offer a series of rituals for the year following a death. These rituals show that mourning and healing in the family and community happen over time. They mark time in the stages of recovery.

In Jewish tradition, for instance, after-burial rituals begin with *shiva,* or "seven," a week when mourners stay home to focus on their loss and friends visit to help and share memories. *Sheloshim,* or "thirty," follows. Mourners return to work but avoid entertainments and social events for three weeks. *Kaddish,* or a prayer for the dead, is recited every day for the first year and then on each anniversary of the death.

Most Islamic communities also provide a structure for marking time. For example, in Afghanistan, close relatives visit the grave 14 days after a burial to relight the lamps on it (or add new ones). The ritual is repeated on the 40th day after burial and on the anniversary of the death. All of these rituals are followed by feasts for the extended family. In addition, some communities hold such feasts every Thursday night (the night before the Islamic Sabbath) for a year.

Chinese and Southeast Asian families mourn differently according to whether they are Buddhist or Taoist. A general practice, however, is to hold a memorial service with a shared meal every seven days for 49 days after the death. In Vietnam, the service and feast are then repeated on days 51, 100, and 265, with a final ceremony on the one-year anniversary of the death.

The West now generally rejects the extravagant funerals of the Victorian era—the glass coach with its black-plumed horses, the paid "mutes" in black who accompanied it, the trail of mourners in black crepe. Nor do many

---

Facing the Holidays

FAMILY HOLIDAYS BRING MEMORIES rushing back. You're likely to find yourself tearing up at familiar ornaments, the smell of the roasting turkey, the tunes of familiar songs. You may dread holidays, but remember that anticipation is worse than reality.

If you can, spend that first Thanksgiving or Passover in the same tradition you're familiar with. It may be difficult, but the continuation of tradition is a comfort in itself. Send your thoughts outward: Your family and friends may cherish the solace of being together; your children may find the holidays a release.

You and your family may decide to follow old traditions or introduce new ones. You might want to organize a special toast to the memory of your mother or father at Thanksgiving dinner, for example.

Or you might make a memorial ornament. Doing this is a way of keeping your loved one part of the family observance of the holiday. You've made a symbol of the progress of grief.

people emulate Queen Victoria herself, who had a nervous breakdown after her not-much-loved mother's death, and went into seclusion for 25 years when her husband, Prince Albert, died. She kept Albert's room as if he were still alive—with fresh water and clothing laid out each day—for the rest of her life.

Yet the elaborate Victorian system—full mourning for the first six months or year, half-mourning for a period thereafter, with many changes in clothing and other symbols—represented an effort, overelaborate though it was, to mark the phases of healing grief. It wouldn't suit life now, but there are private alternatives.

The Stages of Healing

How long does the grieving process take? The Victorians, ornate as always, sometimes distributed lachrymatories—bottles for catching tears—at funerals. It was said that mourning would be complete when the tears in the bottles had evaporated. The truth of the matter is, there's no set time for grief. It can take a few weeks or several years. Most cultures consider that it takes about a year to regain balance.

Many people mark the time and the loss with rituals and memorials of their own. Alice, for instance, had already arranged for a plaque on a bench in her mother's favorite public garden before her father died. "I had Dad's name added," Alice says. "It's just their names with a line from a poem: 'Twas heaven here with you.' I go there when I'm feeling low, their birthdays and anniversaries. It's a great consolation. It gives you a ritual: You go there, think what you have to think. Then you're done with it until the next time."

> *Sorrow has its reward. It never leaves us where it found us.* —MARY BAKER EDDY

Marian and Maggie and their siblings marked the first anniversary of their mother's death by taking her ashes to her Virginia home and scattering them—a great comfort to their father. Of all of them, Marian mourned the most ritually. Once she got home, she says, "I wanted to make an 'altar' in Mom's memory. I had made copies of a large number of photographs while I was in Florida, so I raced around town buying attractive frames, framed the photographs, and arranged them on a lace tablecloth I'd gotten from her. As I recall, I also had a number of candles on the altar. There were about 20 pictures showing Mom at all different ages, as well as her parents and one or two of

PRACTICAL STRATEGIES

Grieving Well

GRIEF CAN ENRICH your understanding and deepen your feelings for the world around you and the parent you lost, but it isn't easy. The following considerations can help you navigate the rough patches:

- ☐ *Talk is healthy.* You may want to talk to your pastor, rabbi, or other spiritual advisor, or you may prefer to join a grief support group (these can be found at religious centers or through a hospice organization, among other places). You may find that you need professional help.

- ☐ *Stay healthy.* Don't rely on antidepressants, sedatives, or alcohol; they only postpone the pain. Make sure you eat reasonably. Above all else, get enough exercise. Vigorous exercise is a great outlet for stress, and it releases brain chemicals that can ease depression.

- ☐ *Reach acceptance.* Try to come to terms with the relationship you had with your mother or father. The memories of friends and relatives will augment the image of your parent. As one man said at

his mother's funeral, "Gosh, she's had this whole rich life that I'm no part of."

- ☐ *Write a memoir.* Put in all you remember of your life with your mother or father. It's saddening, but also cathartic. Make it honest. Write down your parent's qualities—both the noble and the disagreeable; say what made you happy and what hurt. Seeing their life whole helps you say good-bye.

- ☐ *Make memorials.* You might fashion a memorial scrapbook or box, with pictures, letters, photos, and mementos. For one woman, the most important thing was a lock of her father's hair.

- ☐ *Establish a memorial you can visit.* This might be the grave itself, or a memorial plaque at a place that meant a lot to your parent. Parks, public gardens, and public buildings such as libraries and schools can all arrange for plaques. Some people plant memorial trees. Some dedicate money or their own services in the name of a parent to the parent's favorite charity.

---

other ancestors. I kept it up for about six months, then gradually pared down the number of photographs. This happened in waves, and continued for about a year, until it was no longer an altar—it was just one photograph of Mom when she was 16 and very happy. The table had returned to its normal use."

Sometimes a memorial is even more intimate—a thought, a song, something the mourner has made. That was the case with Andrea, a successful artist who cared for her much-loved mother during the final years of her life. Like most caregivers, Andrea felt a sense of liberation melded with grief when her mother died. But she internalized her mother's spirit: "Since she died,

Rock-a-Bye Baby

Carmelita, 69, is a psychotherapist in Oregon and an only child. Her mother, Mabel, had been a member of a spiritual group for more than three decades. In her early 80s Mabel developed kidney problems, then fell and broke her hip. Carmelita persuaded her to move to Oregon, where Carmelita, her daughter, and her granddaughter helped care for Mabel until her death in 2002.

IN TAKING CARE of my mother, I realized that I was not responsible for curing her. There was nothing I could do to prevent her illness or her death. I also realized that she was pulling away from this life. When I showed her a video of my son Robert's newborn, Brynna, she said, "You know I'm not that interested in this." She was focusing all of her attention on the other side. This was liberating. I finally got clear about our relationship. I realized that her primary issue in this life was her spiritual work. When I was a kid, she could be distant and I often felt that I wasn't good enough. It was freeing to see that it really wasn't about me.

My mother talked openly about death. She was never in denial. On her last night she got into bed and took a small amount of morphine the hospice had given her. I sat by the bed holding her hand and she said, "It helps that you're here." Those were her last words. We put on a tape of yoga chants and she slowly faded away.

It was a beautiful death even though it was traumatic for me because I'd never seen anyone die before. I felt it was a privilege to be with her because she was so accepting of her own death. Watching your parent go through death helps you accept your own death. Even so, I experienced a lot of post-traumatic stress afterward. What helped was going to Utah to visit my son Robert and his family. I spent days sitting in the living room rocking the new baby, Brynna, in my arms.

I find that my work is imbued with my love for her. I'm not a colorist, but I I'm now working in the cool colors she always wore; blues and greens were really her palette. Working in those now recalls my mother's passage."

A New Shape to Life

Recovery from grief means recapturing a certain lightheartedness—making it easier to work and love again, to enjoy life's pleasures without guilt, to talk about a mother or father without tears. People are comfortable once more with their lives and families. They keep the lost parent alive in memory, and their families take new shapes. Roles change to fill the void; family members interact in some ways that are the same and in others that are wholly different. A new way of being together comes to pass.

Marian noted these changes as the children united around their father. About a year and a half after their mother died, she says, "I was mulling over some family situation and thought, *If Mom were alive*—and then I stopped. Before she died, I couldn't imagine a world without her in it; now, I realized, we had rearranged the family so completely that I couldn't imagine how it would be to have her back. I am always conscious of the hole her death has left. But the family changed to accommodate it, and we have continued on."

Alice, buffeted by the death of both parents in the space of a few months, took solace in her family, in a support group, and in testifying about elderly suicide before Congress. "At least some use was being made of the situation," she reflects. And she has found peace. "Sure, there are bad moments from time to time," she says. "But life has been good for the last few years. I can tell you that when it is, you don't take anything for granted. You learn to really appreciate the lovely world."

Resources | The Alchemy of Sorrow

BOOKS

Angel, M. D. *The Orphaned Adult.* New York: Human Sciences Press, 1987.

Donnelly, K. *Recovering from the Loss of a Parent.* New York: Dodd, Mead & Company, 1987.

Kübler-Ross, Elizabeth. *On Death and Dying: What the Dying Have to Teach Doctors, Nurses, Clergy, and Their Own Families.* New York: Collier Books, 1969.

Myers, E. *When Parents Die: A Guide for Adults.* New York: Viking, 1986.

Rando, Therese. *How to Go on Living When Someone You Love Dies.* Massachusetts and New York: Lexington Books/Bantam Books, 1991.

Walsh, Froma, and Monica McGoldrick (eds). *Living Beyond Loss: Death in the Family,* 2nd ed. New York: W.W. Norton & Company, 2004.

ORGANIZATIONS

American Psychiatric Association
202-682-6220
www.psych.org

American Psychological Association
800-374-2721
www.apa.org

Association for Death Education and Counseling
203-232-4825
www.adec.org

The Elizabeth Kübler-Ross Center
703-396-3441
www.elizabethkublerross.com

National Self-Help Clearinghouse
212-354-8525
www.healthfinder.gov

Afterword

As I WRITE THESE WORDS, my computer automatically underlines the word "caregiving" as a usage error every time the term appears. I can't resist the symbolism: Could this "spelling error" betray the state of our societal consciousness? Not until our nation implements vigorous policies to help family caregivers care for their aging parents, it strikes me, will support systems such as our computer software—indeed, our entire society—finally recognize "caregiving" not only as a valid word, but as a critical policy initiative.

For we are truly a nation of caregivers. From coast to coast, from town to town, in city and suburb and countryside, families are engaged every day in taking care of those we love. We do it without pausing to label ourselves "caregivers." We don't stop to consider that we are juggling caregiving with work and family, or that the task could potentially jeopardize our own health or employment. We just do it, because we are family and because we care.

Too often it is said that our nation has lost its connectedness, that our youth-obsessed society relegates older Americans to a class of disposable citizens.

I beg to differ.

The reality is that families always have cared—and always will care. In the United States today, more than 33 million people are caring for someone 50 years of age or older. That statistic confounds the stereotype of most older people living alone and neglected. Compare today's caregivers with those of previous generations and you will find that many more of us are doing it, despite the abundance of easily invoked reasons to decline or delegate the option.

The world has changed dynamically in the last 40 years. Roles for women—still the majority of caregivers—have grown far more complex. Women work outside the home in greater numbers than they ever have before. Families are geographically dispersed. Rather than moving across town, adult children move across the country. Families, too, are more complex than in the past. Husbands and wives who were married before their current union bring stepchildren and wide assortments of older relatives with them to the new marriage. The notion of the blended family extends to the world of caregiving as well, where we find daughters caring for fathers, for fathers-in-law, and even for ex-fathers-in-law.

Professionals engaged in providing services to older people (I consider myself part of this group) focus on devising strategies to better reach "caregivers." The biggest hurdle we encounter is often that very designation. "I'm not a 'caregiver,'" we are constantly told, "I'm just doing what a daughter does." Or: "It's my turn to give back some of what I've received throughout my life."

That response, in essence, is the foundation of caring for our aging parents. It's about belonging to a family. It's about nuances in the changing roles of family members over time. It's about the need to balance individual emotions against family history and expectations. And that's just a partial catalogue of the interpersonal dynamics involved.

It's uplifting to contemplate the care that older people receive from their adult children today. Family has always been the backbone of our system for delivering long-term care services. On any given day, our nation's nursing homes have a population of about 1.5 million residents. Meanwhile, more than 20 times that number of family caregivers are tending to the needs of those 50 and up—not a bad ratio. If those family caregivers ceased providing care, we would have nowhere near the number of nursing home beds, assisted living residences, or direct-care workers we would need to provide for our elderly population.

We can take heart that families are there for each other. We should be moved that caring continues, no matter how complex an ordeal it becomes. We must not, however, grow complacent. In fact, we should be appalled. The fact remains that our nation's older parents will be cared for by their adult children with or without formal societal support. The question that needs to be answered is: How much help will there be for our families?

Today, people are caring for their parents with little recognition and scanty financial or service support. Therein lies the dilemma, and the challenge, for us as a nation: In an era when caregiving remains personal—a duty performed house by house, family by family—we need to move it to the national agenda.

But more is needed—much more.

The unpaid work of caring for aging parents has enormous economic value.

The yearly labor costs are estimated to range from \$100 billion to \$257 billion. And caring for aging parents exacts a financial toll on employers as well. Researchers calculate that the lost productivity of caregivers costs American businesses \$12 billion to \$30 billion in bottom-line profits each year. With just a modicum of support from their employers, however, working caregivers could better balance work and caregiving, enabling them to contribute so much more.

And how do you even begin to compute the toll that years of giving care can inflict on the health and well-being of families? Family caregivers are more susceptible to depression. Some of them have suppressed immune systems. It all adds up to significant life stress—which, as research published by the National Academy of Sciences in December 2004 revealed, can accelerate the aging process of caregivers themselves.

Families will always care for those who need it. I believe we owe it to them, which means to ourselves, to foster a society that supports families in this role. But what can we do? The solution is to throw our individual and collective strength behind the following policies. All are long overdue. Each should be enacted immediately to address the needs of caregivers.

Tax credits. Congress should approve tax credits to ease the financial strain on family caregivers and those who need long-term supportive services.

Respite care. These programs offer caregivers much-needed relief by providing them someone to care for their older parents for a few hours or a few days. This critical supportive service should be enhanced so that it is affordable and available in all communities. By availing themselves of the occasional reprieve they so richly deserve, caregivers can avoid burnout—which, in turn, will allow them to continue caring for their loved ones.

Education and training. Sicker and quicker than ever before—that's how today's patients are discharged from hospitals. Better training and education will show caregivers how to provide care properly. Health-care organizations and local offices of aging can identify critical areas to be covered, then offer classes and workshops. For caregivers who cannot get out to a class, long-distance learning options via the Internet could be developed and promoted.

Support groups. No one should feel isolated by their caregiving responsibilities. Peer-to-peer support gives caregivers a forum for relating their own daily struggles and learning how others cope with similar challenges. We must do a better job of linking isolated caregivers with existing support groups, and we need to foster the creation of additional support groups.

Workplace support. To meet the needs of aging parents and the demands of one's job, adequate family and medical leave and flexible work arrangements are essential. Caring for aging parents should not mean sacrificing job status, wages, or professional development. Businesses can be made to understand that neglecting the needs of working caregivers undermines their bottom line by billions of dollars each year. Enacting workplace policies that support our caring traditions is, therefore, both honorable and shrewd.

First, the Family and Medical Leave Act, which guarantees up to 12 weeks of leave and job/benefit protection to workers caring for sick family members, should be extended to cover more workers for longer periods of time.

Second, we should urge employers to take greater advantage of existing tax incentives, such as offering flexible spending accounts for dependent care.

Some companies are way ahead of the curve. Hallmark, for example, was among the first corporations to start a workplace elder-care program; AT&T has followed suit. Also commendable are partnerships between state and local aging offices on the one hand—among them New York City's Department on Aging, the Atlanta Regional Commission's Aging Services Division, and New Jersey's offices on aging—and local employers and businesses on the other. These alliances furnish employees with both resources and professional assistance: They offer information and referral, assessment, and care management.

Housing supports. States and localities must step up as well by encouraging the construction of ECHO units, or Elder Cottage Housing Opportunities. These accessory apartments enable parents to live with their adult children while maintaining a space of their own. ECHO homes are modular units built to share the property of a preexisting home; typically they include a bedroom, a bathroom, some living space, and a kitchen. Because they are laid out on one floor, ECHO units offer accessible living space. But restrictive zoning regulations for this sort of accessory housing need to be changed in communities across the nation. Once they are, families will finally be able to care for their aging parents while offering them maximum independence.

Community services. We must augment the care provided by family with care provided by home- and community-based services. Supplemental care such as home health aides, adult day services, and respite-care assistance provide much needed relief for an entire generation of caregivers, helping them rebalance their work, family, and caregiving demands. It will also permit aging parents to remain in their homes and communities, no matter what their care needs.

Funds for the whole family. The Older Americans Act now recognizes the contribution of family caregivers by giving each state funds earmarked for the family that is providing an older person's care. Disbursed under the federal National Family Caregiver Support Program, the funds can be used for education, training, or respite care. Current funding levels do not even begin to meet the needs of those giving care, but they are welcome—and deserve to be expanded. California, Florida, New Jersey, and Pennsylvania all supplement these federal funds with state dollars, providing enhanced support services.

Easy access to information. Anyone who has tried to navigate the labyrinth known as "Long-Term Care Services" knows how time-consuming it can be. A good referral system would free caregivers to spend less time bouncing around the fragmented system and more time caring for their parents.

The year the first baby boomers turn 65 years old—2011—looms on the horizon. Will we be prepared to meet the needs of this demographic sea change? Are we ready to transform our caregiving initiatives from a personal commitment to a nationwide one?

The words we exchange with one another every day to express our trepidations and aspirations about the future reveal a gaping divide: For today's caregivers, the words that resonate are those such as "duty," "honor," "love," "care," and "home." For today's policymakers, by contrast, the verbal landmarks of long-term care are phrases such as "funding," "labor shortage," "needs assessment," "nursing homes," and "Medicaid." This linguistic divide underscores the enormity of the challenge we face in addressing caregiving together.

—ELINOR GINZLER
Director, Livable Communities
AARP Office of Social Impact

To learn more from AARP about steps you can take to help care for your parent, visit the AARP website at www.aarp.org and click on Care and Family.

Appendix

As you have gathered by now, one of the wisest approaches to caring for your parent is to be willing to consider the future today and to plan accordingly. Planning requires you to come to grips with a variety of issues, so it's understandable if you feel apprehensive about tackling some of them.

Every person's journey will be different. And wherever you and your parents are along the way, the fact that you have taken the time and trouble to learn from this book speaks well of your love for and commitment to them.

To help you with your caregiving responsibilities, the following pages include a number of check lists and other documents you may want to complete and save for future use:

Assessing the Situation. This will help you determine how your parent is doing and anticipate some of the issues you may need to watch out for.

Contact List. Make a list of key people in your parent's life. Keep one copy by her phone, another by your phone, and yet another in your purse, briefcase, or notebook; distribute it to your siblings and other caregivers.

Key Documents. Most day-to-day papers can safely be stored in a filing cabinet or accordion file. However, these documents deserve extra protection, and trusted family members and legal advisers need to know where to look for them.

Inventory. This sheet lists your parent's documents and where to find them. Give specific directions (for example, "top drawer, file cabinet in office") and contact information for all of these locations and people ("Smith& Jones, attorneys, 1234 Main Street, YourTown, 333-555-6666"). The list then goes to siblings, executors, and anyone else your parent wants to inform.

Worksheet for a Family Meeting. Not all families are able to establish regular family meetings, but it's important at the outset to bring people together to discuss your parent's needs, now and in the future.

Reality Check for Drivers. Because your parents' independence is important to them and to you, you will want to help them continue driving as long as they can do so safely. But the operative word is *safely.* This checklist for drivers will help all of you determine whether it's time to make other transportation arrangements.

Monthly Income and Expenses / Calculating Net Worth. These forms will help guide financial planning for your parents now and in the future.

Assisted Living: Asking the Right Questions. This checklist will help you compare residences. Make a copy for each residence you are considering. Think about what is important in a new home for your parent—factors such as location, size, and type of services offered. Call first and ask the preliminary questions; this may help you narrow down the number of places to visit. When you go, take the checklist of questions with you.

Three Stages of Alzheimer's Disease. This list of symptoms will help you plan for adjustments to your parent's care as his or her needs change.

Evaluating Nursing Homes. The need for a nursing home can come suddenly or unexpectedly, such as when your parent is in the hospital with a serious medical condition or injury. However, early planning and visiting, with checklist in hand, can facilitate the often difficult process of choosing the right one. Try to see at least three homes so you can make comparisons. If possible, ask the parent who will be living in the nursing home and other family members to come with you. The visit will give you the chance to view care firsthand; talk to staff, residents, and other families; taste the food and observe the activities. Never hesitate to ask all of the questions listed. If you meet resistance, simply eliminate that candidate and move on to the next.

Statement of Personal Health-Care Values. Ask your parent to give some thought to recording her feelings about various health-care issues. Although this statement cannot take the place of an advance directive, it will be helpful for her to think through her feelings about how she wishes to be cared for at the end of life.

Assessing the Situation

TASK OR ABILITY	INDEPENDENCE INTACT	SOME HELP REQUIRED	DEPENDENCY INCREASING
Cooking Meals			
Home Upkeep			
Personal Hygiene			
Transportation			
Paying Bills			
Other Financial Issues			
Taking Medications			
Other Health Issues			
Remembering Things			
Walking			

Contact List

NAMES	PHONE NUMBERS
Emergency services: 911, ambulance service	
Primary Caregiver	
Immediate family	
Close friends	
Neighbors	
Clergy	
Doctors	
Dentist	
Pharmacists	
Health workers	
Household insurance company	
Car insurance company	
Life insurance company	
Housecleaning service	
Taxi service	
Lawncare / maintenance service	
Other	

Key Documents

LEGAL INFORMATION

☐ *Identification.* Birth certificate, Social Security card, citizenship/naturalization papers, passport or number, marriage certificate, adoption papers, divorce decree, spouse's death certificate, military discharge papers

☐ *Will.* Valid, up-to-date original and copies (including spouse's will). Keep with codicils and letters of instruction in a strongbox, lawyer's office, or with a state registry service. Note: a safe-deposit box may be sealed by the court when its owner dies.

☐ *Durable power of attorney.* Lets a designated agent to make legal decisions if your parent is incapacitated; must be drawn up while parent is considered competent. Check with an attorney for local filing requirements. Your parent and the designated agent. should each have copies.

☐ *Living will.* Lays out a parent's wishes in the event that she is terminally ill and cannot make decisions about her health care.

☐ *Durable power of attorney for health care.* Allows others to make medical decisions on a patient's behalf. Check with an attorney on where originals must be filed and tell trusted people where originals are located. Copies should go to designated health-care agent, family members, doctors.

MEDICAL INFORMATION

☐ *List of medications.* Includes over-the-counter drugs and prescriptions such as for eyeglasses. Includes when prescribed, purposes, dosages, side-effects, and interactions with other drugs. Update often.

☐ *Health insurance policies.* Includes long-term care, Medicare and /or Medicaid information, as well as Medigap policies, with ID numbers, photocopied front and back. Be sure insurance master policy contains correct Social Security number and date of birth.

FINANCIAL INFORMATION

☐ *Income and savings.* Paychecks, bank accounts, credit cards, pensions, social Security, IRAs, annuities, 401(k) plans, military retirement benefits, stock and bond certificates, mutual fund accounts, royalties, partnerships

☐ *Debts and loans.* Credit card, property, bank, personal, credit union

☐ *Property.* Real estate deeds and titles, appraisals, outstanding mortgages, payment and service records of cars or boats, easements or rights-of-way, businesses, rental property , items stored or loaned, rental agreements, housing contracts, name and number of real estate agent

☐ *Business agreements.* Contracts with attorney, accountant, stockbroker, or financial planner, burial or cremation policy

☐ *Taxes.* Copies of federal, state, local income and property tax returns, receipts for at least the last seven years

☐ *Insurance.* Life, homeowner's, car

OTHER

☐ Location of and keys or combination to bank safe-deposit box, home safe, hidden valuables.

☐ Subscriptions

☐ Online passwords and PINs

Inventory

Name: | SSN: | Date:

Address:

Copies given to:

My papers are stored in (address or where to look; note A, B, or C for each item below):

A. Residence:

B. Safe deposit box:

C. Other:

My will (original)	Car insurance policy
My spouse's will	Birth certificate
Durable power of attorney for health care	Social Security card
Durable power of attorney	Passport
Living will	Marriage certificate
Health insurance policies	Children's birth certificates
Life insurance policy	Divorce decree
Homeowners insurance policy	Spouse's death certificate

Employment contracts	Funeral arrangements
Safe combination	Titles and deeds
Trust agreement	Mortgages
Checking account information	
	List of stored and loaned items
Savings account information	
Retirement papers	
	Car ownership records
IRA information	
	Partnership agreements
Other retirement accounts	
	Income tax returns
Credit card accounts	
	Online passwords and PINs
Stock certificates	
Bond certificates	Other
Investment accounts/ mutual funds	
Bank CDs	

Worksheet for a Family Meeting

GROUND RULES

Include everyone. Invite everyone who should be involved and everyone who thinks they should be involved. Include the parent whose care you will discuss. Include close friends of the family or long-time friends of your parents.

Remember the "And Stance." Everyone sees things differently and everyone's "story" is valid. Building a consensus means being willing to meet in the middle. Agree to respect one another's views on those subjects where there is disagreement.

Don't digress. Agree right at the beginning that this meeting is not the place to bring up "old business" (past arguments and hurts). Focus on the needs of the parent whose care you are there to discuss.

Share the load. No one should be afraid to ask for help, so speak up. By the same token, everyone should remember that it's important to volunteer, to ask, "How can I help?"

WHY ARE WE HERE? List the issues that should be discussed at this meeting.

TASK	RESPONSIBLE PERSON	FREQUENCY OR DUE DATE

FOLLOW-UP STEPS (E-MAIL, PHONE, CIRCULATE COPIES?)

Reality Check for Drivers

YOUR PARENTS WANT to continue driving as long as they can do so safely. If they or you observe the following warning signs in their driving, it may be time for them to significantly reduce their driving or even to give it up. Some state motor vehicle departments have programs to evaluate individual driving abilities or offer special licensing alternatives. Contact the state for more information. And work with your parents to find alternative ways for them to get around.

WARNING SIGNS

☐ Feeling less comfortable and more nervous or fearful while driving

☐ Difficulty staying in the lane of travel

☐ More frequent "close calls" (i.e. almost crashing)

☐ More frequent dents or scrapes on the car or on fences, garage doors, curbs, etc.

☐ Trouble judging gaps in traffics at intersections and on highway entrance and exit ramps

☐ Other drivers honking at your parent more often; more frequent instances in which your parent gets angry at other drivers

☐ Friends or relatives not wanting to drive with your parent

☐ Getting lost more often

☐ Difficulty seeing the sides of the road when looking straight ahead (i.e. cars or people seem to come "out of nowhere" more frequently)

☐ Trouble paying attention to—or frequent instances of violating—signals, road signs, and pavement markings

☐ Slower response to unexpected situations; trouble moving foot from gas to brake pedal or confusing the two pedals

☐ Easily distracted or finding it hard to concentrate while driving.

☐ Difficulty turning around to check over shoulder while backing up or changing lanes

☐ Medical conditions or medications that may be increasingly affecting the driver's ability to handle the car safely

☐ More traffic tickets or "warnings" by traffic or law enforcement officers in the last year or two

ADOPTING NEW HABITS

☐ Avoid the following situations:
- *Night driving*
- *Rush hour driving*
- *Freeway driving*
- *Driving in snow or dangerous conditions*

☐ Use alternative transportation:
- *Combine use of car und bus or metro*
- *Ride sharing*
- *Senior citizen transit pass*
- *Community vans*
- *Taxi coupons*
- *Home delivery of groceries, prescriptions*
- *Shop for some items via the Internet*
- *Ask volunteers, friends, or neighbors*

Adapted from "When to Stop Driving," www.aarp.org/life/drive/safetyissues/Articles/na2004-06-21-whentostop.html

Monthly Income and Expenses

ANNUAL EXPENSES

Mortgage/Rent

Federal tax

State tax

Property tax

Other taxes

Utilities: *gas*

        electricity

        water

Telephone/Internet

Food

Clothing

Personal care

Home maintenance

Homecleaning service

Car: *loan*

      maintenance

      gas

Legal/Accounting fees

Insurance: *life*

      homeowner's

      car

Credit card payments

Other loans

Medical care

Dental care

Medications

Pets

Entertainment

Gifts

Charitable contributions

Other

TOTAL EXPENSES

Mother's Income

Father's Income

Combined Income

ANNUAL INCOME

Wages

Business income

Rental income

Pension

Social Security

Interest

Veterans' benefits

Dividends

IRA/Keogh disbursement

Annuity

Trust

Other

TOTAL INCOME

Less Total Expenses

NET INCOME

NOTES

Calculating Net Worth

ASSETS	MOTHER	FATHER	COMBINED
Cash			
Bank accounts			
Stocks			
Bonds			
Mutual funds			
Business*			
Insurance policies*			
IRAs/Keoghs			
Annuities			
Home			
Other real estate			
Personal property			
Automobiles, other vehicles			
TOTAL ASSETS			

LIABILITIES	MOTHER	FATHER	COMBINED
Mortgages			
Car loan			
Credit card debt			
Other debts			
Unpaid taxes			
Other			
TOTAL LIABILITIES			

	MOTHER	FATHER	COMBINED
TOTAL ASSETS (from above)			
less TOTAL LIABILITIES			
NET WORTH			

*Cash value

Assisted Living: Asking the Right Questions

As YOU MEET with staff and tour a residence, pay close attention to how you feel and what is going on around you. Spend time with the staff and residents; ask them what they like and dislike about the residence. Make more than one visit, at least one of them unscheduled. Attach the residence's rate sheet for easier comparison.

RESIDENCE NAME

Check:	☐ First Visit	☐ Second Visit	Date(s) Visited:		
	☐ Morning	☐ Afternoon	☐ Evening		

Circle:	Mon	Tue	Wed	Thu	Fri	Sat	Sun

THE CALL:

How many living units are in the residence?		
Where is the residence located?		
Are different sizes and types of units available?	☐ Yes	☐ No
Do any units have kitchens or kitchenettes?	☐ Yes	☐ No
Are all the rooms private?	☐ Yes	☐ No
Are bathrooms private?	☐ Yes	☐ No
Does the residence offer special care units, such as those for people with Alzheimer's disease?	☐ Yes	☐ No
Is a contract available detailing all fees, services, and admission and discharge policies?	☐ Yes	☐ No
Is there a written care plan for each resident?	☐ Yes	☐ No
What role does the resident have in developing the care plan?		
Are additional services available on the same campus if a resident's needs change?	☐ Yes	☐ No
Can residents choose their own doctors, therapists, or pharmacies?	☐ Yes	☐ No
How does the residence bill for services?		
What if a resident runs out of money?		
Under what conditions would a resident have to leave?		

THE VISIT:

Is the residence clean and cheerful?	☐ Yes	☐ No
Are stairs and hallways well lit?	☐ Yes	☐ No
Are exits well marked?	☐ Yes	☐ No
Do rooms and bathrooms have handrails and call buttons?	☐ Yes	☐ No
Are there safety locks on the doors and windows?	☐ Yes	☐ No
Are there security and fire safety systems?	☐ Yes	☐ No

Is the floor plan logical and easy to follow?	☐ Yes	☐ No
Are rooms large enough for a resident's needs?	☐ Yes	☐ No
Are there enough common areas, such as dens and living rooms?	☐ Yes	☐ No
What special services are available (circle all that apply)		
bank _café_ _beauty salon_ _other_		

THE CONTRACT:

Is the contract easy to read and understand?	☐ Yes	☐ No
Are specific services provided by the residence?	☐ Yes	☐ No
Does the contract include all of the services you are looking for?	☐ Yes	☐ No
What do additional services cost?		
Are all meals served 7 days a week?	☐ Yes	☐ No
Does the contract address levels of care?	☐ Yes	☐ No
How many levels?		
Who determines level of care?		
Are linens/laundry provided?	☐ Yes	☐ No
Are transportation services provided?	☐ Yes	☐ No
Is there a parking fee for residents?	☐ Yes	☐ No
for visitors?	☐ Yes	☐ No
Does the residence offer worship services?	☐ Yes	☐ No
Is there a one-time "entrance fee"?	☐ Yes	☐ No
What is the monthly rent?		
What is the security deposit?		
Are deposits refundable?	☐ Yes	☐ No
Are utilities included?	☐ Yes	☐ No
Is telephone included?	☐ Yes	☐ No
How are rate increases or late payments handled?		
Does the contract cover transfer and discharge policies?	☐ Yes	☐ No
How much notice is given to residents who have to leave?		
Is the living area held if the resident is in the hospital?	☐ Yes	☐ No
For what cost?		
Can residents have a pet?	☐ Yes	☐ No
Can residents have personal furniture?	☐ Yes	☐ No
Does the contract deny a resident the right to bring legal action against the residence for injury, negligence, or other cause?	☐ Yes	☐ No
Can residents come and go at will?	☐ Yes	☐ No
Can personal visitors come and go at will?	☐ Yes	☐ No

Three Stages of Alzheimer's Disease

ALZHEIMER'S DISEASE advances at widely different rates. The duration of the illness may often vary from 3 to 20 years. The areas of the brain that control memory and thinking skills are affected first, but as the disease progresses, cells die in other regions.

As diagnostic procedures become more sophisticated and the public's awareness grows, more individuals will be accurately diagnosed at a younger age and an earlier stage the disease. Alzheimer's disease is considered to be early in its onset if an individual is age 65 or younger when symptoms first appear. However, early-onset individuals may not necessarily be in the early stage of Alzheimer's when diagnosed.

By understanding what to expect as the disease progresses, you can begin to plan ways to adjust your parent's care in the future.

COMMON CHANGES IN MILD AD

☐ Loses spark or zest for life—does not start anything

☐ Loses recent memory, has difficulty with new learning and making new memories

☐ Loses judgment about money

☐ Forgets how to pay or pays too much; may hand the checkout person a wallet instead of the correct amount of money

☐ Has trouble finding words; may hesitate, then substitute or make up words that sound like, or mean something like, the forgotten word

☐ May simply stop talking to avoid making mistakes

☐ Has shorter attention span and less motivation to stay with an activity

☐ Easily loses way going to familiar places

☐ Resists change or new things

☐ Has trouble organizing and thinking logically

☐ Asks repetitive questions

☐ Withdraws, loses interest, is irritable, not as sensitive to others' feelings, uncharacteristically angry when frustrated or tired

☐ Won't make decisions. For example, when asked what she wants to eat, says, "I'll have what she is having."

☐ Takes longer to do routine chores and becomes upset if rushed or if something unexpected happens

☐ Forgets to eat, eats only one kind of food, or eats constantly

☐ Loses or misplaces things by hiding them in odd places or forgets where things go, such as putting clothes in the dishwasher

☐ Constantly checks, searches or hoards things of no value

COMMON CHANGES IN MODERATE AD

☐ Changes in behavior, concern for appearance, hygiene, and sleep become more noticeable

☐ Mixes up identity of people, such as thinking that a son is a brother or that a wife is a stranger.

☐ Poor judgment creates safety issues when left alone; may wander and risk exposure, poisoning, falls, or exploitation

☐ Has trouble recognizing familiar people and own objects; may take things that belong to others

☐ Continuously repeats stories, favorite words, statements, or motions like tearing tissues

☐ Has restless, repetitive movements in late afternoon or evening, such as pacing, trying doorknobs, fingering draperies

☐ Cannot organize thoughts or follow logical explanations

☐ Has trouble following written notes or completing tasks

☐ Makes up stories to fill in gaps in memory. For example, might say, "Mama will come for me when she gets off work."

☐ May accuse, threaten, curse, fidget, or exhibit inappropriate behavior, such as kicking, hitting, biting, screaming, or grabbing

☐ May become sloppy or forget manners

☐ May see, hear, smell, or taste things that are not there

☐ May accuse spouse of an affair or family members of stealing

☐ Naps frequently or awakens at night believing it is time to go to work

☐ Has more difficulty positioning the body to use the toilet or sit in a chair

☐ May think mirror image is following him or television story is happening to her

☐ Needs help finding the toilet or using the shower; also needs help remembering to drink and dressing for the weather or occasion

☐ Exhibits inappropriate sexual behavior, such as mistaking another individual for a spouse. Forgets what is private behavior, and may disrobe or masturbate in public

COMMON CHANGES IN SEVERE AD

☐ Doesn't recognize self or close family

☐ Speaks in gibberish, is mute, or is difficult to understand

☐ May refuse to eat, chokes, or forgets to swallow

☐ May repetitively cry out, pat or touch everything

☐ Loses control of bowel and bladder

☐ Loses weight and skin becomes thin and tears easily

☐ May look uncomfortable or cry out when transferred or touched

☐ Forgets how to walk or is too unsteady or weak to stand alone

☐ May have seizures, frequent infections, and falls

☐ May groan, scream or mumble loudly

☐ Sleeps more

☐ Needs total assistance for all activities

Adapted from *Caring for People with Alzheimer's Disease: A Manual for Facility Staff* (2nd edition), by Lisa P. Gwyther, 2001, published by the American Health Care Association and the Alzheimer's Association.

Evaluating Nursing Homes

IT IS ALWAYS BEST to visit a facility at least twice. Make one of the visits unscheduled, during the weekend or evening, when any staffing problems will be most obvious. You may want to attach the facility's rate sheet for easier comparison.

FACILITY NAME

Address

Check:	☐ First Visit	☐ Second Visit	Date(s) Visited:		
	☐ Morning	☐ Afternoon	☐ Evening		
Circle:	Mon Tue	Wed Thu	Fri	Sat	Sun

THE BASICS

Is the facility **Medicare** certified?	☐ Yes	☐ No
Is the facility **Medicaid** certified?	☐ Yes	☐ No
Has the license ever been revoked?	☐ Yes	☐ No
Is the facility accepting new patients?	☐ Yes	☐ No
Is there a waiting period for admission?	☐ Yes	☐ No
Does the facility conduct background checks on all of the staff?	☐ Yes	☐ No

How many licensed nurses are on duty at each shift?

 RNs LPNs

What is the patient-to-staff ratio?

 Nurse-to-patient ratio? Aide-to-patient ratio?

Does the nursing home have an active family council?	☐ Yes	☐ No

What is the visiting policy?

Is transportation available so the resident can visit the doctor?	☐ Yes	☐ No
Are care-planning meetings held at times convenient for residents and their family members?	☐ Yes	☐ No

SAFETY

Are stairs and hallways well lighted?	☐ Yes	☐ No
Are exits well marked?	☐ Yes	☐ No
Do the hallways have handrails?	☐ Yes	☐ No
Do rooms and bathrooms have grab bars and call buttons?	☐ Yes	☐ No

Are there safety locks on the doors and windows?	☐ Yes	☐ No
Are there security and fire safety systems?	☐ Yes	☐ No
Is there an emergency generator or alternate power source?	☐ Yes	☐ No
Is the floor plan logical and easy to follow?	☐ Yes	☐ No
CARE ISSUES		
Does the facility have a fresh smell?	☐ Yes	☐ No
Are residents clean and well groomed?	☐ Yes	☐ No
Do staff members interact well with residents?	☐ Yes	☐ No
Are residents participating in activities and exercise?	☐ Yes	☐ No
Do the residents have the same caregivers on a daily basis?	☐ Yes	☐ No
Does the staff respond quickly to calls for help?	☐ Yes	☐ No
Is there fresh water available in the rooms?	☐ Yes	☐ No
Does the food look and smell good?	☐ Yes	☐ No
Does it taste good?	☐ Yes	☐ No
Are residents offered choices of food at meal times?	☐ Yes	☐ No
Are residents who need assistance eating or drinking receiving it?	☐ Yes	☐ No
Are there nutritious snacks available throughout the day and evening?	☐ Yes	☐ No
Is physical therapy available for as long as the resident needs it?	☐ Yes	☐ No
Does the staff have special training to deal with dementia?	☐ Yes	☐ No
Are there units or services for special needs, such as Alzheimer's?	☐ Yes	☐ No
QUALITY OF LIFE		
Are residents' rights posted?	☐ Yes	☐ No
Does the staff knock before entering a resident's room?	☐ Yes	☐ No
Are the doors shut when a resident is being dressed or bathed?	☐ Yes	☐ No
Is the facility an easy place for family and friends to visit?	☐ Yes	☐ No
Does the nursing home meet cultural, religious, or language needs?	☐ Yes	☐ No
Are there outdoor areas and help for residents who wish to use them?	☐ Yes	☐ No
Are the residents allowed to make choices about daily routine (such as bedtime, when to bathe, or when to eat?)	☐ Yes	☐ No
Are they allowed to have personal articles and furniture in their rooms?	☐ Yes	☐ No
Is the staff friendly, considerate, and helpful?	☐ Yes	☐ No
Does the facility have a friendly, homelike environment?	☐ Yes	☐ No

Statement of Personal Health-Care Values

ASK YOUR PARENT to give some thought to recording her feelings about various health-care issues. Although this statement cannot take the place of an advance directive, it will be helpful for her to think through her feelings about how she wishes to be cared for at the end of life.

NAME   **DATE**

If the time comes when I cannot act for myself, please consider the following when making care decisions for me.

My priorities for my future health care are:

If I were terminally ill or in a permanent coma, here is what I think about the following medical treatments:

Ventilator

Artificial nutrition and hydration

Antibiotics

With regard to being an organ donor, here are my views:

My thoughts on hospice care and palliative care, including the use of medication for pain:

Here are my views on lifesaving measures such as CPR (cardiopulmonary resuscitation):

Other thoughts:

Glossary

Activities of daily living (ADLs). Everyday functions such as bathing, dressing, grooming, eating, moving from bed or chair, using the toilet, and walking.

Adult day center. These facilities—also called adult day services, adult day care centers, or adult day health centers—provide daytime care to older adults for safety, socialization, and recreation. They also offer help with personal care (and, in some cases, health and rehabilitation services). Transportation is sometimes included in the fee.

Advance directive. Any of a variety of documents that express health care wishes. The term "advance directive" may denote a Living Will, a Health Care Power of Attorney (or proxy), a Durable Power of Attorney for Health Care Decisions, or a Medical Directive.

Area Agency on Aging. A local or regional agency established under the federal Older Americans Act to coordinate and provide services to older citizens.

Assisted living residence. Housing for those who may need help living independently but who do not require skilled nursing care. The level of assistance varies among residences and may include help with bathing, dressing, meals, and housekeeping.

Continuing care retirement communities. These communities offer levels of care designed to meet changing needs. Care levels range from independent living to assisted living to skilled nursing care.

Durable Power of Attorney for Finances. A document in which you appoint another person to make financial decisions on your behalf. The DPA either continues in effect once you become unable to manage your affairs, or it springs into effect at that time.

Durable Power of Attorney for Health Care. Also called a health care proxy, this legal document names an agent to make health care decisions on behalf of someone who can no longer speak for herself.

Eldercare Locator. A nationwide toll-free telephone number (800-677-1116) and online service (www.eldercare.gov) that provides referrals to state and local aging services. It is funded by the U.S. Administration on Aging.

Geriatric care manager. A professional who performs an assessment of a person's mental, physical, environmental, and financial conditions to create a care plan to assist in arranging housing, medical, social, and other services.

Guardianship. A legal process in which a court appoints someone to manage the affairs and property of a person who is unable to act on his own behalf.

Home health care. Services provided in the home, including care and support provided by home health aides, registered and licensed nurses, and physical therapists.

Hospice care. A type of care for the terminally ill and their families, offered by hospitals, long-term care facilities, and hospice organizations, that emphasizes pain management and control of symptoms rather than attempting a cure. See also *palliative care.*

Living will. Also called a health-care directive, this document describes the kinds of care a person does and does not want if he is nearing the end of his life; usually pertains to life-sustaining measures.

Long-term care insurance. Private insurance to cover all or part of the cost of care in a nursing facility or, in some instances, the cost of home health care.

Meals on Wheels. A community-based meal service that delivers meals to the homes of older adults for a modest fee.

Medicaid. A joint state and federal program that helps to pay the medical expenses of low-income people who meet the qualifying standards.

Medicare. The federal program of health insurance for people age 65 and over, and for those younger than 65 with certain disabilities.

Medicare supplemental insurance. A type of private insurance, also known as "Medigap," designed to pay for some costs not covered by Medicare, including deductibles and copayments.

Ombudsman. A person who investigates and resolves complaints on behalf of residents of nursing homes and other long-term care facilities. Also called long-term care ombudsman.

Palliative care. Coordinated services that focus on physical, mental, social, and spiritual needs of those with life-threatening illness and their families. It seeks to maintain the highest level of comfort.

Respite care. Temporary care, delivered by a home health care agent or other provider, designed to give a person's regular caregiver rest and personal time. Such temporary care may be in the home, in a long-term care facility, or at an adult day center.

Reverse mortgage. A loan against a house that allows the owner to convert some of his equity to cash. When the home is sold or the owner dies, both loan and interest are repaid.

Skilled nursing facility. Also called a nursing home, this facility provides skilled care to residents, including rehabilitation for people who have just been discharged from the hospital. It also provides extended long-term care to frail or chronically ill people, who require a higher level of nursing and medical supervision than is available in other settings.

About the Authors

As Editor in Chief of AARP Publications, **Hugh Delehanty** oversees America's two largest-circulation publications, *AARP The Magazine* and the *AARP Bulletin*, as well as the bilingual magazine *AARP Segunda Juventud* and AARP Books. Previously an editor at *Sports Illustrated, People,* and *Utne Reader,* Delehanty has written extensively on psychology and spirituality and is the coauthor with Phil Jackson of the national bestseller *Sacred Hoops: Spiritual Lessons of a Hardwood Warrior.*

A former visiting professor of American Studies at Carleton College in Northfield, Minnesota, Delehanty is a frequent contributor on *The Today Show.* He has also appeared on *Good Morning America,* the *NBC Nightly News,* and other broadcasts. He lives in Washington, D.C., with his wife, Barbara.

Elinor Ginzler has worked in the field of aging for more than 20 years. After overseeing programs at the community level in senior housing and long-term care, Ginzler joined AARP in 1998 to run association programs in health, long-term care, and independent living. She has also supervised AARP's consumer outreach and education initiatives on caregiving, nursing-home quality, Medicare, and assisted living.

Ginzler is currently the Director for Livable Communities in AARP's Office of Social Impact, where she advocates for housing needs of the 50+ population and optimizing the mobility of older Americans. She has lectured on caregiving from Maine to Hawaii and is regularly quoted in the media as a spokesperson for AARP on eldercare issues.

Acknowledgments

CREATING A BOOK, like caring for a parent, requires a demanding team effort, and this book has been no exception. First and foremost, the authors would like to thank all the caregivers who shared their stories with us. We would also like to thank Roberta Conlan for her gifted editing and grace under pressure. We're indebted to Bobbie's team at EdiGraphics, L.C., notably book designer Dorrit Green and writers George Constable, Patricia Daniels, Ellen Phillips, and Robert Somerville. Thanks, too, to researchers Janice Campion, Darlene Koenig, Rosanne (Scotty) Scott, and Jarelle Stein.

A special note of appreciation goes to Allan Fallow for his editing wizardry and to Carl Lehmann-Haupt for his engaging cover design. We also must credit Mary Pipher, who not only wrote a moving foreword but inspired us with her creative thinking about caregiving.

This book would not exist without the support of AARP's Bill Novelli, Tom Nelson, Christine Donohoo, and Cathy Ventura-Merkel. We are also grateful to Barnes & Noble's Steve Riggio and to Sterling Publishing's Charles Nurnberg, Steve Magnuson, and Andy Martin. We were aided immeasurably by AARP text reviewers Pat Barry, Sally Hurme, and Susan Raetzman. Chris Boardwine oversaw the book's production, while Theresa Rademacher honchoed the paper chase. Our profound gratitude as well to Tara Brach, Rosemary Bakker, and Carmelita Thomson for their innovative perspectives on the psychological and spiritual aspects of caregiving.

From Hugh Delehanty: I'd like to thank my brothers, John and Dennis, for their openness and good humor, and my sisters-in-law, Judy and Elizabeth, for their telling insights and support. Thanks, too, to my niece Carmen, for her helpful research, and to my stepson, Clay, for his inspired photography and compassionate wisdom. Most of all, I would like to express my deepest appreciation for my wife, Barbara, who teaches me every day about the transformative power of love.

From Elinor Ginzler: I'd like to recognize Nancy LeaMond, head of Social Impact at AARP, for her inspiration in effecting positive social change. And to my husband, Wally, and our sons, Ben and Daniel, and to all my friends, I give my thanks for the myriad ways in which you enrich my life each and every day.

Index

AARP, xiv, 26, 36, 105, 110
accessory dwelling unit, 133–134
adult day centers/services, 130, 153–154, 211
advance directives
  durable power of attorney as, 161, 211
  living will as, 161
advocate, caregiver as 30-51
  hospital bills / insurance claims
    as part of, 41–42
  legal issues as part of, 46–49
  managing health care as part of, 36-41
  nursing homes as part of, 42-45
  organization as part of, 33–36
  scams/fraud as part of, 45–46
alcohol consumption, 78–79
assisted living facilities, 126, 135–136, 211
Alzheimer's Disease, 96-98
  symptoms list for, 194, 206–207
Another Country (Pipher), xiv
Area Agency on Aging, 211
arthritis, 83, 85–86
*At the Eleventh Hour: Caring for My
  Dying Mother* (Stone), 6

behavior changes, 103–104
board and care housing, 136
body, healthy lifestyle for
  eating habits for, 76–77
  exercise for, 77
  immunizations for, 79
  low alcohol consumption for, 78–79
  nonsmoking for, 78
  prevention of injuries for, 79–80
  safe sex for, 78
bone mineral density (BMD) exam, 87
Brach, Tara, 4, 5, 7, 8
brain
  crystallized intelligence of, 90–91
  fluid intelligence of, 92
  hippocampus as part of, 97
brain, diseases of
  dementia as, 92–93, 95–96
  depression as, 92–95

cancer, 83, 86, 87, 99
caregiver
  as advocate, 30–51
  caring for, 143–144, 147–155
  challenges of, 191
  depression of, 148–149, 189
  diet for, 148
  from a distance, 26–28
  economic value of, 189
  education/training for, 189
  exercise for, 148–149
  funds for, 191
  as hidden patients, 144–145
  housing support for, 190
  statistics on, 14, 187-188
  stress factors of, 145–147, 189
  tax credits for, 189
  workplace support for, 190
continuing care retirement communities
  (CCRCs), 137, 211
Centers for Medicare and Medicaid Services
  (CMS), 140
Certified Aging-in-Place Specialist (CAPS),
  127
children, grief and, 180
cholesterol, 83–84, 98, 99
clearness committee, 152
community services, 150–151, 190–191
companion services, 130
confusion/restlessness, 164–165
The Conversation, 11
  "And Stance" during, 14–15

breaking the ice for, 18–21
as family meeting, 21–25
as open dialogue, 25–26
preparations for, 15–17
sample topics for, 23
Creuztfeldt-Jakob disease, 96, 99
crystallized intelligence, 90–91

dementia
Alzheimer's Disease relating to, 96
behavior changes of, 103–104
as brain disease, 92–93, 95–96
causes of, 96
driving with, 104–105
living with, 101–106
LTCI covering, 67
multi-infarct, 99
vascular, 99–100
Dementia with Lewy Bodies, 98
depression, 92
of caregiver, 148–149, 189
chronic pain and, 95
clinical, 93–94
psychotherapy for, 95
signs of, 94
diabetes, 83, 84–85
diet, 148
Difficult Conversations: How to Discuss What
Matters Most (Stone, Patton, Heen), 13
driving, 17, 104–105, 194, 201
drugs. See Medicare Part D: Prescription
Drug Benefit
durable medical equipment, 211
durable power of attorney (DPA), 62–63,
161, 211
dying, process of
coma as, 165
confusion/restlessness as, 164–165
little interest in eating/drinking as, 163
sensory changes as, 164–165
signs of, 166
slowing metabolism as, 164

ECHO (Elder Cottage Housing Opportunities), 133–134, 190

Eldercare Locator, 66, 211
elimination period, 66
emotional intimacy 158–159
exercise, 77, 148–149

Fair Debt Collection Practices Act, 42
family
dynamics of, 133
meeting of, 21–25, 193, 196–197
members of, 150–151, 165–170, 178–180
The Family and Medical Leave Act (FMLA),
34, 190
finances, 52–69
budget relating to, 56–57
communication about, 53–54
of daily life, 17
financial planner/accountant for, 54,
60–62
government assistance relating to, 58
home ownership relating to, 58
incapacity relating to, 62–63
long-term care relating to, 62–68
net worth relating to, 57
reverse mortgage relating to, 57–58
review of, 55–57
scams/fraud relating to, 59
simplification of, 59–60
fluid intelligence, 92
Fox Chase Cancer Center, 163
fraud/scams, 45–46, 59

geriatric care managers, 26–28, 129–130,
139, 211
geriatrician, 74–76
grief
anticipatory, 177–178
children and, 180
family members and, 178–180
guilt with, 176–177
help for, 175, 183
holidays and, 181
journey of, 174–175
recovery from, 184
relief with, 176
rituals relating to, 180–182
widowed parents and, 179

grief, phases of
    accommodation as, 176
    avoidance as, 175
    confrontation as, 175–176
guardianship, 48–49, 211
guilt, grief with, 176–177

healing
    memorials for, 183–184
    stages of, 182–184
health care representative. *See* Medicare
healthcare. *See* advocate, for managing
    healthcare
hearing, 82–83
heart disease, 83, 84, 85, 99, 100
Heen, Sheila, 13
hemorrhagic stroke, 99
hidden patients, 144–145
high blood pressure. *See* hypertension
hippocampus, 97
HMOs (Health Maintenance
    Organizations), 115
holidays, grief and, 181
Hollis, James, 7
home health aide, 211
home health care, 212
home ownership, 58
homesharing, 134
hospice care, 212
    choice of, 162
    holistic approach of, 163
    types of, 163
hospital
    advocate for, 39–41
    bills for, 41–42
    insurance for, 111
hotlines, 47–48
housing, 133–134, 136, 190
Huntington's disease, 96, 99
hypertension, 83, 98, 100

immunizations, 79
incapacity, 62–63
incontinence, 74
independence, 126, 129
independent living. *See* living, independently

inflation protection, 67
in-home care, 130–132
injuries, prevention of, 79–80
insomnia, 88
insurance. *See* advocate, hospital bills / insur-
    ance claims as part of; long-term care insur-
    ance (LTCI); specific Medicare headings
inventory sheet, 193, 198
ischemic stroke, 84, 99

Jung, Carl, 6

Kabat-Zinn, Jon, 145

lawyers, 47–48
legal issues
    guardianship as, 48–49
    hotlines for, 47–48
    lawyers for, 47–48
    legal services for, 46–47
    representative payee as, 48
legal services, 46–47
Lewy, Freidrich, 98
life expectancy, 13
living arrangements, 16
    changes in, 125–126
    independence as part of, 126
living, in nursing home
    location of, 139–140
    quality care in, 140
    research for, 137–138
living, in own home
    companion services for, 130
    independence in, 129
    in-home care for, 130–132
    meal services for, 130
    safety in, 126–129
    senior centers / adult day services for,
        130, 211
living, independently
    ALF hospitality model, 136
    in ALFs, 135–136
    board and care housing as, 136
    in CCRGs, 137
    homesharing as, 134
    in retirement communities, 134–135, 137
    in senior apartments, 134

living will, 161, 212
living, with adult children
    ADU for, 133–134
    cultural issues with, 132
    ECHO unit for, 133–134, 190
    family dynamics of, 133
    space relating to, 133–134
living, with dementia, 101–106
long-term care
    insurance for, 62, 64–68
    types of, 63–64
long-term care insurance (LTCI), 62,
    64–68, 212
    dementia covered by, 67
    eligibility for, 67
    elimination period of, 66
    flexibility of, 68
    inflation protection of, 67
    nonforfeiture of, 67
    pre-existing conditions of, 66
low-income assistance, 118
lung disease, chronic, 83

managed care, 115–117
McLeod, Beth Witrogen, 4
meal services, 130
Meals on Wheels, 212
Medicaid, 111, 120, 213
medical alert system, 73
medical insurance, 113. See also Medicare
  Part B: Medical Insurance
Medicare, 213, 109-123
    components of, 110–111
    establishment of, 109
    health care representative for, 122, 211
    website for, 110
Medicare Advantage, 112, 115–117
Medicare Part A:Hospital Insurance, 111-113
Medicare Part B: Medical Insurance, 113-115
Medicare Part C: Medical Advantage (MA),
    115-117
Medicare Part D: PrescriptionDrug Benefit
    enrollment in, 118–119
    low-income assistance with, 118
    with Medicare Advantage (MA), 116, 117
    with Medigap, 120

    with Original Medicare, 117
    phases of, 117
    Prescription Drug Plan (PDP) in, 117-120
Medicare SELECT, 122
Medicare Summary Notice, 110, 115
Medicare supplemental insurance, 213
    costs of, 121
    coverage of, 120–121
    Medicaid as, 120
    Medicare SELECT as, 122
    Medigap as, 111, 120-122
    TriCare as, 120
Medigap, 111, 120-122
Merton, Thomas, 5
metabolism, 164
The Middle Passage: From Misery to Meaning
    in Midlife (Hollis), 7
money. See finances
mourning. See grief
multi-infarct dementia, 99

National Academy of Sciences, 189
net worth, 57, 194, 195, 196
nonforfeiture, 67
"Notice of Noncoverage," 113
nursing home, evaluation of, 194, 208–209
Nursing Home Resident's Bill of Rights, 43
nursing homes. See also advocate, with nursing
    homes; living, in nursing home

Older Americans Act, 139, 191
old-old age, xi, xiv
ombudsman, 213
Ombudsman Program, 139
Original Medicare, 112, 113, 116–117
osteoarthritis, 83, 85–86
osteoporosis, 83, 86–87

pain
    chronic, 95
    managing of, 159
palliative care, 213
Parkinson's disease, 88, 96, 98–99
Patient's Bill of Rights, 40
patient's rights, 43
Patton, Bruce, 13

personal health care value statement, 210
personal response system (PRS), 73
PFFS (Private Fee-for-Service) plans, 116, 117
pharmacy, 36–39
Pick's disease, 99
Pipher, Mary, 12
power of attorney. See durable power of
    attorney (DPA)
PPO (Preferred Provider Organizations), 116
preexisting conditions, 66
Prescription Drug Plan (PDP), 117–120
prescriptions. See Medicare Part D: Prescrip-
    tion Drug Benefit
primary care physician, 74–76
psychotherapy, 95

Radical Acceptance: Embracing Your Life with
    the Heart of a Buddha (Brach), 4
representative, for Medicare, 122
representative payee, for Social Security 48
respite care, 154, 189, 213
restlessness/confusion, 164–165
retirement communities, 134–135, 137
reverse mortgage, 57–58, 213
rheumatoid arthritis (RA), 83, 85–86
rituals relating to mourning 180–182

Saroyan, William, 8
saying good-bye
    arrangements made while, 160–161
    closure relating to, 161–162
    emotional intimacy while, 158–159
    by family members, 165–170
    final details of, 168
    signs of dying while, 163–165, 166

scams/fraud, 45–46, 59
senior apartments, 134
senior centers, 130, 152–153
sensory changes, 164–165
Seremelis-Scanlon, Debbie, 163
sleep disorders, 88
Social Security Administration, 111
The Soul and Death (Jung), 6
spiritual/religious organizations, 151–152
State Health Insurance Assistance Program
    (SHIP), 64–66, 110, 121
Stone, Douglas, 13
Stone, Susan, 5, 6
stress factors, 145–147, 189
stroke, 83, 84, 85
    hemorrhagic, 99
    ischemic, 84, 99
    symptoms of, 98–99
    vascular dementia and, 99–100
supplemental insurance. See Medicare
    supplemental insurance
support groups, 151; 189–190

tax credits, 189
transient ischemic attacks (TIAs), 84, 99
TriCare, 119

vascular dementia, 99–100
vision, 80–82

widowed parents, 179
will. See living will
workplace support, 190

Photography Credits

Cover *Butch Martin*/Image Bank, **vii** *Rolf Bruderer*/CORBIS, **xvii** *Clay McLachlan*/claypix.com, **10** Royalty-Free/CORBIS, **30** *Duncan Smith*/PhotoDisc Blue, **52** *Jaime C. Salles*/CORBIS, **70** *Julie Lemberger*/CORBIS, **90** *Josef Scaylea*/CORBIS, **108** *Hiroshi Watanabe*/Aperture, **127** *Joseph Scherschel*/Time Life Pictures, **142** *Dag Sundberg*/Image Bank, **156** *Miguel Salmeron*/Masterfile, **172** *Jim Cornfield*/CORBIS, **186** *Josef Scaylea*/CORBIS, **192** *David Sacks*/Getty Images

*But no matter how they make you feel,
you should always watch elders carefully.
They were you and you will be them.
You carry the seeds of your old age in you
at this very moment, and they hear the echoes
of their childhood each time they see you.*

—KENT NERBURN, *LETTERS TO MY SON*